CLIMB

LIKE A

MZUNGU

DAVID FLINN

CLIMB
LIKE A
MZUNGU

LIVE AN
ADVENTUROUS LIFE

HIGH ADVENTURE PUBLISHING is committed to excellence in outdoor adventure literature.

info@highadventurepublishing.com

978-572-0046

https://www.highadventurepublishing.com

Climb Like a Mzungu

Cover designed by: Miblart
Edited by: Elizabeth Barrett
Photographs from: The David Flinn Collection unless otherwise noted.
Maps: Mapbox and OpenStreetMap data sources.

Publisher's Cataloging-in-Publication Data provided by Five Rainbows Cataloging Services
Names: Flinn, David, 1960- author.
Title: Climb like a mzungu : live an adventurous life / David Flinn.
Description: Newbury, MA: High Adventure Publishing, 2023.
Identifiers: LCCN 2022921442 (print) | ISBN 979-8-9870257-1-0 (paperback : full color) | ISBN 979-8-9870257-2-7 (paperback : b&w) | ISBN 979-8-9870257-3-4 (hardcover : full color) | ISBN 979-8-9870257-0-3 (ebook)
Subjects: LCSH: Adventure and adventurers. | Mountaineering. | Voyages and travels. | Nairobi (Kenya)--Description and travel. | Autobiography. | BISAC: BIOGRAPHY & AUTOBIOGRAPHY / Adventurers & Explorers. | BIOGRAPHY & AUTOBIOGRAPHY / Personal Memoirs. | SPORTS & RECREATION / Mountaineering.
Classification: LCC GV199.92.F65 A3 2023 (print) | LCC GV199.92.F65 (ebook) | DDC 796.522092--dc23

    ISBN (Duplex Cover Color Paperback): 979-8-9870257-1-0
    ISBN (Ebook): 979-8-9870257-0-3
    ISBN (Paperback): 979-8-9870257-2-7
    ISBN (Duplex Cover Paperback) : 979-8-9870257-4-1
    ISBN (Hardcover): 979-8-9870257-3-4

First Edition June 2023

For my children, Eli and Rosalie, it's your turn to be Mzungus.

⁓

*To the memory of Ed Aalbue, Wes and Nancy Pfirman, Patti Saurman,
David Vadnais, Marla Silver-Wheeler, Bill Wilson,
and my parents, Rosalie and Seymour Flinn.*

Contents

Author's Note   1
Guidebook   3
Approach   17
Belay   73
Crux   115
Summit   161
Vista   197
Rappel   229
Campfire   255

Please Leave a Review   303
Upcoming: Travel Like a Mzungu   305
Acknowledgments   307
About the Author   309
Climbing Notes   311
Photography and Maps   313

AUTHOR'S NOTE

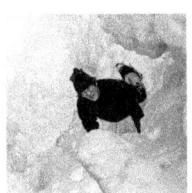

This book is a creative nonfiction piece based on memories of events that happened in my twenties between 1980 and 1990, including places, activities, people, and experiences. I've tried my best to tell a true story using old journals, photographs, friends, and siblings to confirm its accuracy. Some information has been lost to the passage of time. In each of these instances, I have rebuilt scenes or events with the thoughts and feelings of those who shared the experiences with me. Some names and identifying information have been modified to protect the privacy of real people. A few companions have been left out to streamline the story.

While I choose to climb mountains, I encourage you to travel your own path and live an adventurous life.

Joe starting *The North Face Standard Route* on Mount Kenya, July 1989

GUIDEBOOK

JULY 1989

"**M**zungu!*" bellow the children as I climb out of the safari truck, my long legs grateful after being crammed in the back seat. Dust swirls fleetingly, stirred up by all the commotion, as my colleagues scamper into the store. The children circle —wild animals toying with their prey.

Mzungu [ma-zun-goo] comes from the Swahili verb meaning "to wander aimlessly," describing the seemingly pointless travels of early explorers and missionaries. These days, the word refers to a white person.

It must be my fair skin that sets off the children's chanting. Born twenty-eight years ago in Uganda, they don't realize I'm their next-door neighbor, not just another foreigner, but an adventurer, wandering with purpose.

I take off my hat, revealing my blue eyes and thick, brown hair. They stop and huddle closer in anticipation. Mount Kenya's twin peaks of Batian and Nelion glimmer to the east, with patches of snow that sparkle in the midday sun. Pointing first to my chest, then to the mountain, I say, "Mzungu nenda mlimani." *Whiteman goes to the mountain.*

The horde murmurs, "Jasiri, mzungu, jasiri," as they break up and drift away, realizing no handouts are coming. I don't feel *jasiri* (brave).

Turning to enter the store, I notice a small boy, about six years old, standing nearby, not yet ready to leave. His clothes are worn and mud-splattered, and his black skin contrasts with the brown dust wallowing at his bare feet. I squat and gaze into his eyes. He tilts his head back, nervously pivoting on his left foot, ready for flight.

The wind gusts, unbalancing me. The young boy watches warily as I rise slowly and say, "Rafiki yangu," calling him *my friend*. I wave and head into the store. My climbing companions are at the counter, haggling over prices while I wander the aisles and snag some *chapatis* (African tortillas). Noticing a lonely tin of crabmeat on the shelf, I grab it on impulse and plunk my goods on the counter.

The lads retrieve the bag of provisions and head out to the vehicle, Tusker beer bottles clinking. Paying the bill, I thank the shopkeeper, "*Mzuri sana*, bwana." Cross-cultural communication is a lost art.

Returning to the truck, dust billows behind me. Joe lounges on the tailgate while Andrew and Francois engage the children. Noticing my rafiki standing nearby, I head over and say, "Naitwa David. Twende, nemba salama rafiki." *My name is David; It's time to go, be safe, my friend.* He smiles and runs off with his pack. As they go, they scream in unison, "Mzungu!"

TWENTY-EIGHT YEARS EARLIER, in November 1960, I was born royal blue, with my umbilical cord wrapped around my neck. The British doctor at Kampala's Mengo Hospital quickly unwinds it, allowing me to gasp my first precious breath. As oxygen courses through my body, the bluish tint turns the usual pink, and the African nurses smile and relax.

Uganda is on the equator, so the night is warm, crickets chirp, and doves coo. Dad sits on the edge of the bed as Mom cradles me in her arms—a cozy welcome into an exciting new world.

My parents came to Mbale, a small town near the border of Kenya, in the fall of 1959 as Anglican missionaries. When my birth date drew near, they traveled to Kampala over the bumpy dirt roads to the only western hospital in the country.

My Dad and I visit the equator in Kenya. Photo by my
Mom, Rosalie Flinn, August 1961.

We're the lone Americans, smack dab in the middle of the British
Empire, joining doctors, scientists, and schoolteachers trying to bring
first-world benefits to the wildness of Africa.

Consistent with immigrants everywhere, my parents flock together
with the British to celebrate Christmas, Easter, and Thanksgiving holidays. When living in a strange land, familiar cultural rituals help take the
edge off daily life among the Ugandans.

Every Sunday, Dad scoots over to St. Andrews Cathedral next door.
The church has a modern design with a large, welcoming space.

My father and I were at a political rally in Mbale,
Uganda. Photo by Rosalie Flinn, April 1962.

He helps the local deacon with the 9 a.m. mass, but his knowledge of the Lugandan language is limited. Since the bulk of the locals wish to learn English, Dad's 11 am service is always full.

Three years later, my sister was born in the summer of 1963. I'm happy to have a sidekick, and she's a cute little thing. I get to babysit, trying to keep her from eating the lizards that rummage around our flat. My family has settled into life in Africa. We take trips to different parts of Uganda and Kenya when my parents aren't busy with the church, wandering around like good mzungus.

One day in early 1965, my friend Michael and I play outside my house. The jacaranda and flame trees are in full bloom, glorious with intense reds and purples, juxtaposed with orange-brown soil.

Five-year-old Michael speaks English, teaching me Swahili and Lugisu, the local tongue.

My Mom and I in Mbale, Uganda. Photo by my Dad,
Seymour Flinn, June 1963.

Because Mbale is on the border between the Nilotic and Bantu language groups, English is commonly used because it is easy to learn. Who would have thought the mzungu tongue would mitigate tribal rivalry?

With buckets and shovels, we move the dirt to build a city for our Corgi trucks. Engrossed in construction, we don't notice the group of teenagers that slowly materialize.

"*Unafanya nini na* mzungu!" they yell, demanding to know why Michael is playing with me. They surround us, chanting, "Mzungu, mzungu."

Michael is quiet, continuing to bulldoze the road to his majestic dirt castle. I ask what they're blathering about.

"They're bored, bothering us. They'll leave soon."

Looking up, my pale skin is covered with brown dust, my blond hair glistening in the afternoon sun, blue eyes wide open, calmly looking at one of the older boys standing over me. I smile and volunteer my shovel, inviting him to help.

He kneels and says, "*Mjinga* mzungu." I have no idea he's calling me stupid. We look into each other's eyes as the breeze rustles the jacarandas, and a smile forms on his lips. He gets up, tousles my hair, and yells, "*Twende!*"—Let's go—to his pack. They drift away as Michael and I continue to plow the dirt.

～

MY FAMILY IS ready to leave Mbale after the birth of my brother Andy in November 1965. From the nearby Tororo airport, we fly back to the United States. Thankfully, our departure occurred just before a major purge of foreigners.

My friend, Michael Masaba, and I in Mbale, Uganda.
Photo by Seymour Flinn, January 1965.

Since the country's independence from the British in 1962, Ugandan lawmakers have been negotiating with the Buganda king to establish an acceptable administration. Unfortunately, it would take twenty years to resolve the situation.

We return to Wilmington, Delaware, where Dad's family has deep Revolutionary War roots. Like my forebears, who came from England and France, I'm also an immigrant. It's a new world to learn, full of strange things like snow, asphalt, and lots of white people.

Dad's away trying to find a job, and Mom's bogged down with Lissa and Andy. Being the first one through the gauntlet, I'm the parenting experiment. Will I listen? Eat yucky vegetables? I do an excellent job since my parents often leave me alone.

On a sunny day in the summer of 1966, pulling weeds and trying to build a wall around some uncooperative ants, I become aware of a subtle gurgling. While building forts is a good thing, the bubbling noise piques my interest.

The Cathedral staff of Saint Andrews and I were at the Tororo Airport the day we left Uganda. Photo by Seymour Flinn, December 1965.

Tromping across the road and into bracken woods, I discover the Brandywine River a few blocks from our house. Oh, what a great place! The river chortles, ducks quack as they land, puffs of wind rustle leaves, and the sun dapples across the rocks.

There must be frogs out there, amongst the fish wallowing in the pools. Hey, what about turtles? I pick up a stick and meander along without a clue that this river once cooled the furnaces at the DuPont gunpowder factory where my ancestors worked during the war.

Time stands still for me, engrossed in the fun of exploring. At the moment, the subtle sounds of nature soak into my body. Time slips slowly by, trapped in the eddies and currents. Meanwhile, for my father, it races rapidly, threatening to overwhelm him in one horrible crescendo.

Naturally, I'm scared when I hear Dad yelling my name. He runs to find me on a rock, white water rippling by, totally pleased with myself.

Uh-oh. Dad looks mad. I wonder what all the fuss is about.

"David, come here right now. You could fall in and get hurt."

A bit perturbed since Dad never yells, I begrudgingly hop off the rock to join him. The scolding continues as we march back home. But the wilderness continues to ripple through my soul. The explorer in me has awoken.

THE TRUCK DOOR slams as Francois jumps in, and Joe starts up the engine. Nanyuki is a small village that has atrophied like the rest of Kenya. My Lonely Planet guidebook notes that after World War II, the British built buildings in the style of civilized London. While suited to the climate and pleasant to look at, things fall apart.

Africans don't seem to care about fancy things. They're more practical, living in the moment, and don't manicure their world. As we drive out of town, I notice the paint peeling from the sides of buildings, shingles missing from roofs, broken glass windows, and trash swirling around the street. It takes getting used to, but realizing it's small stuff, I don't sweat it.

The farmland transforms into a forest, and the houses thin as the trees take over. We leave the pot-holed streets behind and bounce up the dusty road to Sirimon Gate, the entrance to Mount Kenya National Park. I'm grateful for the Mitsubishi four-wheel drive that shortens our approach.

Africa reaches up and grabs the vehicle, stopping it dead in its tracks. The mud swallows the tires, and we bustle out to free it. Fifteen minutes later, we realize that it's hopeless.

So much for four-wheel drive. We unload our kit and get cracking. We'll deal with the truck when the climb is done.

The trees of the timberland forest are sparse, transitioning into chaparral as we hike higher. The view of the valley flickers through the fog as it rolls and swirls around us, eerie in the silence but refreshing as the hot sun occasionally blasts through, only to disappear again.

I stop, panting, and turn to Joe. "Wow, we're much higher than I thought. Didn't expect the impact of altitude. No running up this trail."

Joe is wiry, a few inches shorter than me, but with a nicely cropped brown beard and mustache. His studious look is capped off with wide, thin-framed plastic glasses.

"We started at almost nine thousand feet," Joe laughs. "Should have hired an elephant to haul our stuff." Mount Kenya tops out at 17,057 feet. Yikes, only 8,000 more to go.

"Hey, Joe, you never told me where you're from." I met my colleagues in Nairobi at the Kenya Mountaineering Club. None of us knew each other but rallied for the sake of the climb.

"I grew up in northern California, in Berkeley, of all places." He stops, huffing a bit, sucking in oxygen. "Life was good, my parents happy, pretty basic stuff. You mentioned you used to live in Uganda?"

"Yeah, not too far from here. My Dad was a missionary helping the church."

"Wow, that's wild. When did you leave?"

"My father's contract was up in late 1965, and then we headed back to the States. Life in America was still strange years later. Growing up in Greenwich, Connecticut, many high school classmates drove BMWs worth more than my father's salary."

I was preoccupied with belonging and being accepted. A gangly four-eyed nerd who used sports to bond with his peers. Clueless. A wide receiver playing football who refused to wear glasses because they could break when tackled. As if I ever got the ball.

"I hated high school," Joe replies. "Everyone was trying to impress each other. Too much boasting and bantering for me. Glad I joined the Boy Scouts to escape to the woods. Where did you learn about the outdoors?"

"My middle-school bud, Larry. His dad took us backpacking. A hardworking, rugged guy at home in the woods. Luckily, he showed me a better way to avoid school social drama. The crackling of a campfire and smores dripping with chocolate, sealed the deal."

"Amen to chocolate. You got any handy?"

Pulling out a Kenyan version of the Cadbury bar from a pocket attached to my hip belt, I pass it to him. We plod on, hoping to catch Andrew and Francois, galloping ahead. The trail winds through large chunks of volcanic rock scattered by glaciers with remnants of snow tucked away on their northern sides.

As we pause next to a boulder, I ask "So how did you get to Kenya?"

"This spring, I was looking for job at a large advertising agency. They offered me a freelance opportunity to photograph the truck in the wilds of Africa for Mitsubishi North America."

"So you're here on a boondoggle?" My jaw drops processing this news. And I thought I was good at convincing companies to pay for my trips.

"Well, yeah, it's stupendous having an expense account. But I need to get to the game park after this climb. Although Africa appears to be a long way from Los Angeles, my boss is impatiently waiting for DHL to deliver my exposed film."

Crossing a stream that trickles down the valley, I say "In that case, better not send them any pictures of the truck stuck in the mud."

"Not a chance of that, I need to keep this job. Especially since the truck makes getting around Kenya so much easier." It beats traveling by matatu, the infamous African private taxi. Joe continues on while I gaze at the unique shrubs that line the stream.

An hour later, we catch up with the other two at the ridge top, where the glorious peaks of Mount Kenya flit into view, mist swirling.

Andrew looking northwest over the plains on the Sirimion trail of
Mount Kenya, July 1989

The lobelia shrubs, an alpine wonder, are scattered along the path, different from their desert cacti cousins. They sprout out of the ground, surrounded by scrub grasses, volcanic rock, and hoar frost that nestles in the shadows. Batian, the taller of the two peaks, pops us a glimpse and disappears back into the clouds.

Dumping my moose of a pack to forage for a jar of peanut butter, I open it with a flourish, offering some to Joe. "Have a snack and enjoy the view. I'm psyched to be here with you guys."

Joe passes the PB to Francois, who slathers it on his chocolate bar, munching as he says in his French accent, "The mountain is amazing, beautiful. I'm off to the hut. Anyone else?" He throws on his pack.

"I'm game." Joe jumps up, and poof, they're gone.

Andrew takes a photo of the shrub next to us. "I just love these lobelia." He has bouncy curly hair and a clean-shaven face as I do. He's a few inches shorter, and his enthusiasm makes him a great teammate. I like his glacier glasses; very snazzy as my Mom would say.

I agree. "These trees are right out of Dr. Seuss. Like the Joshua tree in California." The groundsels resemble giant artichokes, rainwater pooling in their leaves.

Andrew nods. "Totally stellar. Nothing like this in the UK. I'm happy to stroll and enjoy the shrubbery." His English accent is crisp and clear.

"What brought you to Kenya?" I ask while taking a closer look at the nearest groundsel.

"After graduating from the University of Reading in England, I've been working in Nairobi for three years. I'm taking a short break from my research for this climb."

"Wow, so this is just a long weekend for ya, huh?" What a life to get a job in Africa.

"It's bonny excellent to get away. Nairobi is like all cities, one big rat race. I'm glad to unwind amidst these lovely plants." He stops to peer into a lobelia. "Incidentally, what brings you here?"

Francois snapping pictures of the shrubbery with Mount Kenya in the distance, July 1989.

I join him in examining the large shrub. "I'm going back home to Uganda; this is just an excellent diversion."

"You used to live in Africa?" Andrew seems puzzled to learn an American has roots here.

"My folks were missionaries for the Anglican Church when I was born. And now I'm back!"

"Seriously? That's cool. Welcome home!"

Another lobelia looms nearby, over ten feet tall. Snap goes my camera. Surrounded by my new friends and stunning scenery, I'm blown away by my luck. Six months ago, camped out on Dad's couch, the guidebook described what I could see and do in Africa, cautioning about the hazards while highlighting the rewards.

Although books help provide direction, it's up to me to travel my own path through life. Looking up at the clouds swirling between Mount Kenya's twin summits, I realize it's been an extraordinary journey getting here.

As the mist entwines the mountain, the lobelia stand watch. This grateful mzungu is ready to climb the most badass peak in Africa.

Ken approaching Huntington Ravine, Mount Washington, February 1986

APPROACH

JANUARY 1980 – JANUARY 1983

W ith a running start, I jump into the bow of the canoe. Gathering speed, fending off rocks using my paddle, the metal bottom lets out a high-pitched squeal as it plows through the snow. Risking a glance behind me, John is balanced precariously on the stern. At our current speed, careening down the ski hill in the dark, with the wind whipping through our hair, flipping the canoe over would be disastrous.

The moon peaks out from behind the clouds, glistening on the snow, reflecting a pale-yellow stripe down our path. Imagining a roller coaster, I hang on and howl when reaching the bottom of the hill. Suddenly, a road jumps in our way, and the canoe throws sparks as we bounce across the pavement. More asphalt draws near, and we launch, aluminum screeching, to the other side, stopping in the snow. Raising our paddles, we yell "Yes!" in unison.

It's January 1980, halfway through sophomore year, and tonight is my introduction to the Syracuse University Outing Club (SUOC). John is president and sure knows how to throw a party. The club, a coed collegiate equivalent of the Boy Scouts, encourages students to appreciate the great outdoors by exposing them to rock climbing, caving, canoeing, hiking, and skiing.

The meeting is hosted at the E-Room, an equipment room in the basement of the ski lodge on the edge of campus. The lifts have been quiet for years, the machinery long since rusted, downhill skiing having moved on to steeper terrain. Rarely used by the university, SUOC has full reign of the lodge, brainwashing beginners with stories of glory in the wilderness.

After the excitement of my first SUOC adventure, we stow the boats away. Naturally, there's a beer keg, and the party starts. Sitting on a canoe, I start chatting with Eric.

"How did you learn about the outing club?" he asks.

"It's a long, sordid tale. Nothing as thrilling as canoeing down a ski slope."

"We have time. There's a lot of beer in the keg." Eric adjusts his glasses and smiles.

"I went to school in Connecticut but didn't do much outdoors. A few church downhill ski trips, a backpack or two. Mainly neighborhood sports. High school drama was way too stifling. I had close friends, but most of them moved away."

"Any girls, man?"

Groaning about the girl question, it's time to chug my beer. Eric is handsome, with a solid lumberjack frame and a smile surrounded by a bushy beard. Girls must fall at his feet.

"Nah, nothing happened. I had Coke-bottle glasses for years. Surrounded by girls in the French Club and Yearbook Committee, but too shy. And the prom? Forget that." There it was, the whole uncomfortable virgin topic. I hope we don't dwell on it.

Eric nods. "Well, I had one girlfriend, but we drifted apart. How did you get to SU?"

Grateful he doesn't drill into my girl-free world. "My family moved to upstate New York my senior year, and I stayed with church families to finish school. Clueless, I applied to three architecture programs, not realizing it's one of the most grueling majors on the planet. The College of Arts and Sciences at Syracuse accepted me."

"Well, you must have some smarts. I transferred to the Forestry School after finishing my associate's degree in New Paltz and now going for Forest Engineering. The outing club rounds out the experience. Do you live on campus?"

"Yeah, up on Mount Olympus in Day Hall. Fortunate to meet good people, lots of girls. They know I'm sweet; that's what they tell me; I'm always stuck in the friend zone. Still better than living in a monastery."

"Ah, the benefits of dorm living. I punted and found a place off campus. College is wonderful; everyone has an open mind. It's electric, none of the silly high school games." Eric finishes his beer.

Nodding in agreement, I say, "And there're a zillion things to get sucked into—sports, book clubs, jobs, dancing. Last year, I organized downhill night skiing trips. Too freaking cold, and barely able to see the poorly lit runs."

Eric laughs. "Downhill canoeing is way more fun. So, last question, what's your major?"

"Now, that's a complicated answer. Last year I studied Arts and Sciences, and now I'm in the School of Art, hoping to make it into Industrial Design. Abandoned my books for oil paint and colored chalk."

Eric waiting to climb at Seneca Rocks, West Virginia in March 1982.

Eric cracks a grin. "And those artsy girls. Nice move."

Standing to stretch my legs, "I'm stoked to have met you. This party has been awesome. Time to head out; got an art history exam tomorrow."

"I'll bail with you. Need a ride down the hill?"

"That would be amazing; saves waiting for the bus." As we head to the exit, John stands by the door, nursing his beer. Shaking hands, I say, "Thanks for inviting me. Looking forward to more adventures."

His elfin smile lights up his face. "I'm glad you showed up. Tuesdays are trip signup nights, so keep that in mind."

Unfortunately, the following weekend, a girl pitches over in a canoe and tragically snaps her leg. After the ambulance leaves, the tobogganing season is over. John promises the campus police that the canoes will remain on the river. We need to maintain a low profile and let them worry about the football team tossing beer kegs off dormitory roofs.

MY FIRST CHANCE TO run a river comes a few weeks later. Most SUOC boats are banged up, but that's to be expected when used as toboggans. Kayaking magazines describe whitewater rivers full of frothy waves with big rocks that want to crunch boats. This river is supposed to be mellow. Better be.

February is a strange time to paddle a river, but John explains the rationale to me over beers at Hungry Charlie's, the pub for post-SUOC-meeting revelry. Lucky for me, New York's drinking age is 18.

"You need to practice the real thing before Spring," he lectures. "The best time to kayak is when the rivers are raging due to the winter thaw. You want to have fun, right?"

It's hard to dismiss the logic, but I have more questions. "Couldn't we start in a pool or someplace a bit warmer? Perhaps go skiing instead of kayaking?"

"Bah. You need to get into the swing of things, and this Class II river will be a piece of cake." John changes tack. "You handled your first canoe ride famously. You're a natural."

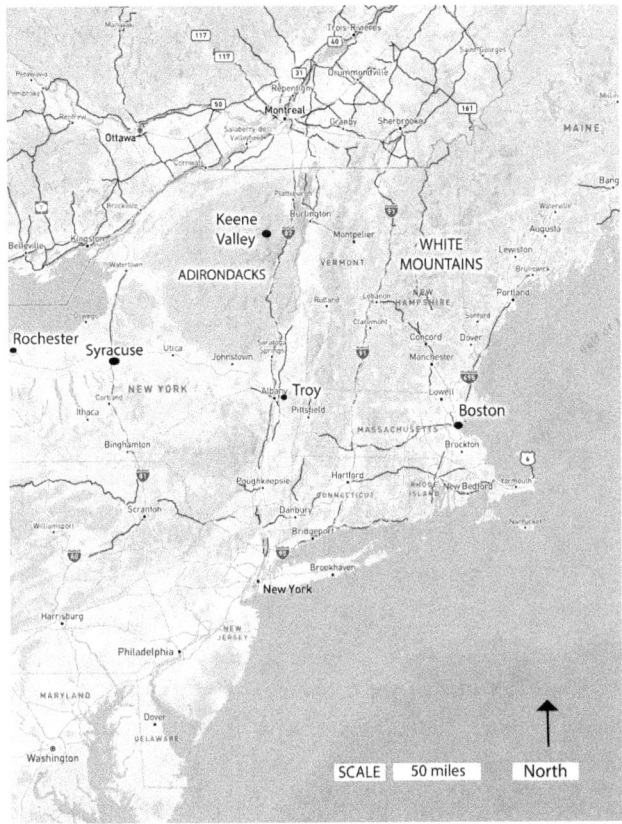

I lived in Syracuse, Rochester, Keene Valley, Troy, and
Boston throughout this story.

Going for passion works, as I agree to show up on Saturday.

After helping unload the boats from John's Pontiac station wagon, it's time to gather my gear. The wetsuits are a smorgasbord of sizes with strips of duct tape in odd places, providing more mental than practical warmth.

I haul my boat to the edge. The winter-gray sky blends with the dark water around me. Squeezing into the kayak cockpit, I launch into Chittenango Creek[1], getting comfy. Trying to relax, wiggling my big toes in the neoprene booties that, thankfully, have no holes. Paddling upstream, I wait for the other three beginners to join me.

"Okay, people," John calls, "gather around. We need to review a few points before getting y'all going." Like ducklings attending their father, we careen around and line up facing him. "You seem to have the basics of paddling; that's good. But before we proceed downstream, you need to demonstrate that you can evacuate the boat if it capsizes."

Losing one's balance can cause a kayak to flip upside down, which is a frightening thought. While inverted and without exiting the cockpit, I'm supposed to use the paddle to roll back up. It might be possible in a pool, heroic on a frozen river.

The dorky spray skirt has elastic to keep it snug against my belly, meant to bond me to the kayak and prevent water from gushing in and sinking the boat. Yes, I go there and ponder waves crashing, dragging me to the bottom, bouncing off rocks and tree stumps. In theory, the helmet is supposed to prevent a broken skull.

With a suspicion forming in my mind, I ask, "Do you expect me to dump over, upside down, and wiggle out of the kayak?"

"Yes! That exactly." John laughs. "Seriously, if you flip over in white water, I need to know you can get out safely. No drowning is allowed on SUOC trips."

"Ah, right. It's freezing out. There's no other option?"

"Since you missed the pool training sessions last fall, you need to show me a release, or else you'll have to stay here."

A splash spooks me as one of my colleagues gets right to it, tips his boat over, dunks himself, pulls the spray skirt, and pops up, gasping for air.

"Don't let go of your paddle and grab the boat! You can't lose them in white water," John says. "Excellent. Swim back to land."

A wailing builds inside me, but I do the exit flawlessly. Staggering back to shore, like a drowned dog freezing, I wonder what I've gotten into. Jaws chattering, I slither back into the kayak and head downriver. Eventually, my wetsuit warms up, allowing me to enjoy the adventure. The river gurgles and the eddies are chock-full of ice, reminding me of wind chimes as they gently nudge my boat. Getting the hang of things.

After paddling for a mile, it starts snowing. The icy water chills my hands clutching the paddle, and I try to imagine a friendly, roaring fire. As if that isn't enough, I can't feel my toes. Wedged into this tiny cockpit, my long legs don't appreciate the awesomeness of kayaking and have gone to sleep.

The snow trickles down in the calm gloomy sky as we finally reach the take-out. I crawl away from the river like a salamander, barely able to walk. It takes twenty minutes for my toes to return to my body. Later that night, all is well at SUOC's best party house, equipped with a sauna in the basement. It's rickety-looking, but the cavers know a lot about gas-fired furnaces.

The outing club has four primary cliques: cavers, climbers, water rats, and normals. The first three splinter off into their factions, while normal members stick to skiing and hiking, creating a fascinating example of group dynamics. Rivalries exist, each clique bragging about its glories. The refreshing part is that nothing is personal; it's all bantering and boasting. I appreciate these tribal intensities, competitive but not nasty.

After the sauna brings me to a cozy inner glow, a back rub by a caving girl caps off the evening. I can't remember her name, but I'll never forget the soft, strong fingers caressing my back. Sex has been non-existent; being touched this way is fantastic. I love this place. Coming out of my back-rub fog, John sits nearby.

"Yo, Flinny, life is good, eh?"

"Life is magnificent," I reply blissfully, lying on my tummy, arms by my sides, feet spread wide, warmth coursing through my skin.

"Good to see you enjoying the SUOC lifestyle. A snowy day on the river, followed by a toasty sauna. Almost makes us forget about studying." He shifts, placing his beer can next to his knee.

I roll over and sit up next to him. "Thanks for a great trip today. I've been wondering, why do you love kayaking? Can't see anything squished into that low cockpit."

"Ah, good question. The short answer is that it's the same for any sport; you gotta put in the time. Being a beginner is hard since nothing is in sync. Relax, learn, and it grows on you." John sips his beer.

"Okay, I get that you need to be good to have fun. But what keeps you going, especially after getting tossed in the water, bouncing off huge rocks inside nature's washing machine?"

"The thrilling rush of a big wave forces me to focus. My worries fade away, and I emerge revitalized, ready for the next adventure, whether in the wilderness or in the classroom."

John's enthusiasm is intoxicating, stimulating my mind with the possibilities, but my legs have declared that the kayak is not for me.

～

IN LATE MARCH, I receive a letter from the Industrial Design department. Cradling it between my fingers, its thin, crisp type beckons opening. Heading back to my empty dorm room, I perch on the bottom bunk and fondle the envelope, my belly crawling with anxiety. Fingers sweat; destiny awaits.

Fifth on the waiting list. Dang. Not bad, considering there are forty slots for two hundred applicants. It's rare when anyone backs out, so I'm toast. It's great to be close, but this far away sucks. The room is quiet as the letter slips to the floor. While a bold attempt, I wasn't good enough. The competition has been at it for years, not a mere six months. My architecture skills are solid, but my creative drawing stinks. Being results-oriented, I look at it simply: I tried but failed. Now what?

It takes me a few days to get the courage to call home and check-in. The dorm pay phone is near the elevators. Luckily, no one else is camped out chatting.

"Hey, Dad, how are things?"

"Busy as always at church. The usual political drama, but it seems the chaos is under control."

Dad has been at it for three years. His parish is in Troy, New York, the poor part of the city. The previous rector was a drunk, the church barely functioning. It's a depressed city with fierce race wars, so my siblings attend private school. I thought we left the battles back in Africa.

Then I tell him. Silence. Crickets chirp. I can't bear it. "I'll meet with my Arts and Sciences advisor after the semester to figure out my next steps. I don't think art school is for me."

Dad's not mad. Bet he knew how it would go. "Get a degree; that's all we want. College is important."

"Thanks for not being angry. I'm committed to graduating, but what major is the question. How is Mom feeling?" I worry since she hasn't been working much lately.

"She's still tired. The doctor says it's arthritis, and that's why her hip hurts."

"What does Pop-pop think?" My grandfather is a big deal in the Delaware medical world, running one of the largest hospitals in the East. "He must know someone who can help her."

Dad sighs. "He's working on it. In a few days, we have an appointment with an arthritis specialist."

"Can I chat with Mom?"

"She's resting. I can have her call you when she's able. Hey, here's your sister." Dad hands the phone to Lissa, and we catch up, but I'm distracted and worried about Mom.

THE SEMESTER ENDS in early May 1980, and I move into a big Victorian house ten blocks from campus with six other characters from the dorm. The house phone has a humongous cord, allowing me to chat with Mom in my room.

"I've decided to switch my major to Geography," I tell her.

"Why Geography?"

"Creating maps seems cool, and I can get a job in the Cartography lab, thanks to my drafting skills. My advisor recommended this approach, and I agree it's a great idea."

"It does seem logical, especially with your architectural background. How do you feel about it?"

"I'm happy to have a solid plan to graduate, even if it means one more semester to make up for the art school credits. I'm drawn to maps and nature, so Geography makes sense." Continuing to chat with Mom, I dance around the girl questions and don't tell her about the crazy parties we have.

It's a hot and hazy summer in Syracuse. My housemate Steve and I both have rooms on the first floor. He's going to the Forestry School and is from Long Island. He's taller than me, topped with a large bushy afro and a thin mustache.

He works at the hospital downtown, tormenting rats for some odd research purpose. I'm a delivery boy for Acropolis Pizza at night. We go hiking a few times but mostly hang around Syracuse, enjoying life outside of the dorms.

The transition to Geography is not so bad. School is school, and when drawing maps, using ink is not that different from paint. Working in the Cartography lab ten hours a week helps earn some cash.

In October, the climbers invite me to the town of Little Falls, home to Moss Island,[2] on the Erie Canal. We siege the fifty-foot crag, rigging three top ropes to get folks climbing quickly. Our climbing leader is Bob, a rugged Wildlife Bio major with an enormous brown beard, reminding me of a young Santa Claus. He explains that each climb has a name, indicating a sequence of moves called a "route."

We start on the classic *Jeff Loves Eileen*, the words of graffiti spray-painted on the wall by a passionate Jeff years ago. Bob is assisted by his girlfriend, Marla, who wears tight yoga pants. She has big hair, glorious brown curls, an elfish smile, and a twinkle in her eyes: tiny, barely over five feet, a gymnast in high school.

Bob and Marla launch into teacher mode and explain the main principles of climbing: anchors, ropes, and belays. Anchors can use trees or are constructed with gear called protection. Today we are using trees as anchors, which Marla calls a *top rope*.

A new friend, Gaston, is climbing, with Eric belaying him. We've learned safety requires a rope that keeps the climber from falling. Think of taking a leashed dog on a steep walk: the owner is the belayer, and the climber is the dog. As the climber moves up, the belayer draws in the rope, keeping it taut.

A figure-eight knot tied into my harness, Fall 1987.

If the climber slips off, the belayer locks the rope as the owner tightens the leash.

"You got it," says Eric. "Climbing is too easy for you with those super-long arms." After a few minutes, Gaston waves from the top, indicating he's done climbing. His bright orange tights make me squint.

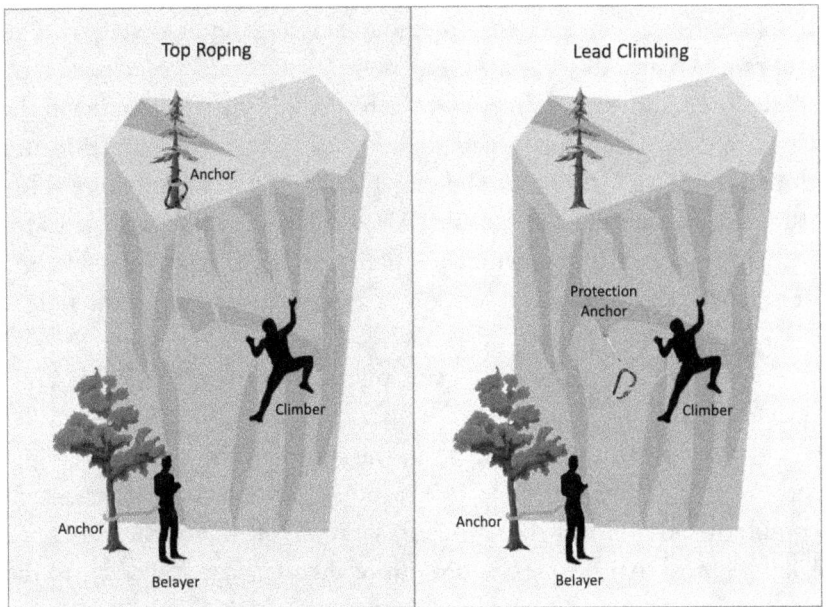

Top roping and lead climbing are the main types of roped climbing.

Marla helps Eric adjust the rope and hands me the end. Remembering my lesson, I tie a figure-eight knot that attaches the rope to my harness.

Marla looks up and says, "You tied it right. Great! Up you go, and remember to think about your feet. Look down and find the right spot."

"Thanks," I murmur, cautiously stepping up to the rock wall.

The climbing harness fits me snugly like a diaper. The dog leash slithers to the top of the wall, where it goes through a ring called a carabiner, anchored to a huge tree. Eric—the dog owner—has hold of the other end of the rope.

Wedging my foot in a crack, I stand and get on with it. The rock feels rough against my fingers, but I appreciate the solid texture. Wiggling my tips into the crack seems sensible, and my feet pivot sideways to fit the horizontal ledges. I move one limb at a time, making progress, searching for significant footholds to stop and shake my arms. This is fun.

The danged rope gets in the way, since it tends to follow the crack, almost as distracting as my sweaty palms. Growing up, I always climbed

27

trees, but this is way different. Instead of standing on branches, my toes are crammed into this crack. At least there are decent ledges to rest on.

Before I know it, I'm sitting at the top beside Gaston, soaking in the view over the Erie Canal. He's four inches taller than I am, thin but ripped with wiry strength, and has blond hair trimmed short. He's studying Wildlife Biology, crushing his grades but not exactly sure of his path, like many of us. Sometimes he pretends he's Gaston Rebuffat, one of mountaineering's legends, using a French accent to imitate his idol.

"Do you like climbing?" I ask.

"Yeah, it's cool. I love the giant puzzle, never following the same, boring line."

I agree. "It's fun. Different from the speed rush of downhill skiing, more serene. There's a lot to think about, and I like the physics and complexity: climbing, belays, anchors, gear, all of it. Not thrilled about falling. Heard that people can slip out of their harness and crater to the ground."

"Splat city kitty." Gaston laughs. "Yeah, falling can be a bummer, but the rope makes it less terrifying."

"Ha, you admit it's scary."

"Absolutely. But heck, I could get hit by a bus walking to class tomorrow. I'd rather be in control of my destiny." Gaston stands, reaching for another rope. "Time for a rappel!"

Zoom. He motors down the cliff, a marine bouncing out of a helicopter, gliding in total style. Rappelling—the opposite of climbing—requires sliding down the rope. A figure-eight friction device, a tricked-out paper clip, controls the descent.

I peek over the cliff edge. Big air unnerves me. Imagining Wile E. Coyote, with legs whirling to find traction, my mind maps the trigonometry in an instant, fear fluttering in my tummy. Climbing up is one thing; going down is another. I should walk off and leave the exposure behind.

Years earlier, I stood on a house deck twenty feet over Maine's calm, deep-blue ocean. Vertigo crept in as the dread of falling swelled, the ocean beckoning.

Gaston always dresses colorfully. Notice the rope tied
through his harness. Moss Island, Little Falls in 1981.

Gripping the railing, part of me wanted to jump, to spite it, to refuse to succumb to fear. To show I dared to take the challenge and push the envelope. Be a man.

I'm scared of heights. Of falling. Of dying and going splat city kitty, mashed under the wheel of fear.

"Flinny," Gaston yells. "Stop spacing and get going." The rope ripples impatiently.

I breathe deeply, clip in, turn around, and don't look down. My mind chills, and my body takes over, welcoming the exposure, the rush of this experience animating my being.

Snug in the diaper, walking backward, my weight pulls the rope through the paper clip. Screw being scared; it's time to just do it.

I HEAD HOME for the short Christmas break, thrilled to score Dad's old Ford Maverick. Tan with two doors and automatic transmission—

the perfect cruising machine. It's great to have wheels and the freedom to drive on SUOC trips.

In late January of 1981, I sign up for ice climbing in Ithaca, only to discover John's car has broken down, and we can't fit the horde in the Maverick. Milling around the E-Room, we opt for plan B.

Weeks ago, John rigged a garden hose to drip water down the hay silo attached to the ski lodge. Imagine a twenty-foot wall of ice providing the perfect practice climb. After a few hours of engineering attempts, we conclude rigging a top rope is a fail. Plan C leads us to grab a keg of Genesee Cream Ale, and our discussion turns to spring break.

SUOC sponsors a trip to Franklin, West Virginia, an outdoor adventure playground, every March. Seneca Rocks, a premier climbing mecca, is minutes away. The region has the best caving in the East. The Potomac River is nearby for the water tribe, while the Dolly Sods Wilderness provides great backpacking for regular folks.

Cruising south in John's station wagon, stuffed to the gills with caving, climbing, and canoe gear. Surprisingly, nothing flies off the roof, and we pull into the Thorn Spring Park driveway right before dark. During the ride, John tried to convince me to go caving. Sitting around a campfire outside our cabin, the cajoling continues.

"I get that you prefer climbing," John says, "but you should try caving. SUOC is about experiencing all the sports. Besides, we'll rappel into the cave."

Cautious reply. "Well, I want to climb *The Gendarme* at Seneca Rocks."

"You will, but caving is wild. Think of it as more rope practice. Right, guys?"

When John gets on a roll, he's tough to resist. His logic appears sound: better to try it to make sure. Yep, I agree to go.

The name "Sites" is more appealing than caves with names like *Hell Hole* or *Schoolhouse*. The entrance is a hole in the ground—not that I'd stumble into it, a scene from a Hollywood horror movie. Two hundred and twenty-five feet down, the bottom is covered with dirt and rumored to have a bat-poop pyramid.

We anchor a Bluewater nylon rope to an enormous tree and use a kick-ass device called a descender's rack. The rope slides through six rungs, applying friction with the caver's weight to control the descent. It's a beast meant to handle all kinds of mud and muck.

With six of us on the trip, I'm the third to head in. The first half of the rappel is cake, walking backward down a hundred-foot section. Suddenly, the notch arrives, and, poof, I'm launched into space. Adrift, slowly spinning around, a timid spider hanging to a thread, my carbide lamp unlit, eyes yearning for light. At night, the outdoors can seem dark. Being in a cave a hundred feet down is really dark, like super-duper dark. My eyes trick me into thinking bats are nearby, but my ears tell me there's nothing but air. I spot my friends' ghostly glow as they encourage me down.

Off the rope, sitting in guano, waiting for the others. Realizing my mistake, I move to a pile of clean dirt to work on my lamp. Carbide rocks the size of blueberries mix with water to generate gas, which a striker sparks to ignite the flame.

Finally, my lamp lights, exposing the long way up, the rope jerking as another caver descends. The cavern is as big as a house, surrounded by drab, brown, and dark walls, with an occasional sparkle of white crystal.

My five caving buddies, John in the middle, after 16 muddy hours in
Sites Cave, West Virgina in March 1981.

We spend hours wandering around on a "route," assuming John knows where we are going. My carbide lamp gives off enough light to keep claustrophobia at bay.

The best aspect of having company is the ability to engage in distracting conversation.

"Hey, this formation is awesome," I say. "It appears that muddy water drips from the ceiling to form the bottom, building a huge hourglass."

"That is correct," John replies. "The top part is called a stalactite, and the bottom is a stalagmite. It's hard to believe it may be over a million years old."

"Here's another one," someone says, pointing their lamp to the far right of us.

My colleagues' voices and banter help push the claustrophobia away, making it tolerable. John knows this and ensures we don't spend time alone. I'm trying to forget his earlier stories about swimming or spending days inside a cave.

Caving is what you'd expect: cold, dark, muddy, bats, balrogs, dwarves, and Gollum. I spent hours in high school reading *Lord of the Rings*, drawn into the fascinating world of Middle Earth. I'm in the Mines of Moria, slowly getting comfortable.

Sites should be called Sights. It's fantastic to walk upright, gazing at incredible rock formations. Typically, caving involves crawling around in the mud and bashing skulls against a low rock ceiling. Guess the long vertical rappel skipped all the tight passages and slinking stuff; I can relax and enjoy myself.

After more exploring, we finally make it back to the rope. John is a purist and hasn't let anyone whizz in the cave. Bouncing around, barely holding it, I beg to be first, having to go so badly. Gibb's ascenders are a complicated but remarkable ascending system. One on my right foot faces inward. The next one attaches below my left knee and the last at my right shoulder. These three points connect to the rope and allow me to climb.

First, putting weight on the knee, then draw my foot up, move the knee next, finally the shoulder, and back to the knee in a cycle. Designed to inchworm up the rope, the ascenders hold me in place; as I crank, my brain focused on the need to pee, leaving no room for fear.

Popping out, yanking on the rope to indicate I'm done, then dashing to the surrounding trees for relief. My sanity returns with the loss of bladder pressure, and I notice the sun is down.

Yikes, we were inside for sixteen hours. No wonder I had to pee like a racehorse. This trip convinces me that climbing in the sun is better than crawling around in the dark.

It's fascinating, this whole clique thing. The outing club has a tussle between climbers, cavers, and water rats. Another division forms between the Syracuse students and the Stumpies who go to the Forestry School, a state-run campus next door. One would never know you've crossed the boundary, like stepping into your sister's room, the twilight zone.

Stumpies are the granola children, hippies with dogs running around, frisbees in hand, beards for men, and fur on the girls' unshaven legs. I gravitate to this crowd, repelled by the dolled-up girls at Syracuse with their tight Jordache jeans.

After the West Virginia trip, I'm elected Vice President of SUOC. The responsibility includes managing the weekly meetings and helping with the annual budget process. I'm secretly happy at the recognition; it's dandy to be wanted. Being part of the inner circle is a great feeling that my effort is appreciated. It's wonderful.

With junior-year finals approaching, my housemate Steve and I dream up the most excellent plan. After discovering that Rick and Billy are graduating and driving west for summer jobs with the Forest Service, an idea percolates in our skulls.

At Hungry Charlie's, the post-SUOC meeting watering hole, I beg Billy for a ride to Wyoming, explaining that we'll hitchhike around the west, visiting friends. Steve and I want to see the sequoia trees found in the Sierra Nevada of California. It seems a good plan as any.

With bated breath, waiting for Billy's answer, topping off his beer with a small, imploring gesture. It's his car, after all. He reaches for the mug, takes a big swig, then nods his head in agreement.

Yes! The Trip to Kiss Sequoias is coming together.

Hanging out in the E-Room after a run to Little Falls in early April, it's time for some fun. The party swells with dozens of Deadheads, Stumpies, and the full complement of climbers, cavers, and water rats, all brimming with wool sweaters and hiking boots. Nary is a disco song to be heard, and beer is swilled with gusto. Most of the walls have predictable posters of European ski resorts and Yosemite Valley, augmented with ice axes plunged tip-first into the wall.

I stroll over to Eric. "This is wild. Love this outing club. Somehow everyone gets their studying done and still has time to party."

"Ready for your trip out west?" Eric asks.

"Absolutely. I'm worried Rick and Billy will bolt out of town without us." I guzzle my beer.

"Well, that can be resolved. Camp on their porch," Eric chuckles. "Hey, what's that noise?"

Lounging against the wall near the kitchen, I look around. "It's getting louder. And closer. What the hell?"

Suddenly, a Stumpie barges up the outdoor stairs with his chainsaw roaring. The panicked crowd crushes against us to get away from the crazy loon. He stops at the door and turns it off, grinning madly as a wild man; he runs his hand along the metal, the blade removed for this stunt. Eric and I shrug and trudge past Chainsaw Guy, heading for the keg.

Having grown up in a staid high school town, the greatest gift of SUOC is the warm, welcoming embrace. My friends become my extended family, an invisible connection forged by wilderness adventure.

Regardless of personality, SUOCers are inclusive, providing the comfort of belonging. I get to choose these people as my best friends, and they choose me. This is my tribe, and it unknowingly launches me on my path to going mzungu.

~

THE BEAST IS READY. Billy's white station wagon, overloaded with four six-foot-tall dudes, heads north to Canada. While traveling west, the two possibilities are I-90 across the United States or the Trans-Canada Highway. With the option for potent Canadian beer, our route choice is obvious.

When arriving at the border, three things happen. First, the officer asks where we were born. Mentioning Kampala, Uganda, earns me a "Are you kidding me?" look.

Then he asks about firearms or weapons, and we snicker to ourselves, thinking about the Roman candles buried in the back. Oh, nothing, officer. The final straw is Billy's turntable in the rear window. "Over!" the officer yells, pointing to a parking area.

It takes forever to uncover the issue. It seems odd, but Canada is worried he'll hock it for cash. It's some customs thing. He needs to pay a $250 deposit or they'll confiscate the stereo. Disgusted, Billy gives them a check, and we bolt to Toronto, visiting as many breweries as possible to assuage our trauma.

The Beast getting unloaded to repair the rear shock, near Soo Locks
in the Upper Peninsula of Michigan, June 1981.

The first stop is Molson's for Bradors and Porters. Next to the Old Vienna Brewery and a dead end at Labatt's. Stocked with three cases of the best beer this side of Germany and tins of Skoal, we are ready to roll.

Somewhere in Ontario, the Beast blows a shock. We bounce along, nearing the border of Michigan, hoping to make it across before the car breaks down.

"Let's toss firecrackers at the buggers!" I yell over the music, "Can't let the cops push us around ."

Steve chimes in, "Let's show these Mounties some real American stereo justice."

Billy slows the car, asking, "You wanna? I can pull over."

Rick shakes his head, eyeballs rolling.

Wisdom rules, and we cross over like everyone else and stop in Soo Locks, Michigan, to buy a new shock. The repair begins at a nearby scenic park after emptying the Beast. I can't believe this much junk can fit into a car.

After a swim in the conveniently located lake, we push on, spending the night in Wausau, Wisconsin, on the side of the road. We never thought of staying in a motel. Sleeping out under the stars is the SUOC way.

Saturday takes us to the Badlands, where we bake in the sun, ogling at the vibrant red, orange, and yellow colors in the arid land. We blast to the Black Hills and camp under a much more excellent grove of Ponderosa Pine trees.

After dinner, we head into Deadwood and cruise the bar scene. It's fun to think we're modern cowboys, sitting in the seats of Jesse James and Billy the Kid, quaffing mugs of beer and shots of whiskey. Too much playacting for me, and feeling woozy, I head back to the car and crash.

"Flinny, wake up, you clown!" Steve's voice stirs me from a comfortable slumber. "You're lucky you bailed. Fifteen minutes after you left, the cops checked IDs at the bar."

Rubbing my eyes and sitting up, "Holy crap, my spider sense must have been going gangbusters. Thank God." I'm the young one, still not twenty-one.

Rick laughs. "You would have been dragged off to jail, for sure."

Steve anxiously waiting for dinner outside Soo Locks,
Michigan in June 1981.

I move over to let him sit down. "Sometimes too many drinks are a good thing."

The next day we tour the Black Hills, Custer State Park, and Mount Rushmore. Monday takes us past the Devil's Tower, where Rick and Billy drop us in Buffalo, Wyoming.

After a round of hugs, they drive off, the Beast riding a bit higher as smoke belches from the muffler. With the easy travel over, Steve and I are on our own.

STANDING on the side of the road, the reality of our plan dawns on me as another car zips past. I imagined buzzing around carefree, bumble-bees hopping from car to car, darting from town to town, the miles ripping by.

"Sorry, man," I say to Steve. "Hitchhiking seemed like a good idea back in Syracuse, enthralled by *Zen and the Art of Motorcycle Maintenance*. The lure of the open road, charting my own path to create structure in a chaotic world. I didn't plan on having to wait for a flipping ride. Expectation is failing to match reality."

"Yeah, it's a drag standing around chewing tobacco to pass the time," Steve agrees. "Beats sitting in Organic Chemistry with some boring TA droning on. Don't worry; someone will stop." Steve's the best; he always has a sunny outlook.

I scuff my boots against the asphalt. "Of course, two big scruffy guys with backpacks have nothing to do with our luck." A gust blows dust in my face.

I spent Thanksgiving at his parent's house last year. It was a madhouse, packed with relatives in a comfortable home in Queens, an easy subway ride from Manhattan. Not having this experience growing up, I loved the chaos of the large Italian family. Most importantly, I learned spaghetti sauce is called "gravy."

Finally, we get a ride in a tricked-out Bronco, loud disco Bee Gees blaring. The guy riding shotgun nods off, ripping a snore as he snoozes. The driver reaches over and jabs him in the ear. After asking where we're from, he pontificates, "New York, yep, New York. That place, it's a jungle." They let us off outside Cheyenne, where we spend hours waiting for the rain or a ride. The ride wins.

A California girl picks us up in a Toyota. She wears Red Baron sunglasses and drives us to the mountains. Camping under lodgepole pines with a smattering of Douglas fir, the sagebrush smells pleasant when smushed. A hearty spaghetti meal follows. We sleep by a raging river roaring as loud as a freight train.

In the morning, blisters the size of mongooses appear on my heels. I diligently paste them with Band-Aids before putting my boots on.

On our next hitch, the driver proudly discloses that he's been arrested for dozens of speeding tickets.

It gets weirder as we score a ride with a Hunter Thompson-like fellow whose truck is stocked with beers. "Damn Christians! I guess it's all right if you want tunnel vision," says the crazed swimming pool salesman from California. We appreciate the free beer but are glad to get out of the car in Jackson Hole, where the trail and rain begin.

I was hanging out in the Tetons in June 1981.

We spend the day bushwhacking. Too proud to say I'm lost; at least my trusty map and compass give me a clue to where we are: somewhere in the Tetons.

I've never seen such a dramatic skyline as the sun goes down. Clouds encircle the jagged mountains; knife edges beckon the climber in me.

The rain descends, enclosing us in fog and drizzle, the glory of the vista dripping away. The mud gets worse, threatening to swallow our boots.

We reach an opening in the forest the size of a runway, fallen dead lodgepole pines scattered like matchsticks. Halfway across, stepping over a big tree, I glance up to see a moose ten feet away. His antlers are huge. We both have bug eyes, watching each other, wondering what to do.

Steve is quiet as we ponder our way out of this predicament. The downed trees make running impossible. Luckily, the moose snorts and steps away.

"Whoa, excellent," Steve says. "I could have reached out and touched his antlers. Almost peed in my pants."

"Did you see the size of his nose? Way more exciting than swatting mosquitoes! Dang, I hate this rain. Can't it stop for a day?" I ask the universe.

"Lots of luck with that prayer. I bet my underwear is growing mold as we speak."

"Don't need that visual."

Our slog continues for hours, but we find the trail and stagger like zombies. Our food supply is low, and my attempt at fishing is a total failure. Drenched with rain and jittery from the moose scare, we're toast, dreaming of pizza.

My poncho is useless; I'm sick of being wet. Bedraggled like a drowned rat, this is getting old. Our tarp barely keeps us dry; my down sleeping bag is a lump of useless muck.

Stopping to wring out my shirtsleeves, lo and behold, I stumble upon a cooler. Unbelievable! Not hidden in the bushes as it should be, but smack dab in the middle of the trail, a glistening white Styrofoam gift from the universe.

We open it to discover steak, wine, cheese, Champagne, bacon, eggs, hot dogs, lettuce, and orange juice.

It seems the Ponderosa God is looking over us starving children. Mouth watering, I'm about to rip into the juice when a fellow in his late twenties jogs down the trail.

We apologize and mumble sympathies, but he isn't too upset. Instead, he gives us some hot dogs, cheese, and eggs.

I've learned to beware of temptation when cold and delirious. But still, he shouldn't have left the cooler in the middle of the trail, waiting to be pillaged by bears or starving hikers.

Tired of being cold and damp, we dump the hiking and return to hitching. "What's up with that dude and his cooler," I say as another car whizzes by, ignoring us.

Steve yawns. "I still can't figure out where he came from with all that food. To think of carrying a Styrofoam cooler for miles. Talk about glamorous camping."

"I'm fond of his style. Beats ramen noodles and peanut butter any day."

As another car ignores us, Steve belts out a comment that makes me chuckle. I can't imagine slogging through that rain-infested swamp of the Tetons without him. Even in the worst downpour, trying to keep a fire going to dry my sleeping bag, Steve is cracking jokes and making me laugh.

A boisterous and bubbly woman in a car smothered with Arizona WABC bumper stickers gives us a lift to Yellowstone, where we sweet-talk a rookie ranger into giving us a ride.

She dumps us off in West Thumb, and we camp at Duck Lake. I catch zero fish but enjoy a fine sunset in Yellowstone Park. The days start to blur into each other as we flit from car to car.

~

I'm trying to score a ride with a "Beyond Eureka" sign
in Northern California in June 1981.

"HEY, SISTER DEAR, HOW ARE THINGS?" Wedged into a tiny phone booth, I'm pleased to hear Lissa's voice.

"My job stinks, the boss is a bum, but it's not that bad. Where are you?"

"Steve and I are stuck in some God-awful small town in California. I had to walk a ton to get here. At least this diner has a phone. Glad to hear you're working. Someone has to since I'm screwing off. How're Mom and Dad?"

Lissa sighs. "Mom's back from the doctor. It's not arthritis. The doctor says it's something else. Dad doesn't tell me anything."

My usual bouncy self goes somber. Lissa is three years younger, has glorious strawberry-blonde hair and blue eyes, and melts the hearts of all the boys.

I used to call her Pest and pound on her as a big brother should. But I've grown up and learned to appreciate having a real friend. "Darn, it's not fair. I hope the cancer's not coming back."

"I overheard Mom and Dad talking about it. I'm a bit scared, David."

"Me too. Hey, is Mom home? I'm hoping to say hi."

"Nope. They're both at some church dinner. Psyched that they let me stay home. Those affairs are dull."

"No boys your age, right?" I guess, smiling. "Well, I'll try back in a few days. Time to get going. I love you!"

Placing the phone gently in its cradle, I face the grimy glass of the phone booth, the sun trapped behind the clouds in the west, thinking of Mom.

Standing on the highway, getting super weird looks as the hours ebb by. Wondering why I'm doing this for the tenth time. Pondering dire thoughts that maybe it's time to jump on a Greyhound bus.

And so we did. After relaxing at a friend's house in Berkeley for a few days, Steve and I get a sweet ride outside Monterey north of Big Sur. The van driver from Philly invites us to stay with him as he heads south to Los Angeles. We drop Steve at the airport days later to fly home for his job.

"It's been a blast, man," I say after giving Steve a goodbye hug. "You're the best travel buddy I ever had."

My fuel truck with the Hughes 500D fire patrol helicopter at the Wind
River Indian Reservation, Wyoming. August 1981.

"Ha, I'm the only buddy you ever had." He punches me in the arm.
"You're lucky to have me. Be solid, and I'll see you back in Syracuse."

Steve grabs his pack and stomps off into the terminal. He stops at
the door and turns back to wave. He's right. I'm lucky to have such a
wonderful friend, and I miss him already. Well, sort of.

Van Man and I drive to the Grand Canyon. After being a tourist
gawking at the sights, I say goodbye and hitch north, heading to
Yellowstone.

Outside of Lander, Wyoming, a radical change in plan occurs. I'm
picked up by a Bureau of Indian Affairs fire patrol helicopter pilot. A
few minutes into the drive, he offers me a job I can't refuse. He needs a
new fuel truck driver with an upcoming move to Montana.

I ponder this crazy opportunity for fifteen seconds and commit to
five weeks before school starts. The next day, his company flies me
round trip to Denver to sign some papers, and two days later, I'm on
the job.

Stationed on the Wind River Indian Reservation, I work eleven
hours a day, seven days a week. While it entails lots of sitting around

waiting for a forest fire to start, I'll clear $1200 before heading back to school. Pay off my debts and still have $500 in the bank. Sweet.

At the airport one day, after filling the truck with Jet A fuel for the chopper, I call home.

"Hi guys," I say when Mom and Dad get on the phone. "Happy twenty-second wedding anniversary!"

"Thanks, David. It's good to hear your voice. Are you safe and sound in Wyoming?" Mom asks.

"Yes, I'm still here. And it's funny you should ask. This morning I celebrated your marriage with a kerosene bath."

My parents immediately stammer in unison, "W-what? Are you okay?"

"Yeah, I think so. When refueling the chopper, I forgot to tighten the pressure value on the filtration system. As soon as I started pumping fuel, gas sprayed out in an eight-foot radius, soaking me."

"You're not wearing those clothes, David?" Dad asks hopefully.

"The folks at the airport let me shower in their bathroom. I'm not the first one; it seems to happen frequently. Glad no one lit a cigarette nearby!"

"You're fortunate, and I'm glad you're safe," he says.

I continue chattering, telling them enough to make them comfortable, and they relax, happy I'm not hitchhiking anymore. Most parents prefer their kids to study or work. Hitching around the West is not high on their list of Experiences I Want My Child to Have.

One fine bluebird day—sunny with a clear blue sky—the pilot takes a couple of Shoshone up in the chopper, where they shoot an elk from the sky and land to retrieve the carcass. We sit around later, slugging beers and munching freshly grilled venison. Afterward, the Shoshone lads head home, and I'm left dousing the fire, watching the sunset's last pink and orange glow fade over the hills.

In mid-August, the chopper moves to Crow Agency in Montana. The gig is the same, but a local takes me to a Crow Pow Wow. I'm the only mzungu in attendance; I didn't even think about bringing my camera.

Overwhelmed is an understatement. A bit nervous at first, but I felt comfortable and welcome. So much to observe and absorb. Many folks are decked out in full garb, happily singing traditional Crow songs and marching around the huge bonfire.

Grateful for the trust in giving me a glimpse into their world. It seems so natural; I'm drawn to their connections with the earth and the desire to celebrate their heritage. I wonder if they have Pow Wows in Uganda.

Time flits by, and weeks later, I find myself on a plane out of Denver. Watching the clouds scud by the window as I reflect on the past few months. I loved the pace of traveling, hopping from car to car, meeting different people, building trust one hitch at a time, and making friends instantly. Schmoozing to obtain the best drop, avoiding town centers—the literal no-hitch zone—and plodding to the edge of town. Freeway entrance ramps are optimal, where cars go slowly, making it easy to see me and pull over. There's much to learn about life wandering around using my thumb.

When the landing wheels emit a loud clunk, as if they are falling out of the plane, I realize summer is over. Back to school and the real world. Bearable knowing that my adventures will continue, eager to climb like a mzungu.

My senior year kicks into full stride as classes and SUOC fill my time. After a bunch of day trips to Little Falls, it's November, and time to head to the Gunks in New Paltz, a three-hour drive southeast of Syracuse. I'm still learning and getting used to top-roping, but my first foray into lead climbing will be a major development.

The Mohonk Preserve is a large, privately-owned park chock full of trees, trails, carriage roads, and some of the best climbing in the East. The Shawangunk Mountains form a ridge of quartz and sandstone, like a stack of pancakes, making for steep and overhanging routes. The horizontal cracks provide great holds and excellent anchors.

We're roping up at the Uberfall[3], the prime area in the Trapps region, a short slog from the road. The easy approach makes it a dream for climbers, the gateway to single and multi-pitch lead climbs. A pitch is a section partitioned by belay anchors, constrained by the length of the 150-foot rope.

Weaving a webbing harness around my torso and legs, I anchor the belay to a massive tree at the base. Since the club doesn't have protective gear, the leader must supply their own equipment.

Woody graduated from law school a few years ago but is happy to travel on SUOC trips. He's a great climber, and his focus and energy are welcome. Not to mention his gear.

The lead climber is exposed to a nasty fall without secure protection —temporary anchors that look like colossal machine nuts. Small pieces of nylon rope allow a carabiner to connect the pro to the rope. I get why Gaston calls climbing a puzzle; lots of nuance and tricks are required to make things safe.

I belay Woody as he grinds up the route. When it's my turn, it's like top-roping; the real work is for the lead climber. The rock is excellent, and the route can't be too hard since it doesn't take me long.

Turning around at the belay starts the ol' caterpillars a-crawling. Vertigo threatens—one hundred feet straight down—as climbers mill around like bugs on the ground. But the fantastic view makes the exposure worth it. Glad Woody's with me; I wouldn't want to be here all by myself.

Afterward, we visit the famous Rock and Snow climbing store in downtown New Paltz. John Bouchard, a rad climber from New Hampshire, presents slides of a bold ascent on the *Eiger North Face* in Switzerland. His alpine-style approach took only an impressive 15 hours, rather than the usual three days.

Fascinated, I ask what he carried with him on the climb after the show. He laughs and says, "Candy bars and sweaters!" I gather taking less stuff is the way to go. Lighter is righter.

~

AFTER A FESTIVE CHRISTMAS AT HOME, January 1982 kicks off with an ice-climbing bang. Supposedly, it's similar to rock climbing, with the same concepts of anchors, ropes, and belays.

Eric getting the hang of things, Lick Brook Falls, New York. Note the use of ice leashes. February, 1982.

And then there are these things called crampons and ice axes, used to create holds by poking them into ice.

It's a cold Saturday as we trundle down the road, arriving at Tinker's Falls[4] thirty minutes later. Approaching the ravine, the walls steepen slowly, ending at a cute 40' waterfall brimming with frozen wonder.

Thirty feet wide with a ten-foot vertical section, the ice looks like celery stalks stacked on top of car-sized broccoli crowns. Up close, the solid blue ice shows its strength, compared to the fragile white icicles that shatter when whacked with an axe.

To the right of the ice pillar, Bob and Marla guide us up the scraggly trail to the ravine rim. They rig a top rope around a lovely birch tree, planning to lower us into the ravine to climb. They don't want to mess around with rappelling to ensure we tie in correctly and get the hang of climbing. After, we can try the more advanced stuff. But first, a speech.

We gather around our teachers, fifty feet away from the edge, to avoid any chance of toppling off the 100' ravine wall.

Bob says, "Climbing ice is straightforward since you already know the basics. Your ice axes are sharp, so please be careful not to whack the rope."

"Focus on your toes," Marla adds. "It's easy to fixate on the axes; remember to set your feet shoulder-width apart and keep them side-by-side. Then swing away."

Bob continues. "Place your first axe high, like trying to hit a nail with a hammer." He demonstrates against a tree but is careful not to damage the trunk; he is a Stumpie, after all.

"Once the axes are planted, hang on your arms, bend your knees, kick one boot into the ice, then the other. Once set, pull up on the two tools, and stand."

Marla says, "You need to be robotic, moving your hands first, then your feet. Very different from rock climbing."

Bob concludes, "So that's it for the lecture. Gaston, how about you first, then Flinny, followed by Eric."

The ice flows down the eighty-degree slope, a carpet six inches thick, with the occasional tree hanging on for dear life. We give it a whirl; of course, Gaston is a natural.

It's a bit awkward to get the hang of it, but I quickly learn to appreciate the wonderful *thwack* of the axe finding its home in the ice.

Dangling like a monkey, sticking my butt out, using the crampons take some practice. Marla's right; it's easy to get distracted whaling away with the ice tools.

Stepping on knobs of ice is easier than kicking; the sharp crampons bite quickly. Nearly fall after an aggressive leg extension. My right foot blows off, but I'm still hanging on, thanks to the tight rope. Phew.

On the way back to the cars, I ask Eric his thoughts on climbing ice.

"It's almost as good as rock. Great that I can create my own holds. Danged gear is heavy, though."

I settle my daypack, shifting the snowy rope looped over my shoulder. "Well, yeah. Anything more profound?"

Eric steps over an open spot in the frozen streambed, "I like the construction aspect of it. It's fun flicking my wrist, using the leash to pivot the axe into the ice." He demonstrates with his empty hand.

Gaston climbing the ravine ice flows at Tinkers Falls,
New York. January 1982.

I reply. "Gotta try your trick next time; I was focused on my feet. One thing I don't care for is waiting to climb in the frigging cold. Like hitch-hiking, too much standing around."

Gaston says, "There is that. Perhaps you should try soloing. No more waiting." Soloing is another form of climbing, leaving the ropes behind to save time and hassle. With the risk of plunging to the ground, splat city kitty.

I comment, "Heavy thoughts. I'll stay on the rope, thank you; no need to go hog wild." The end of the micro-hike is near; the road noise is getting louder.

"Sounds like you're going on the next trip, then?" Eric says.

Gaston pipes in. "Absolutely! I'm looking forward to trying one of the ice pillars."

Two weeks later, we head over to Lick Brook Falls.[5] The 140' *Upper Falls* is an insanely steep portion of fat blue ice, huge bulges of cauliflower at the bottom, topped with vertical carrots. Come to think of it, more like Nature's very own upside-down ice cream cone.

We watch some radical dudes go for the pillar. I'm not ready to climb such a monster. Fortunately, we wander down to the *Lower Falls* and set up a top rope.

The waterfall of ice flows like a staircase, vertical in places with broad landings to rest. It's exposed, and I feel great out in the wild with no trees nearby. I don't know why, but I feel safer without the bushes and rocks around me. It takes a lot of concentration to climb; I have to put my past and future worries aside and focus on the now.

Eric's trick works. Holding the shaft with my fingers and the ice axe leash tight around my wrist allows me to flick my hand forward, sending the axe in a smooth arc, resulting in a solid thunk.

After my third try, the sequence of my hands and feet is starting to jell, where I'm in rhythm and having fun, splayed out like a gymnast on a balance beam.

THE BEAUTY of Chapel Pond unfolds at the parking turnout. A ten-yard stroll brings me to the snowy edge of the pond. Nestled in the High Peaks of the Adirondacks, I'm mesmerized.

Gazing to the right, the water drains out into Chapel Pond Canyon. Turning around behind me, the Washbowl Cliffs loom across the street; the hardest rock climbs around. Another ninety-degree pivot to the right, the famous Chapel Pond Slabs can be seen through the trees.

The cliffs directly across the pond rear up off the ice, steep and forbidding. *Chouinard's Gully*[6] is the prominent ice line where Bob, Marla, and I are going, my first multi-pitch ice climb.

Marla after a great day ice climbing at Tinkers Falls,
New York, January 1982.

The day is gloomy gray, typical for winter in the mountains. We gingerly cross the ice, and I wonder if it's safe. The thought of falling in causes my stomach to rumble. Luckily, things calm down once we tie into the rope.

Bob is a confident Wildlife Bio Major. And it's clear he's going to work with animals. His white Samoyed "Bow" is the most mellow dog in SUOC. Bob is focused and driven to be the best, whether in school or climbing. Definitely from the "work hard, play hard" crowd.

Bob belaying Marla on *Chouinard's Gully* in Chapel Pond
Pass, Adirondacks February 1982.

He leads and sets belays with trees and ice screws as protection.
These half-inch wide tubular metal cylinders are six to eight inches long.
The screw threads on the outside twist into delicious fat ice and create
an illusion of security. In theory, ice screws will hold 1000 pounds, but I
don't want to test it.

The best part is the continuous nature of the ice flow. Top-roping is
okay, but this longer climb gives me the true feeling of the sport. Instead
of a short, repetitive activity, this is a real adventure.

Stopping to remove Bob's ice screw, I'm feeling good. The sucker is
cranked in solid; a truck could hang off it, but a total bitch to get out.
Guess that's the point. Making the mistake of looking down the gully, I
can't believe I climbed so far. My belly gurgles, so I get back to business.

The value of teamwork becomes apparent when I get perplexed, and
Marla boosts my confidence. The spruce thicket at the top leaves no
room to hang out, so we thrash down climber's left (looking up at the
climb) to avoid messing around with three rappels.

Sitting in the snowbanks covering the boulders on the edge of Chapel Pond, I feel awed by my accomplishment. Recalling my twinge of fear at the ice screw, I ask Bob if he was scared on the lead.

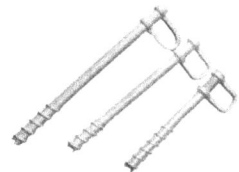

Salewa ice screws from the 1980s. Note the loop to clip a carabiner into a sling and rope.

"It's a tough thing to admit, but yeah, a little. The challenge in climbing ice is that the leader really can't fall. To prevent making mistakes, I go into the zone and avoid any mental distractions."

Marla says, "I'm glad you didn't mention you were scared."

"Men aren't supposed to show weakness, right? According to James Bond, never admit defeat, and you'll always get the girl." He reaches over to give Marla an affectionate bear hug.

Wow, what a life. I'm a little jealous—a girlfriend who likes to climb. Bob does have it made.

MARCH ROLLS around with the annual West Virginia trip, where I plan to stay clear of caving. Driving down with Eric and two girls makes the eight-hour ride zip by. It's great getting to know them; they're sisters by the time we get there. It's great not getting all sex-crazed and weird. Heck with all that.

I spend four days on Seneca Rocks learning how to set up top ropes. We siege the west face of South Peak and trundle up the *Old Man's Route* to a vast ledge as basecamp.

Then onto the summit to rig ropes on *Critter Crack, Le Gourmet,* and *Crispy Critters.* Around the corner, someone named a route *Tomato.* Guess the first ascenders were hungry.

The sedimentary rock is similar to the Gunks but uplifted 90 degrees, white-boned granite that feels gritty as sandstone but with solid holds. Lots of exposure; the entire cliff is only 250 feet wide at the base. The top of South Peak forms a knife-edge ridge that narrows to the width of a sidewalk. Over 300 feet high, it's safe but airy; I've no desire to risk a tumble.

The trip's highlight is climbing *The Gendarme*[7], a snippet of rock that juts up twenty-five feet, detached from the main cliff. Located in the center of the prominent gunsight notch, a SUOC leader establishes a top rope on *The Gendarme*, and now it's my turn to climb.

I've watched the others do it, but my belly crawls with tension, threatening to unravel. Partly a fear of failure, of being ashamed to fall in front of my friends. Mostly it's just plain scary.

Steadying myself, with hands on the rock, looking down at my feet, closing my eyes, and exhaling deeply. Knowing that if my friends can do it, I can, too.

Look down, use your feet, focus. Wedging my toes into the three-inch vertical crack, my hands clasping the flakes on the sides. *It's easy; you can do it.*

The Gendarme (it fell in 1987) in the gunsight notch of the South Peak, Seneca Rocks in West Virginia, March 1982. Note that the book's front cover captures me on top of *The Gendarme*.

I launch, motoring quickly to pull over the top. Crouching down, the exposed summit is barely two feet wide. Gaining courage as I rise, hands outstretched in success. It feels incredible to stand on top of a pinnacle 200' off the deck. Ready to fly like an eagle.

~

PEER PRESSURE GETS me elected SUOC president for the next school year. The club knows I graduate in December, but they don't mind. I'm told this happens all the time. The glory of being a top dog must have got to me.

The warden at Dad's church found me a summer job as a supervisor on a work crew. It's a bit awkward bossing around people twice my age. Very weird. Making money, but I miss the everyday life of school and climbing.

Finally, it's time to head back to Syracuse for my last semester. The geography courses are interesting, and I knuckle down to finish my final papers. Luckily, I get a break and dash to the Adirondacks in October with Bob and Marla.

There's no better place than the Chapel Pond Slabs for long run-outs, low-angle friction, and hundreds of feet of pure fun. Boulders are scattered around the base of the slabs, a few over twenty feet high. There's a collection I call the Three Trolls, similar to those Bilbo found in *The Hobbit*.

Bouldering is a form of climbing that requires no ropes; the climber versus the rock. A fifteen-foot fall would snap an ankle, so I stay mellow and down-climb when I get scared. We sleep at the base, near the boulders, classic car camping. We can't belay from the car, but the road is only a few hundred yards to the Slabs.

Saturday morning dawns with a bluebird sky, perfect for climbing the *Regular Route*[8]. Bob does the leading, Marla goes second, and I climb last. Slab climbing is a ballet where balance is the ticket.

Marla is my kind of teacher. She grew up in a Washington D.C. suburb, and due to her compact frame, was an excellent gymnast. Burned out by the competitive nature of the sport, she gravitated to climbing and is excellent at teaching the importance of friction.

The French company EB produced the innovative Super Gratton in the 1970s.

Unlike my climbs up till now, slabs require elegance, and brute strength is almost useless. Friction is the key, using my weight to force a precise foothold. Like ice climbing, sticking my buns out forces my toes into the smidge of a dent in the rock.

Luckily, a few weeks ago, I bought some EBs from another SUOCer. The tight-fitting climbing shoes are essential on the long route, a full day of eight pitches. Rappelling would have taken way too long. Fortunately, we can hike off to climber's right.

Back at camp, we scrounge for wood to make a small campfire. Finally, I get the flame to catch and sit back on a small boulder, satisfied.

Marla comes over and hugs me. "Dave, any thoughts about today?"

"It was spectacular, so wonderful to have a long, sustained climb."

Marla laughs, "That's a bit vague; how did you feel?"

"Climbing takes all my attention. Every foot placement or handhold needs to be precise. Now I feel alive, energized, and ready to deal with the real world. The art of balance fascinates me, as does the capacity to trust my body to do the right thing."

Marla pokes the fire. "Exactly, just like gymnastics. It's all about the right kind of movement, a dance. I love the whole process. The planning, traveling here, and then the climbing."

Bob jumps in, "I love the doing part. I believe I'm achieving something that no one else can."

Marla adds, "Climbing's a philosophy where I treat my life as one big climb. Today was yet another cog in the wheel of climbing my life."

"Life climbing, I like that," Bob says.

Live to climb, climb to live—life in a nutshell.

And I'm the squirrel, gnawing on the nut, trying to break in and reward myself with the riches.

◦

NOVEMBER IS THE BIG MEETING, and I'm nervous. It's up to me to bag the loot. The president needs to lobby the university annually to justify the budget request. Club tradition uses personal transportation, freeing up university money for equipment. The meeting goes well, I answer a few questions, and the board approves the $8000 cash. Sweet.

Celebrating at Hungry Charlie's with pitchers of beer, the tribe is in full force. A brown-haired girl sits next to Marla, and I plunk myself between them. She's new to SUOC, and her green eyes sparkle. The beer helps me chat normally and not be all shy as usual.

Filling her mug, I say, "We're going to the Adirondacks over New Year's. Skiing into Avalanche Pass to camp and climb *The Trap Dike*. Are you interested?"

Katy owns her neophyte status with style. "I hope to try cross-country skiing. I've done a lot of downhill."

"Well, you came to the right place. We have tons of skis." Finishing my mug, "You sure you don't want to try ice climbing?"

Katy chuckles. "You sound like Marla. Lots of subtle hinting. You guys are a cult."

"Great idea for this year's T-shirts: 'Join SUOC, the outdoor cult.'"

We continue chatting about the usual things, and the pitchers are soon empty. The crowd thins out, and it's time to go. "Katy, it's nice to meet you. Hope to see you out on skis after New Year's."

"Ditto. And you're not bad for a politician."

I give Katy and Marla hugs as they depart. The rest of the crowd teases me, but I don't care. Cute girls make everything better.

IT'S my second lap up the mountain, and I'm toast. No food since breakfast and my pack is stuffed with sixty-five pounds of climbing gear. I'm tired of being a porter. The lack of snow on the trail makes for an ominous premonition for New Year's Eve 1982.

Flummoxed by the unusually warm temperatures, Bob, Marla, and I moved our Adirondack trip to New Hampshire, bringing along six beginners. It's my first ice-climbing foray on Mount Washington, notorious for its annual death toll of at least one mountaineer.

Taking a break, munching on a Hershey's bar for an energy boost. The night is cool, the moon hidden behind the mountain. Wedged between rocks in the trail next to my boot, ice sparkles in the headlamp light. The thin crust of frost crunches loudly when I continue up the path.

My mind wanders with the realization that I've graduated and need to figure out what to do with my life. In high school, I caddied at Round Hill Country Club. That's no future. I could be a guide. Sell gear to the masses? Better to use my Geography degree and get a job building maps. Maybe find a sugar momma and play all day. My body plods up the trail while the possibilities mount in my brain.

Finding the right fork in the trail, I continue the grind to the Harvard Cabin, my Last Homely House, a basecamp to explore Mount Washington's winter wonderland.

With my career still unsettled, the glowing porch light beckons me like a moth to the flame.

Rhea and Bow, Marla's and Bob's famous white dogs, greet me at the door. The vibe is bouncy and upbeat. After easing the mammoth pack into a spot in the corner, I proceed with welcoming hugs to my friends. The cabin is cheerful, the wood stove at the back of the wall purring away.

The caretaker's closet of a room and tiny kitchen are nestled in the rear, the open space filled with two picnic tables and a few chairs. The sleeping loft is upstairs, where the heat settles and makes for a wonderful night's sleep that keeps winter at bay.

"Marla, where are the others?" I ask, starting to fill a large pot with water for pasta.

"Bob took them up *Pinnacle Gully*[9] this morning. Thank goodness they got an early start. Three on a rope is slow. That must be why they're late."

Firing the stove and waiting for the water to boil, I look over at Marla. "You're not worried about them, are you?"

"Heck yeah, I'm worried sick. They should be back by now." She sniffles. "I know they're prepared, carrying bivouac gear and headlamps. Still, something could have happened to them."

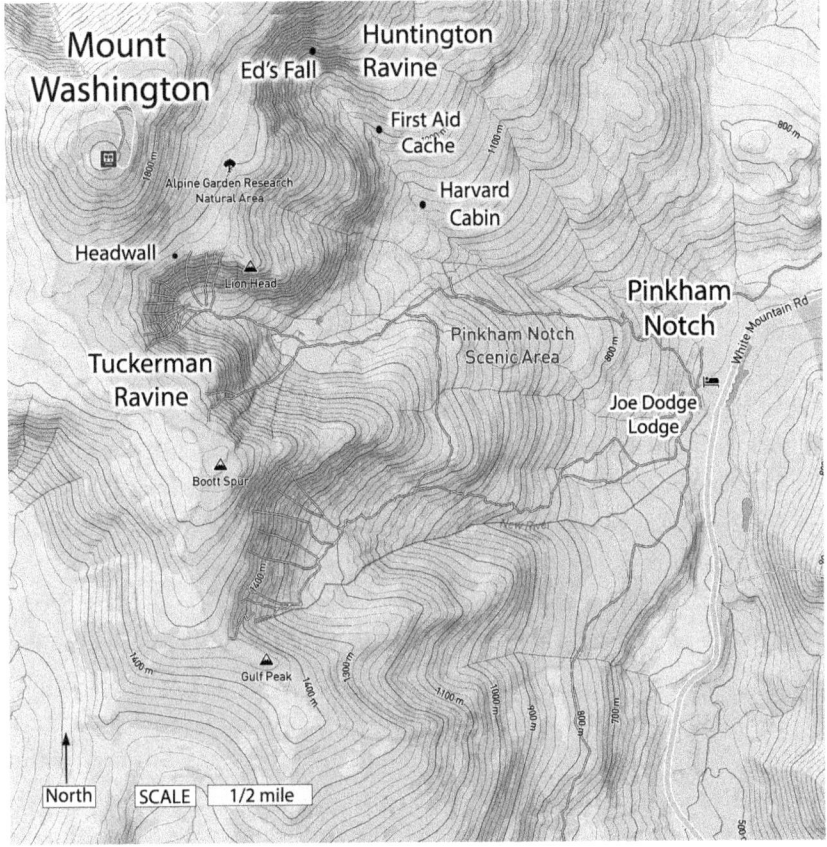

Mount Washington is a playground for wilderness-loving outdoor
adventurers, including ice climbers.

"I bet they waited for the moon to rise. Climbing down must be a
bitch without snow. Bob would sit tight and wait for the extra light." I
hug her. "Let's eat something; I know I'll feel better."

She smiles half-heartedly, reaching for the spaghetti sauce. It's
wonderful being close to her, absorbing her life glow, making me happy.
Platonic, yeah, but who cares? Life's too short not to seize the opportunity. Marla could be my sister, a friend to cherish and appreciate. My
bowl is quickly emptied as I scarf down the pasta.

Since our climbers have not returned, the leftovers wait on the stove.
Being New Year's Eve, out comes the booze, and the fun starts. I try my
luck at checkers with Ed, a Freshman and one of the beginners.

"Have you ice climbed before?" I ask him, placing my piece forward on the board.

"No, not yet. I've practiced rock climbing at Little Falls, but never on ice. Heck, it's the first time I've been further north than the Catskills."

"Not many mountains in Brooklyn, I imagine."

My smirk turns into a pout as Ed jumps my double black piece with his red. "It's a bummer that winter missed the Adirondacks. At least it made it here to Mount Washington."

"Marla took me up to Huntington Ravine today. We saw ice high in the gullies."

As Ed jumps another of my pieces, my frown deepens. "I wonder if we can play in the ravine and practice glissades and self-arrests."

"It looked possible to me. Marla mentioned it's a good place for us to start tomorrow."

"I'm looking forward to it. It's my second year on ice, and I'm happy to take it slow and easy. Never been here before, either." Finally, I make a move.

Ed grabs his piece and jumps me. "The ravine is awesome. Raw, intense, barren. We'll have fun. Psyched to be here on this grand adventure!"

Pushing back from the table, I smile and stand. "Well, that does it for me. I always lose at checkers. It's potty time."

Stepping outside to visit the outhouse, its outline profiled against the mountain, moonlight peeking, throwing blades of light throughout the forest. Breath fogs my headlamp, adding to the spooky sense of it all. The door groans as its opens. I sit and respect the pee. Girls hate it when guys spray all over the seat. Fantastic to see Ensolite foam as a toilet seat liner against the chill. Ingenious to use a sleeping pad for tushy warmth.

The photo of a woman ice climbing decorates the inside of the door —motivation in all the right places. Smiling, I wonder if she would be interested in me. Perhaps soloing *Pinnacle Gully* to ski off the headwall, I can be her badass boyfriend.

Returning to the cabin, the moon lights up the landscape, and pools of ice sparkle in their reflections. It's a memorable evening, a brisk twenty degrees, with no wind. The creaking trees reminds me of their struggle to keep the water inside their bark from freezing.

Back in the hut, Marla is getting worried. "Dave, we need to go look for them. It's taking too long."

The hut manager agrees. "It would be good to have someone take a peek. No need for glory; simply see if everything's okay."

"How many should go?" I ask.

"Three would be good. Safe but fast."

Marla and I chat with the others, and the search party is quickly organized.

"Head up to the first aid cache in Huntington Ravine and look around," I tell the group.

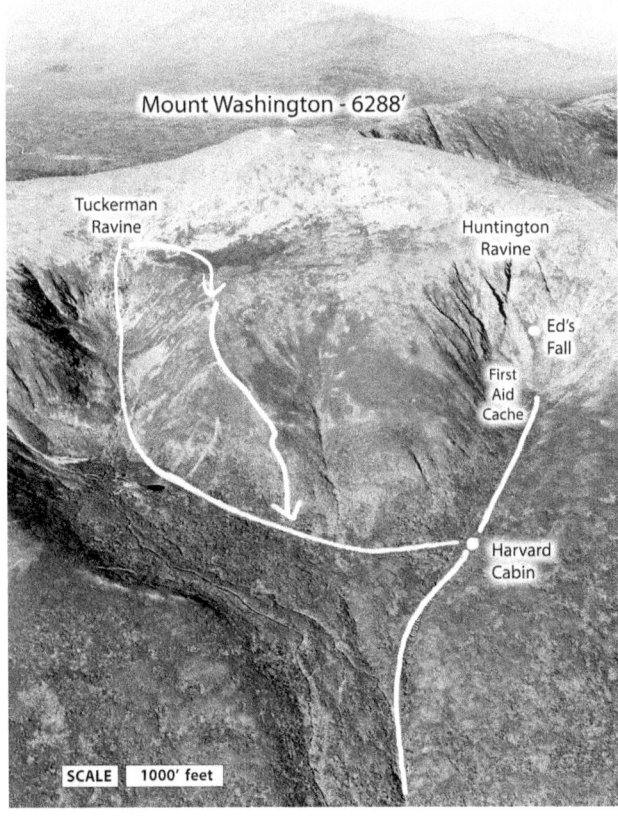

Looking west towards Mount Washington's Tuckerman and Huntington Ravines in New Hampshire.

Marla adds, "We need to see if they are in trouble. Bob knows what he's doing."

The searchers get ready. Ed borrows my headlamp, and off they go, leaving heavy ice tools behind.

"Come here, Bow Bear." Marla reaches up and grabs the large white Samoyed. Bow is the most mellow and wonderful dog, always cuddly with six inches of fur, a small polar bear. Rhea weasels in, never happy to have Marla give attention to another. "Oh, Dave, I'm worried. I need to go look for them."

"Let's wait a bit more. The lads should return shortly. Fifteen more minutes, then we'll go." I try to speak with confidence. "They'll be back, I'm sure of it. When is the question."

Dire thoughts trickle through my mind as the wind rustles through the trees. Standing on the cabin porch, looking back toward the ravine, the moon glowing as it nears full. I've never been up in the mountains in winter. The harsh alpine conditions bear down on me. This is not my intimate Chapel Pond in the Adirondacks.

Ice crunches, and one of the searchers runs up, panting, out of breath. I follow him into the cabin as he tells of lights to the right of *Damnation Gully*.

"The other two are trying to reach the three climbers. I figured I should run back."

"You did the right thing," the hut manager says. "I'll grab the portable Motorola radio and head up there. Anyone else?"

Marla jumps up. "I'm coming."

They leave quickly, and I'm reeling, sleepy and warm, trying to adapt to the situation. Still exhausted after my second run up the mountain, I opt to stay in the cabin, reluctant to become another tragedy. My worries unravel in my gut.

❧

SOMETIME AROUND MIDNIGHT, Ed fell. What happened is pieced together from everyone's stories. The remaining two in the search party tried to reach the three climbers, scaling a talus slope to avoid the dense alder and spruce thickets.

A hundred feet from the climbers, Ed slipped down a forty-five-degree ramp and fell off a twenty-foot cliff. The remaining searcher yelled for help. Bob directed the two climbers to continue to the first aid cache and began looking for Ed.

Bob found him lying face down on the talus below the cliff. When the last searcher arrived, they moved Ed to a more comfortable spot out of the alder brush. They cut off his backpack to administer first aid.

Bob noticed lights coming up the ravine and yelled to them. Marla and the hut manager raced up.

Seeing Ed's condition, he handed Bob the radio and ran back for the Stokes litter rescue basket at the first aid cache. Marla stayed with Bob as he talked with a Pinkham Notch ranger station paramedic.

They kept Ed company for an hour until the first EMT arrived, dashing out of his New Year's celebration and up the trail in less than an hour. More rescue volunteers came trickling up to help and begin giving Ed oxygen.

By 2 a.m., they began hauling Ed down the talus slope in the litter, trying not to jostle him. Thirty minutes later, the paramedic sent the exhausted and hypothermic Bob back to the cabin with Marla. No one from our club could help anymore.

THE SUN GLIMMERS off the loft wall, reflecting light into my eyes, and waking me. Marla and Bob slumber nearby. Life appears as it should be.

"Marla," I whisper, "it's time to help Ed. We should get up."

Even in her exhausted state, she opens her eyes, realizing I don't know. "Dave, Ed didn't make it. After you conked out, Ed died. His injuries were too severe. I'm sorry."

I'm crying, shocked by the news. Oh, no, please God, no. My mind ceases to function correctly, barely processing that Ed is gone. I pray he didn't suffer long.

Climbing downstairs to eat some cold oatmeal, the hut manager is thoughtful with his kind words. Full of anguish, sitting on the bench doesn't help me relax, so I grab my boots and trudge into the ravine.

Stumbling up the winding trail like a zombie, a rock jumps in front

The JustRite headlamp required 4 D batteries and was used by many SUOCers.

of my boot, causing me to stumble. The incident forces me into the moment, aware of the ravine unfolding before my eyes. The ice gully rivulets glow in the sun, bright white and blue contrasted by the ominous gray rock surrounding them. I hear boots crunch and look up the trail.

Four rescuers are carrying Ed, and I join them. The litter is heavy, the trail to the Harvard cabin a mess, chock full of boulders, ice, and brush to thrash through. The five of us have trouble carrying the litter, but no one speaks. The ravine is still, with no wind, just the echoes of our boots scuffing the rocks.

Back at the Harvard cabin, more marvelous people come out to help. Noticing my JustRite headlamp wedged next to Ed's body, with its cracked lens, I carefully stash it in my jacket pocket. The experts will take care of Ed. It's time to be with my friends.

The cabin is somber. Coffee percolates on the wood stove, and we sit quietly, listening, waiting. I get up and check the fire, stuffing in another log, something to do. Bob and Marla cuddle nearby, the white dogs emulating rugs underneath their feet. Grabbing the coffee pot, I fill my mug, relishing the simple ritual.

Bob is quiet; his face drawn, barely moving, not his usual cheerful self, the full brunt of the epic literally in his lap. The rest of us are statues, barely moving, dealing with the tragedy. After lunch, most of the crowd choose to bail. The cabin crouches over us, the open wood beams dark and protecting. The window dims as the sun moves west, gray in the late-afternoon light.

"Are you guys planning on leaving?" I don't need a ride; my Maverick is parked below, waiting for me.

Bob sighs and mutters, "I can't go yet. It doesn't seem right."

"The weather is glorious," Marla says. "Leaving today seems too quick. Ed's soul is still here. I need to stay and say goodbye."

Arching my back, stiff from sitting too long on the bench, I move over to a chair. "Death is something I've never faced before. I'm with you, Marla. Ed must still be here." Nothing has prepared me for this; I need time to process my feelings before returning to those who don't understand. What a horrible way to start the new year.

The cabin is dark, a lantern flickering, its smoke wafting toward the wood stove's heat. Quiet as a tomb, time to go to bed and let this awful day drift by. The hut manager's door is shut. Before heading up the ladder, I check the stove and give Bob and Marla a hug. The only window frames the midnight-blue sky with a few glittering stars. Trees swaying in the breeze, limbs creaking.

Sunday dawns clear and bright, temporarily washing away the melancholy clouds of yesterday. Cooking breakfast in the dark cabin, we sip coffee, trying to focus on everyday, mindless stuff.

I stand and stretch. "It's hard to believe I was sitting here thirty-six hours ago, laughing and playing checkers with Ed. Getting to know him, grooving on his enthusiasm at being with us."

Marla unfolds her legs and places her feet on the floor, reaching out to poke Rhea with her toe. "Yeah, he is, well, was so sweet. We had a great time tramping around the ravine and exploring. It's so sad." She wipes a tear from her eye and pulls Rhea onto her lap, the fifty-pound dog happy to oblige, craving the attention. Bob slowly and methodically combs Bow's white fur.

I pace around the small cabin, stepping over packs and ropes. Sadness is hard enough without sitting around all day. Being out and moving helps me understand my feelings. Wallowing is tough on me. I'm a climber and want to act.

Stooping to scratch Rhea's ear, "Guys, I can't stay here doing nothing. Ed is gone, but I feel he'd rather have us get out and have fun. Wanna wander over to Tuck's?"

Bob looks up, rustling Bow's fur back into place with both hands. "Yeah, sounds like a plan. It would help take my mind off things. This cabin feels like a mausoleum. Marla?"

"The dogs need a walk," she says. "Let's go."

We dress for the cold and stroll over to Tuckerman Ravine, bringing our ice axes. The mzungu in me whispers that we could play around on the headwall or practice our glissades in the snow. Do something.

Ice crunches under my San Marco mountaineering boots. Skiers flock here to ski the Headwall, but not today. As we approach the Hermit Lake Shelters, the ravine opens wide, the sun glistening, the sky deep royal blue. Despite the gloom of losing Ed, the stellar weather helps soothe my soul.

Terrible conditions didn't cause his accident. It was a beautiful New Year's Eve filled with a glorious full moon, mellow wind, and clear skies. If the weather had been bitter and nasty, with a full-on nor'easter blowing snow, no one would have gone climbing, preventing the horrible chain of events.

"Wow, the day is intoxicating. The ice is glowing, perfect for ice axes." Rhea comes near; I squat down to pet her.

Bob approaches the beginning of the ice flow as Bow barges through his legs, almost knocking him over. "Bow, you brat! Holy cow, the ice is amazing. Bright blue, better than most ice I've climbed."

Marla joins him. "It does look lovely. Wait, you're not thinking of climbing, are you?" She reaches over and hugs him.

"Hey, what a great idea." Bob smiles. "If you don't want to go, Flinny, are you in? Come on; this might be our last chance to climb the Headwall. It's usually filled with gobs of snow. We can do it."

I push up from my knees, letting Rhea chase Bow. Being out of the cabin has freed my fears. The warm sun melts my sadness, the perfect weather an irresistible siren call. Dropping my pack and pulling out the rope, I nod. It's time to climb in perfect conditions.

There's something about the raw essence and potential energy of ice that's primal. Deeper than a "call to the wild," thwacking ice axes into frozen water fascinates me. I love to work my arms and legs in rhythm to dash up a waterfall.

What motivates an ice climber can be mysterious to others. Many approve of Sir Edmund Hillary's famous quote, "Because it's there," as an answer, glorious in all its ambiguity.

The *Tuckerman Headwall* from the Hermit Lake Shelters. Bob and I
climbed 600' straight up the center. January 1, 1983.

"Be careful, you crazy boys." Marla punches Bob in the arm. "I
know you need action to process your feelings, but please come back
to me."

"I'll be fine. Flinny will keep me safe. The ice is absolutely primo."

I give Marla a big hug. She has no desire to climb, content to hike
around with the dogs. Rhea is having fun, running around in circles,
barking as she goes. Her behavior is renowned in Syracuse; everyone
knows Rhea. Definitely a great distraction, seeing her whip around in a
frenzy, belting out an "Ah-rooooo" as she spins.

"Bob, you're on belay. Climb when ready!"

"Climbing!" Bob steps up, swinging his axe into the blue ice,
hearing a satisfying *thump* echoing throughout the bowl.

At the base of the *Tuckerman Headwall*,[10] tying into the rope is
comforting, the connection a conduit from which I draw strength.

Watching Bob from the corner of my eye, the dogs play like wolves, Rhea running in circles, yapping at Bow.

The headwall is a skier's playground, but today the scrawny bushes and rocks highlight a strip of blue ice thirty feet wide, our own Yellow Brick Road.

"Ice!" Bob yells as a chunk breaks off and careens down. Instinctively, I lower my head, where the orange Joe Brown helmet intercepts the projectile. Would Ed have survived if he had worn a helmet? It's possible. Is climbing going to bring him back? No. But I can't rewind time lying around and pining, either. I'm ready for this and hope my spirit is also.

We're halfway up, below the remaining vertical part of the headwall. It's our third rope pitch, and Bob leads. The sun has passed over our heads, warming the summit and leaving us in the shade. The horrible night is far from my mind as my Forrest Lifetime axe thunks into the blue ice.

My legs relax, using the front points of my crampons to stand on knobs of ice, calm as I unwind Bob's remaining ice piton on the pitch. Called a *Snarg*, they create a dubious anchor, but they are fun to whack with an ice hammer.

Out to the northeast, the sun lights the ridge, and the downhill ski trails glisten at Wildcat Mountain. Yanking on the rope gives Bob the signal that I'm about to start climbing. A double-check of my harness and a tug adjusts my axe leash.

My right foot stomps on an apple-sized lump of ice. Putting weight on the apple, my foot slips off. Another kick follows without the usual satisfying *thunk*. Instead, a tinkling metal sound causes me to turn and watch the crampon slide off my boot and bounce down the ice five hundred feet to the rocks below.

Time to freak out: high up on the headwall, gripped, stupefied, and scared. I messed up buckling my crampon, or perhaps the strap broke. Yell to Bob, but the wind whips my voice out and away. Frozen in place, I'm about to join Ed. My mind starts to chirp about being a bonehead. Things are not looking good.

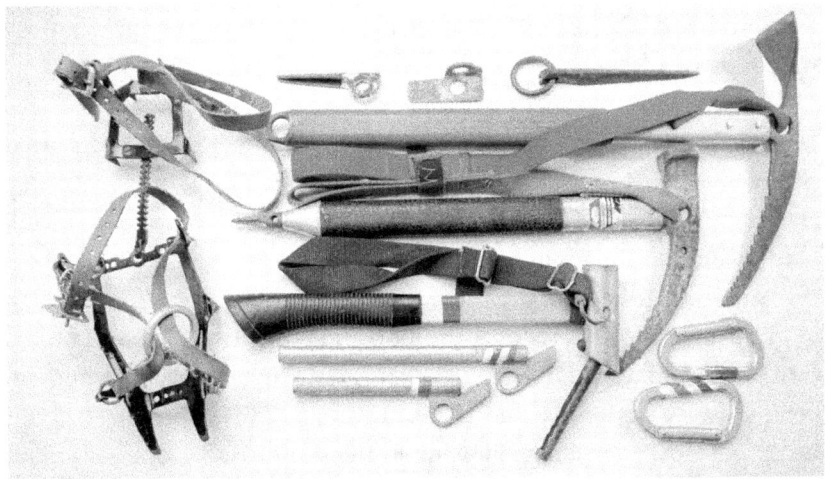

From the left, adjustable crampon, rock pitons, Mountain Technology ice axe, Charlet Moser ice hammer, two carabiners, Lowe Hummingbird tubular hammer, Lowe Snarg ice pitons.

It's all mental games in the end. A jerk on the rope snaps me out of my funk. Bob's wondering why I'm not moving—untethering my left hand from the ice hammer, I gently reach up to tug on the rope. My lifeline returns me to the present, away from mental noise. Refocusing, I determine my best option is up. Time to get thwacking.

My three years of training return. Use my feet. Dozens of beginners hear this mantra at Little Falls, the SUOC rock climbing crag. *Focus! Stop grabbing wildly for holds and use your feet.* The vision of a beginner flailing around on an easy rock slab, finally getting their balance, makes me smile.

Before the invention of crampons, men and women climbed glaciers by cutting steps. Ice axes have an edge designed just for this purpose. I bash at the ice, creating a step for my right foot.

I can't blame my situation on others; losing the crampon is my fault. I must own it and save myself. Bob didn't drag me up this climb. I'm responsible for getting out of this mess.

Finally, the headwall angle slopes off, and I mosey up to Bob and his belay.

"Flinny, what the hell took you so long? Man, it's cold when the wind kicks in."

Smug and safe on the comfortable ledge, I proudly stick out my right foot and declare, "Have a gander at my missing crampon."

Bob has a double-take and exclaims, "What the hell?" again.

"Musta kicked it off. I finished taking out the Snarg and started climbing when my right foot slipped. Heard a jingle, and, poof, my crampon flew away. Crazy! I cut steps to get here; totally cool. Thank God I didn't lead that pitch."

"You're an idiot. Get over here and take the belay. Sheesh!"

Luckily, the ordeal is done, and Bob and I crest over onto the Alpine Garden. An hour before dark, the sun is sinking toward the horizon behind us. We sit down for a welcome rest.

"Look at Carter Dome glowing in the sun. Lovely," Bob says as we munch on candy bars.

"It's wonderful. It sucks Ed's not here with us."

"Oh, he is." Bob sips from his water bottle.

"I barely knew him, but I will never forget the few times we spoke. Still glad I didn't fall and join him in heaven. That would have been bad."

Bob stands up, groaning, and slips on his pack. "Yeah, you owe me for losing your crampon. Didn't need that stress. At least it ended up okay. Ready to head out?"

"Sure, let's go. I've had enough drama for the year."

We head north along the ravine rim and navigate down Lion Head to the base of Tuckerman Ravine. It's been a fine day. Well, up until the crampon-tossing incident.

I slowly fill in more of my feelings as time goes on. Of all my worst fears, this one had come true. I had read about being grateful for life but never understood.

Ed is gone physically, but my memory, especially his laughter and smile that night, endures. And his desire to help others at the cost of his own life. Ed, these mzungu qualities of yours will always remain with me.

ED'S MEMORIAL

Recorded in the camp log at the Syracuse University Outing Club's Sheep Shed, Long Lake, New York on February 18, 1983, by John.

This Sheep Shed is dedicated to the young, wild, and free spirit of Edward Aalbue, who died during a winter camping trip. He lost his life while traveling down his path in search of happiness.

We're all looking for something that will lead to joy in our own lives. For some, it's making a lot of money, finding an enjoyable job, or raising a family. For others, it's skiing across a frozen lake, kayaking down a wild river, or crawling through a dark cave. For Ed, it was climbing a mountain. The only way his death has any meaning is if we let it influence us when we encounter a fork in our own road. Ed's the lucky one, for he's finished his journey and has accomplished his goal. We, however, are still searching, still hoping to find that something.

You must be prepared to face future responsibilities that lie around the next bend, but don't let them stop you from enjoying new experiences that you will encounter today along your journey, because you might not be here tomorrow. Do what you like to do and have a good time doing it. Blessed are those who dream dreams and are ready to pay the price to make them come true.

We'll catch ya up there, Ed.

Love,

The SUOC Family

Bob leading the *Regular Route*, Chapel Pond slabs, October 1982

BELAY

MAY – AUGUST 1983

Every first weekend in May, SUOC makes a pilgrimage to the white-water derby in North Creek, New York. Nestled in the heart of the Adirondacks, the Hudson River begins its journey at Lake Tear of the Clouds, a mosquito bog on the shoulder of Mount Marcy. Draining west to Lake Colden, Calamity Brook flows south to Henderson Lake, the official start of the Hudson.

When logging began in the 1850s, the lake became a vast holding pen for large trees sent downriver to the sawmills at Glens Falls. One hundred years later, kayaks and canoes replace logs floating down the Hudson.

The spring sun has beaten back Father Winter as we ditch our skis and ice axes for rock and river fun. It's been a few months since Ed died, and life ripples onward, carrying me downstream. Work and climbing brings stability, helping me forget that awful night.

Last month, I moved to Rochester for a cartography job, keeping my outgoing SUOC President duties even though I finished in December. Membership is for life; it doesn't matter that I'm no longer a student.

Of course, it turns out I graduated right in the middle of the biggest recession since World War II. High-paying jobs are tough to get, but minimum wage in my field is better than working at the pizza house.

To get a jump on the weekend, I leave Rochester early Friday in the Maverick—stopping at Eric's house outside Rome in a tiny blip of a town called Remsen.

He had better luck than I did, landing a computer mapping job near Rome Air Force Base last summer. Maybe due to his Forest Engineering degree, but his kind and helpful nature was key; everyone likes Eric.

"How's the love life, dude?" I pull out of his driveway and head north.

"Ah, not on fire. Lots of possibilities but no action. You?"

Accelerating onto the entrance ramp, I reply, "This girl Katy, but getting our schedules to work is tricky. Especially with this move to Rochester." I navigate the topic to more mundane things. My mushy stuff is hard to talk about during long car rides, especially since I've never even kissed her.

Cruising the curvy mountain roads, I confess, "I'm not planning on boating this weekend. You mentioned there's climbing nearby?"

"Tons of climbing, but Poseidon rules the weekend. His disciples, the river rats, require our presence at the race." Eric turns down the radio as the Grateful Dead's "Ripple" starts playing. "Too mellow."

"How did the derby become a thing?" I swerve to avoid a semi that crosses into my lane. "Whoa, sorry about that."

Eric doesn't blink. "When logging ceased in the 1940s, the state devised a clever way to monetize the river. Dams were developed to create flood conditions for white-water rafting. The Hudson's water level rises by almost three feet due to the morning discharge from the Abanakee Dam, ten miles upstream."

"Now, that is my kind of government," I say. "Our taxes at work."

Eric laughs. "My property taxes, you mean." He takes a drink from his coffee cup.

I chuckle. "Death and taxes, no way to avoid either. Can you find a more bouncy song? I need some car music. You know, loud!" Blinking, I refocus my eyes to stay awake and avoid deer on the road. "Does this race have any significance to the Kentucky Derby?"

"Astute observation!" Eric says. "The timing of both events is a mere coincidence. No horsepower where we're going, only waterpower."

"Is it dangerous?" I wonder.

"The dam release creates big waves that, under the right circumstances, can form widow-makers—Class V whirlpools that reach out and grab you."

Whitewater has a grading system, with Class I as flat water and Class VI as life-threatening. Big deal. They copied the idea from climbing.

"I think I get it. Stay in the kayak and avoid being a Pinball Wizard."

Eric agrees. "Bouncing off boulders is not good. Don't flip over."

"And you call this fun? I'll stick to climbing any day." I slow down, nearing the top of the hill, looking out for moose.

Eric drains his coffee cup. "We're almost there. Watching paddlers race through the slalom gates while the rest of us drink beer and eat grilled snacks is the best part. A beer foam SUOC trip is graded a Class VII spectator activity."

"Bohemian Rhapsody" blares out of the cassette player, and our heads bounce along as we belt out the lyrics at the top of our lungs.

THE BARN IS OLD, a cabin next to the marsh, a tributary to the Hudson. We're the first to arrive, opening the place for the summer and getting ready for the arrival of the paddlers. The surrounding fields have scattered pine trees amidst thick grass, sprouting in the spring thaw. A lovely Christmas tree scent wafts from new growth on the nearby spruce trees.

The outhouse is fifty feet away, and a stream parallels a stone wall. Due to the risk of giardia in the water, giant jugs adorn the porch for drinking and cooking. The barn oozes with rustic charm, our SUOC campground.

Chores complete, we gather around the campfire, waiting for the others. Barely hearing the stream's gurgle, I lean over, reaching out to Eric with my beer. He taps my can. His parents bought the Barn years ago, complete with a propane stove and heater to provide the semblance of authentic living. Thanks to the musty smell and rumbling snores of folks sleeping in the main room, I choose to crash outdoors in the comfort of my tent.

As I add another log to the fire, lights from the road shine brightly, and a car careens into the driveway. John's wagon, loaded with boats, barely misses the rock near the gate. Other cars pull in and park haphazardly in the driveway. Everyone is happy to be out of the big city and ready for a roaring good time.

Waking the following day, the sun peeks over the trees, lighting my tent with its glorious glow. The coffee urn is loaded; hopefully, someone plugs it in to start the heavenly brew. Barely hungover, I plunk in my contact lenses and stretch my long legs. It's time to crawl out of the tent and head inside.

Volunteering for duty, I flip pancakes in the air with the spatula, the cakes large and fat, just what hungry paddlers need. At long last, it's my turn to eat, relaxing in a beat-up beach chair at the blackened fire pit, wolfing down my cakes slathered with real maple syrup. College students have standards too.

While most folks have come for the race, I spy another climber who might be convinced to punt the derby.

"Hey, Woody, are you interested in climbing today?" I ask.

He gives me a long, pondering look and says, "Sure, why not? What's on your mind? Moxham Dome?" Woody's the leader I met at the Gunks last fall. Four years older, thin-rimmed glasses nestled on his nose, and an unshaven face gives him a Warren Harding look. But Woody's more reserved than the famous and boisterous Yosemite climber.

"I'd like to do something different, more adventurous," I reply. Moxham Dome is across the road from the Barn.

Woody jumps up. "We can abandon the tribe and paddle to Rogers Rock on Lake George. I've always wanted to climb there. We'll honor the spirit of Poseidon but avoid the frothing, freezing water relished by our kayaking buddies."

What could be more fun than paddling to a climb? We join the hustle and get our kit together and tie a beater aluminum canoe to my car. Perhaps the same one I used back at the ski lodge years ago.

After tossing our packs into the boot, off we go, leaving the paddlers to their river. Our adventure starts at the Rogers Rock Campground, forty-five minutes to the east.

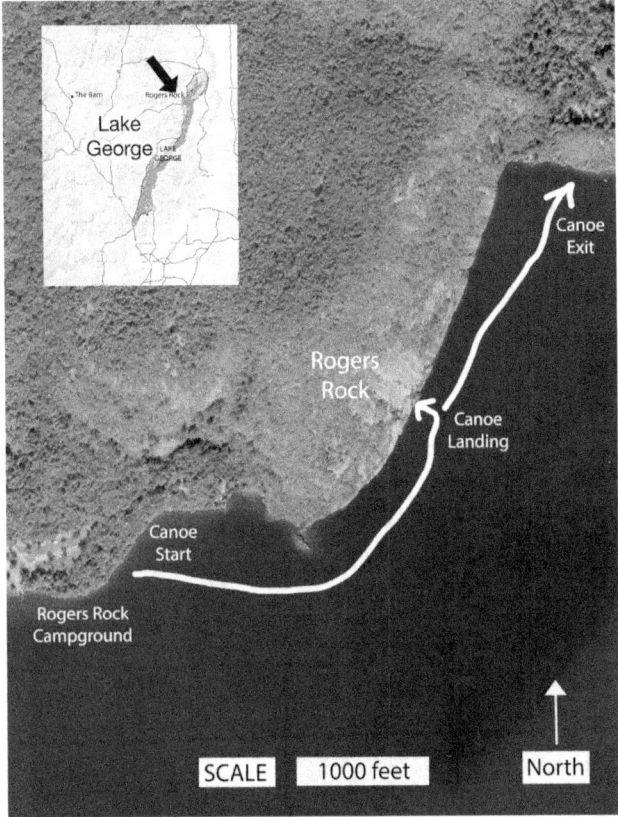

Rogers Rock, on the west side of Lake George, New
York, requires a canoe to reach the climb.

Parking at the empty boat launch, squinting in the bright sun, I try
to free the canoe. "Can't believe you tied the boat so vigorously. These
knots won't budge."

"You lack power in those feeble arms, Flinny. Better start working
out if you want to climb 5.10." Rolling up his red sweater, he miracu-
lously unties the canoe, and we huff it down to the lake.

"It doesn't get better than this," I say, stowing my pack. "No wind,
blue sky, perfect weather for a day of climbing. No slogging for miles in
the bugs, simply a short mellow paddle down the lake. This is the kind
of approach I love."

The boat noses up to the slab of Rogers Rock. We consider
climbing out of the canoe, but wisdom has us depart on the three-foot-

wide ledge of boulders and hardy birch trees. Legends abound of Rogers Rangers escaping the British Army by sliding down the slab in 1758. The rock is two football fields high, angled at seventy degrees. No sledding this with our canoe.

Woody putzes with his rack, a carpenter's tool belt. Instead of a hammer and nails, he organizes pro, carabiners, and slings.

Pro is short for protection, metal forged to fit snugly into rock fissures. The first climber places the pro; the second climber removes it. Moons ago, in the 1940s, climbers drove pitons—tricked-out nails—into cracks.

Woody and I use newer tech, the era of "clean climbing," minimizing our impact on the rock. Besides the damage caused by pounding metal, driving pitons takes too long.

At the start of *Little Finger,*[1] I wrap a sling around the lovely birch tree near the canoe as our anchor. It's made of nylon, the same stuff as a dog leash.

"On belay?" Woody stands after tightening his laces. He shakes out his hands in anticipation, releasing tension in his arms.

The canoe landing near *Little Finger*, Rogers Rock, on Lake George, New York. Photo by Justin Hodges, July 2018.

George is belaying Jamie at Owl's Head, Cascade Pass, Adirondacks. Note the figure-eight belay device anchored to the sling with a carabiner. October 1983.

"Working on it. Give me a sec." Using a carabiner attached to the sling, I thread the rope through the figure-eight to secure the belay. This system can hold Woody safe in case he falls. "There you go, belay on." My right foot perches against a nearby boulder as I hold the rope snugly.

"Climbing." Stepping over the rope, he scoots up the shallow fissure in the center of the slab. As he climbs higher, I let the rope out. If he falls, I'll brake with the figure-eight, but Woody needs to place pro for temporary anchors.

The first pitch is a thin crack amidst a sea of slab, a low-angled carpet made of stone. Tufts of grass, peppered with an occasional pine tree sapling, fight for survival. Lichen hangs fiercely to the face of the smooth rock.

"Don't flash this sucker," I call to Woody. "Place some pro, please." He's a vigorous climber, and I've seen him dash up routes, leaving me in the dust.

Stoppers were made by Chouinard Equipment, the predecessor to Black Diamond and Patagonia. September 1987.

Woody does the right thing and laces the crack with all kinds of protection, making a safe line of rope up the rock. Without pro, I'd have nothing to arrest his fall.

On the second pitch, I belay from a narrow perch facing south, with an unrestricted view down the lake. The four-foot-deep ledge is created by nature's freeze-thaw pattern, water eating away at the cracks, loosening boulders, and sending them crashing into the lake.

I'm chilling in my shades, the canoe lightly screeching against the rocks one hundred feet below. Woody takes rope slowly but steadily. He pauses to futz around with a Stopper —a brand name of pro—and finally gets it placed. A tug, tug, and another tug on the rope lets me know he's about to climb. His sweaty hands reach for the chalk bag before he moves on.

The sun bakes the rock, radiating heat. Woody hasn't moved for fifteen minutes, probably looking to place pro, occasionally yelling something. The worst part of belaying is the long waiting game, not knowing what's happening, and trying to pay attention.

The lake glistens and the rising waves of luscious noontime heat take me to the ultimate Zen belay. All warm and snug in my harness, I nod off to the soothing, rhythmic sound of lapping waves.

I dream of my front porch, the sun glowing through the gaps in the trees, pondering my future. School is over, and life is complicated by my move to Rochester. After four and half years of studying and climbing, it's time to focus on working. Sitting next to me, Katy comes into focus. She smiles, and I reach out, relishing the feel of her hand in mine. Life is good.

A jerk on the rope startles me; my eyes pop open in a panic. Losing my balance, I instinctively swivel back to the slab, barely able to avoid a face plant.

"Hey, Flinny, stop napping! Pay attention!" Woody yells down.

Regaining my stance, I yelp, "Got ya'. Belay on."

Looking down the slab, vertigo churns inside me; caterpillars hatch into butterflies, fluttering around my stomach.

Squeeze the rope, close my eyes, inhale slowly, and exhale fully. Blinking in the dazzling sun, the rope slides through my fingers, back in the groove again. The butterflies carry Katy away as I return to my belaying job.

Finally, it's my turn, and I use friction from my EBs—awesome climbing shoes—to my advantage.

Woody leading casually on *Little Finger*, Rogers Rock.
Note the pro in the crack, attached to the rope with a
carabiner. May 1982.

Vertical climbs stress using fingers, while slabs are all about the feet. I can feel the slight depression in the rock, my weight firmly planted in the divot. The joy of friction climbing builds confidence, a dancer levitating up the slab.

While I pull the last piece of pro and dash to the final belay, Woody gathers the rope. Sitting next to him on the sun-warmed boulder, I remove my Joe Brown helmet and toss it next to my pack.

"That was the best. Thanks for doing all the leading." High above the lake, gazing south towards the village of Lake George, I see nothing but water and trees. "Sorry about spacing on the second pitch. A bonehead move." My feet relish their freedom from the cramped climbing shoes.

"Musta been that late-night partying." Woody punches my shoulder. "A downside of all that beer-guzzling. You can't keep it together on a long climb."

"Well, yeah, I'm sure it didn't help. How did you feel leading on the sharp end?" Lying back, using my pack as a pillow, relaxing like a cat soaking in the afternoon sun.

"Sweet climb, even if you took a nap. I had trouble messing around with pro, but my rack worked perfectly. Wasn't scared at all."

"You bummed we missed the white water race?"

"Heck no. Climbing beats freezing in a kayak," Woody says. "Do you have any chocolate?" He reaches for the snack bag between us.

"Help yourself." My toes wink in the warm rays. "A great climb after a chill paddle. This is the life."

The bushes sigh in the slight wind, and the waves lap the rocks below. After a climb, nothing else matters, and the world's problems diminish, seeming so trivial. Letting it all go and wallowing in the wilderness is a refreshing escape that energizes me to keep going.

The wind puffs, rustling the snack bag. Woody slowly coils the rope. I'm dozing in the sun, enjoying another Zen belay.

Ten minutes later, a sharp gust jolts me awake. It's time to get cracking since the weather appears to be turning. I sit up, collect my scattered things, and lace up my EBs while Woody waits patiently.

We traverse fifty feet to the north and arrive at the rap point. Permanent anchors built for everyone's use are a significant aspect of well-established climbing areas. Our double ropes cut the standard six rappels into three, saving us a ton of time.

A lovely birch tree is lassoed with a sling and a two-inch welded ring of metal. I thread five feet of one rope through the ring, and Woody ties the ropes together with a fisherman's knot. Our anchor is secure and ready.

Woody coils the two ropes, knotting the bottom ends with a figure-eight knot. He swings the ropes like a life preserver ring, letting them fly, blown by the wind down the slab.

Climbing up, the rope is protection; going down, it's our lifeline.

"Happy to rap instead of thrashing through the woods festering with ticks. See ya down there, Woody. On rappel."

I slide down the rope like Batman, using the figure-eight device attached to my harness. Some love the rappelling thrill, but I'm leery of relying on my equipment, preferring to control my destiny, not expecting some dodgy anchor to keep me alive.

Waiting at the next rap point while Woody slides down, I soak in

the vista from this hard-to-reach vantage, grateful to have one rappel done. Thankfully, the ledge is flat as a parking lot with a bomber birch tree— because the tree will hold fast if a bomb goes off.

"Getting breezy," Woody says. "Okay, I'm off." He clips into the sling with his carabiner. These vocal queues are part of our safety ritual. I think Woody may be securely anchored, but it's better if he explicitly confirms it. I grab the ropes and pull on the left one.

"Rope's running clean. Step to the right, so it doesn't hit ya." One last tug and the ropes cascade down with a zipping sound, piling up in a tangle at my feet. "Sweet. An easy

The rappel is controlled by friction from the rope passing through the figure-eight. October 1987.

retrieval. Two more raps to go." A stuck rope would add tons of drama to our grand day out.

"I'll toss 'em again." Woody coils the two ropes and lets them rip. "Dang, caught in the trees. Guess I'll go first to clear them."

The lake is amped up at the final rap point, water boiling like a teakettle. Putting on our jackets, the wind gusts reach twenty knots, causing tree branches to tremble.

Thirty minutes later, back at the canoe, the waves swell over two feet high. The friendly and gentle lake is now Class III whitewater.

"Holy crap. There's no way we'll paddle back to the car in these waves."

Woody nods. "We're screwed. Downwind is our only shot. It's not going to be fun, but we need to get the hell out of here."

My boots are soaked by the waves crashing against the rocks. Fear starts to spawn in my stomach as I fidget with my backpack, prolonging the upcoming ordeal. I'm not ready for this. Unfortunately, circumstances force our hand. Therefore it's better to dive right in and get it over with.

Creeping into the bow, the canoe bangs against the boulders, and the grinding metal makes me wince. My stomach wobbles and water sprays on my face, distracting me from being scared as I concentrate on keeping the canoe upright.

Woody perches in the stern while I use my paddle as a rudder, bracing against the next washing-machine swell as we cruise away from Rogers Rock.

Thank goodness we avoid going parallel to the waves. That would be nuts, capsizing us in seconds. I've never been in white water before. My mind goes blank, focusing on the paddle to keep the canoe perpendicular to the humongous surf, capped with frothing white bubbles and droplets spraying.

Zooming the quarter mile north across Echo Bay in twenty minutes, we beach the canoe at Windmill Point in a neighborhood. We're lucky; we could have landed in a snake-infested bog swarming with black flies.

Too chilly for rock paper scissors, we draw straws with twigs. After pulling the winning short one, I stay with the canoe while Woody hitches back to the car.

Woody rapping off a tree on Moxham Dome near the
Barn, Minerva, New York, May 1982.

Huddling out of the wind, my mind withdraws, and my body enjoys the munch of a well-deserved granola bar. Freezing due to soggy boots, I'm grateful we didn't capsize. The fear of waves swallowing me alive ebbs as I drift along in the moment, watching the storm slowly blow down the lake.

Wearing all my clothes, nuzzling deeper into my jacket, trying to convince my body it's warm. My teeth chatter when the wind blows, and I'm in limbo, a hibernating bear waiting for spring.

A car door slams and my eyes flutter open to a welcome sight.

"Whoa, what a dramatic ending," I say to Woody as we tie the canoe to the top of the car.

He grins. "Ah, our spectacular adventure has wrapped up perfectly. There's nothing better than a good scare to appreciate a fine day. But dang, I'm starved. Love PB&J, but burgers and beer sound great."

"Next time, we should stick to Class VII." Beer foam is always better than gnarly whitewater.

~

It's a long ride back to Rochester. The cassette player cranks Deep Purple, the grinding chords of "Highway Star" keeping the freeway tempo. I drink bad rest-stop coffee, thinking about Katy, my elusive honey. Why don't I visit her in Syracuse? My stomach rumbles.

After getting home, I call my folks instead. "Hey, Popster, how are things?"

"Oh, busy as you can imagine. Bustling around the parish, dozens of services and sermons, too many meetings."

"Your sermons are great. People love how you relate the Bible to real life. Last time we talked, you wanted to open an outreach center. How's that going?" Dad loves organizing people. I can't figure out how the heck he corralled Ugandan villagers to church. Years before we arrived, many were animists, worshipping a different kind of god.

"Purring right along," he answers. "The vestry approved the center last week, thankfully. The community around the church is poor, and outreach will greatly help." He pauses. "How are you feeling after losing your friend on Mount Washington?"

"It's been rough at times. I can't believe it's been five months already."

Dad sighs. "Death, especially when unexpected, is hard to bear. I'm so sorry you have to live with this. Is there anything I can do?"

"February was tough, but I organized a memorial service in Syracuse that allowed me to process my feelings and accept his loss. Moving to Rochester also helped in a way, you know, the distance and all."

"Time can heal all wounds. Hey, how's the new job?" I appreciate

Dad asking about Ed, but it makes me sad. Happy to transition to more banal stuff.

"It's fun. I'm working on a tourist map for Columbus, Ohio. The Chamber of Commerce hired us, funded by ad sponsors. It's old school, though. I would prefer computer mapping." And to rake in more money. The minimum wage barely covers the gas for the seven-hour drive to the Adirondacks.

"I'm proud of you. At least it's in your field."

Because my family contributed to my education, I feel responsible to repay them by succeeding professionally. You bet Dad's happy I'm not screwing off like a dirtbag climber.

"I'm learning tons, that's for sure," I answer. "Is Mom home?"

Dad sighs. "No, she's out showing a house. Life of a real estate agent, always on the hustle. I'll tell her you called."

Mom works for Century 21 part-time, and I'm worried she might be pushing it. Ten years ago, she had breast cancer. The doctors say it's coming back.

"Thanks, Dad. I'll call you guys again soon." Love you.

As MAY WINDS DOWN, Bob and Marla convince me to join them at Wallface over the Memorial Day weekend. Nestled deep in the heart of the Adirondacks, its remote location makes it a magnet for hard-core climbers. Bagging *Diagonal* or *No Man's a Pilot* is a rite of passage to join SUOC's elite. Four miles of hiking to the cliff is a serious commitment with a limited chance of rescue. Be prepared as the Boy Scouts say.

Since no one is around to go with me, I leave early on Saturday, heading east to Rome, the gateway to the wilderness. Glad to get out; I felt trapped in the big city. The piano intro for the Door's "Break on Through" catches my attention, teasing me with its recommendation.

Pulling into the Tahawas trailhead at noon, parking next to Marla's VW Bug, smothered with Grateful Dead logos and a bumper sticker declaring "Save the Earth." I creak out of the driver's seat, guzzling the last of my coffee.

The terse description in the guidebook confirms the long approach.

Mother Nature rules in all her glory. Chock-full of trees, bugs, and the occasional black bear. The perfect place to get away and recharge.

I stuff my things into a backpack from the Eureka factory outlet. Equipment manufacturers know outing clubs such as SUOC are lucrative targets for sales. Last weekend, when it rained, I went shopping for deals. The best part of an upcoming trip is the easy justification for buying more gear.

The fresh green maple leaves rustle in the breeze and frogs croak in the distance. The bugs are nasty, motivating my departure, and soon I'm meandering around the muddy stream of a trail. Mucking through, grateful for my leather hiking boots. *What a mess. Is this really a trail? More of a swamp.*

My foot makes a sucking sound as it leaves the mud's clutches. Shortly, I reach a bridge across Calamity Brook. Black flies begin to swarm, and the hankie tied around my head, soaked in DEET, works overtime.

The approach allows me to process my transition to the working world. My academic success in college was measured by grades, which demonstrated how good I was. At work, I'm paid for my time, but there's no challenge, no way to gauge my worth. Fortunately, climbing allows me to compare myself to others. While work is dull, the climbing game adds spice.

Slogging along the remaining three miles to the base of Indian Pass, bearing left when the dirt path turns into boulders, I stagger into the climber's campsite at mid-afternoon. Bob and Marla's tent is snuggled in the dirt clearing, with "SUOC" prominently stamped in black ink.

The pack thumps to the ground, my aching back happy the approach is over. I waddle to the creek to cache a few beers in the cool water. It's quiet at camp, and since there's still daylight, I don my daypack and head up to Summit Rock to catch a gander of Bob and Marla.

They complement each other in so many wonderful ways, the perfect couple. Bob's got the drive and Marla the nurture. Even their dogs mesh their personalities; Bow Bear is mellow like Marla, while Rhea is bouncy, more like Bob. Thankfully, both dogs were left home on this trip, or else I'd get to be the babysitter.

I'm lounging in the sun less than an hour later. Gazing at the big wall in front of me and studying my trusty guidebook—*Climbing in the Adirondacks* by Don Mellor.[2]

Hearing a faint noise, something large bounces down the cliff, a ball in nature's pachinko machine. Craning my neck, I see Bob starting the final pitch of *Diagonal*. Waving like a lunatic, bellowing out numerous yells, but they never hear me.

Dusk is settling in when I reach the tents, with barely enough light to forage for firewood. No sign of Bob and Marla as I chow down on a delicacy of ramen noodles topped with yummy Chinese food flavoring. The fire is toasty, wood spluttering nicely, sparks crackling and shooting around, beacons for my missing buddies.

Restless, I wander away from the warmth of the fire, looking for some sign of my friends. Twenty minutes later, I return and sit down on a log, pondering my options.

Wallface has no defined summit trails, only herd paths. It would be nuts to thrash through miles of shrubbery in the dark. I remember Mt. Washington when we lost Ed. Bet Bob wants me to stay put. Not sure if they even know I'm here. Hopefully, the fire will help them find their way back. At least it's cooking a few bloody mosquitoes.

The coals mellow to a dull red as I visit the bathroom bush, scouring the cliff, the cloudy night sky void of the moon. Crawling into my sleeping bag, grim thoughts wander through my skull as I pluck out my contacts and put them away for the night.

I'm worried about Bob and Marla but don't know what to do.

Six months ago, Ed went searching for our friends, and that turned out horribly. Crashing around in the dark can easily make things worse if I get hurt. Sleep is a long time coming.

Dawn peeks through the tent fly, and I wearily motivate into the cool morning. My trusty Optimus 8R is purring away nicely, and soon, I'm guzzling coffee, awakening my senses with the caffeine buzz.

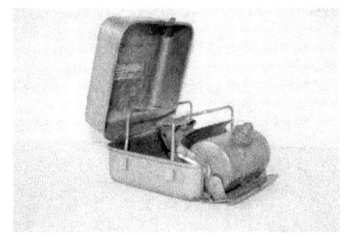

The Optimus 8R stove is compact, works in all seasons, and uses white gas.

Before I can gather my wits to look for my friends, the bushes rustle, and Bob and Marla waddle into camp, looking worn out and haggard. I jump up and hug them fiercely.

"Wow, you guys made it. Wonderful to see you! Let me boil more water." I extend my mug.

Bob dumps his pack, relaxes on the log, and gratefully slurps the coffee.

Marla sits next to him. "So happy to be back. We had to bivy under a huge rock, waking up to find the path five feet away. I didn't sleep well."

"She lost her boot on the climb," Bob says. "Which made for a dramatic bushwhack. It slowed us down, and then it got dark. Forgot to bring my headlamp."

Marla removes her tattered climbing shoe, rubbing her poor mashed toes back to life.

"When you were near the top, I heard a huge crash. Did you trundle your boot?" I ask.

Marla smiles sheepishly. "Yeah, it slipped out of my pack as I climbed the last pitch." It's common for climbers to approach climbs in their hiking boots and switch to climbing shoes for the steep stuff.

"You guys hungry? I brought extra bagels if you want." All the anxiety from the night burns away as I celebrate their return with an extra dollop of brown sugar in my oatmeal. The stove does its job just in time before the raindrops splat down.

I let the coffee pot cool and fill my mug. Leaning over to Bob, I top him off. "Rut roh, climbing will be grim if this rain keeps up."

He takes another sip. "To heck with climbing; I've had enough drama for the month. Tired of epics. What a year."

His words take me back to Mount Washington. I hope it rains cats and dogs.

"Time for Gore-Tex." Snagging my parka as the rain tempo increases, promising more. "Hey, y'all," I say, putting away the stove. "Let's bail and head to the Sheep Shed. At least there's shelter and a wood stove. Beats driving back to Syracuse in grotty weather."

"I think that's a great idea," Marla says. "We'll be soaked after the four-mile walk back to the cars."

Wallface Cliff in Indian Pass of the Adirondacks, with *Diagonal* highlighted. Photograph from adirontrek.blogspot.com.

We motivate as the drizzle thickens. Because Marla has to hike out in one of her climbing shoes, Bob and I lighten the load by carrying some of her stuff.

It sucks to miss out on climbing, but thankfully misfortune is narrowly averted with Bob and Marla's return. Usually reaching the summit is the ticket, but having my friends back is the best.

"How ya' doing, Mom? I'm calling from a pay phone in Long Lake. Staying at the Sheep Shed a few miles away since the rain chased us out of Wallface."

"I'm well, Davidite. Tired as usual, but you know, the doctors say it's the side effect of the cancer treatment. I'm still able to get to church and sell some houses."

The rain increases, splattering on the trash can nearby, making it harder to hear.

"You're almost finished, right?"

"Yes, this is the last week of chemo. It's better than ten years ago; not as painful. I'm glad to be done with it. Hospitals are such dreary places."

"Dad mentioned you guys are heading down to Maryland to celebrate. Sorry I can't go this time, you know, with my job and all."

"No worries, David. I'm proud of you for working hard. I know you love climbing, but having a good job is important. And getting married. I want to hug some grandchildren, you know. How's Katy?" My tummy lurches. Oh no, I should never have mentioned her to Mom.

"Ah, she's good. I haven't talked with her in a while. We're both quite busy. Hey Mom, Bob, and Marla are waiting for me. Plus, the rain is coming down harder. I'll call you later in the week from Rochester. Love you!"

Gently place the phone back in its cradle and exhale slowly, realizing I'm holding my breath. What is it about girls that get me all worked up?

Bombing down the muddy track to the Sheep Shed, a rustic cabin on the Cedarlands Boy Scout property. The Scouts gave SUOC permission to use the cabin under the agreement to keep it in shape.

It reminds me of the Harvard Cabin and the Barn with its warm loft and big open room. The hexagon shape of the Sheep Shed is unique. Probably a dreamy architect was having too much fun.

The drizzle continues as I pull up next to Marla's Bug with the fire pit going wild. Bob has built a rager, a perfect welcome. Bustling out of the Maverick, I scoot over to the campfire, warming my toes, happy to be drying out.

Finally able to relax while my friends snuggle on a log, the sprinkles subside. Peeking over the flames, I say "Last night, I felt powerless, wondering what the heck happened to you guys. Can't imagine what was going through your minds."

Marla shrugs. "I was numb and exhausted, but being with Bob kept the nightmares at bay. Guess I'm getting used to epics."

Bob adds, "Compared to the ordeal on Mount Washington, this was tame. Yeah, it was uncomfortable, but we did the right thing, waiting for morning."

"About that. I still feel terrible that we didn't go to Ed's funeral." I follow a spark as it rises to the gray sky above.

Bob reaches for another log. "It happened so fast, his fall, holding him in my lap. That night still haunts me but I don't know what else I could have done. Didn't hear about the service in time. Wish I had gone. It would have been good to talk with his parents."

"Processing his death hasn't been easy as I mosey on with life. Closure from his funeral might have helped."

Hugging her knees, Marla says, "Survivor's grief is the struggle of living through a disaster without your friend. At least that's what my Psych teacher said. I'm so sad that he's not here. I wish I never talked him into coming with us."

"Dealing with loss is more challenging than climbing," I reply. "We're taught to reduce risk but rarely how to cope with the consequences when things go wrong. Unfortunately, we're learning the hard way."

Marla gets up and sits on Bob's lap, giving him a big hug. The fire crackles happily, without a care, reflecting our somber mood.

~

Another work weekend at the Sheepshed, Long Lake, Adirondacks in October 1982.

"Yo Flinny, let's climb *Diagonal*.³" I can tell it's Woody from his terse introduction. Always a lawyer, getting right to the point.

"You must have heard from Bob and Marla that I was rained out."

"Yep. We should go. The weather this weekend looks great. You can lead the easy pitches." I've not done multi-pitch lead climbing, only seconding. Time to amp things up.

Jumping in the Maverick Friday after work, I bomb over to Syracuse to corral Woody. He packs sparingly, leaving the tent to me.

Buckling his seat belt, "Nothing personal, but it's better to be safe than sorry. By the way, Jim and JC are going to meet us. They're going for *No Man's a Pilot*."

"Cool, more the merrier," I reply. Both are climbing leaders with tons of experience. Met them at Little Falls earlier this year. "What's it like on Wallface? After getting skunked last weekend, I'm looking forward to getting on the crag."

Woody responds with a glassy look in his eyes. "It's majestic. The biggest wall in the Daks is waiting for us. Lots of awesome climbs to bag, but I want to lead *Diagonal*. It's 5.8 on the crux, easy-peasy. A five-star route, according to the guidebook."

The drive passes quickly, and we get to the trailhead right before dark. I wrestle my gear from the boot and get packing. Anticipating the hike for its ability to wean out my work stress.

Headlamps on, we grind out the miles to the climber's camp. Should have left my tent last weekend and saved carrying the extra weight. Because Woody isn't much of a party animal, we skip the fire and head to bed.

It's an early rise and he's raring to go. Another tent is pitched across the clearing; I can only assume it's our friends. Suddenly, I hear a rustle, then a whine, followed by a loud bark. Their tent shakes, the zipper opens, and Tosh dashes out. He's a formidable Husky, scary if he senses danger, but he's off to chase a rabbit.

"Ready, Flinny?" Woody shoulders his pack as Jim and JC emerge from the four-person tent.

Jim shakes his head, eyes bleary. "Any coffee? We got in really late. Must of been three in the morning."

Climbing Grades

Yosemite System	French System	Description
5.0 - 5.3	1 - 2	Easy
5.4 - 5.7	3 - 4	Moderate
5.8 - 5.9	5a - 5b	Difficult
5.10 +	5c +	Extreme

Grades from *Climbing in the Adirondacks, a guidebook* by Don Mellor, 1983.

"Sorry, man, you can use my stove to make some more." I point to the fire ring where my trusty Optimus 8R cools.

Woody starts walking away. "We'll see you up there. Let's go, Flinny; these slugs will take forever to get ready." Tosh rushes back into camp and leaps on JC, knocking him to the ground.

Chuckling, I follow Woody, waving goodbye.

We enter the talus slope after a brisk five-minute walk, where boulders vary in size from baseballs to pickup trucks. Hopping from one to another, hoping they don't tip, tumbling me into the depths. Supposedly there are caves up here. Just my luck to fall into one, never to be seen again.

My fingers cramp tying into the rope and I close my eyes, taking a deep breath. Woody is straightforward and calm about my first lead climb.

"Don't overthink it. You know what to do. It's an easy pitch. Climb until you find two pitons and rig a belay."

Donning my trusty EBs, the firm soles are designed to hold my balance on a pea-sized nubble of rock. Following Woody's advice, I start climbing, not letting my fears get to me. I'm more worried about the flying pests.

They buzz around as I start the pitch. If you've never met a blackfly, you're lucky. Mosquitoes are bad enough, with a long proboscis that sneaks into your skin to suck your blood. Black flies are half the size, but all teeth, chomping skin, leaving gouges.

Swatting one chewing on my wrist adds another carcass mashed into the dirt caked on my arm. Puffs of chalk rising from my hands help dry out my sweaty fingers. I can't avoid adding blood to the mix, thanks to the rough rock ripping away my skin, a stoic non-living black fly.

Compressing my fingers, stiffening their tips to grip the horizontal quarter-inch wide ledge, I wiggle my index finger, finding a smidge more room to improve my hold.

I continue this parade, alternating chalking up, black fly smashing, searching for holds, and placing protection. It's a compelling puzzle; finding the right pro to fit the crack is fun. Living the Lego dream.

When the rope runs out, it's time to build the belay. I find the tiny ledge, barely enough room for my feet, and the friendly pitons provide a solid anchor.

Pulling in the slack, I yell to Woody that he's on belay. He flashes the climb in minutes, making my plodding attempt look tame. He smiles as he continues past me, leading the next pitch to the famous *Diagonal* ledge.

It doesn't take me long to reach Woody. It must be due to climbing second. No need to fear; simply climb. But now, the exposure threatens to unwind me.

"Don't look down, Flinny. Just focus on the big ledge. See, it's like a freeway. Just scamper up and place some pro once in a while. You'll find the belay trees at the end of the ramp. You can do it."

It's great to have his support. The angle is relaxed and the width of a bus makes it easy to forget the 300' cliff to my right.

The following two pitches go quickly; I barely remember whether they were hard. Topping out, I'm exhausted but ecstatic from my first multi-pitch lead climb. Thanks to Woody, I kept my wits about me, happy to have conquered the jitters.

Gazing south to Lake Henderson, the start of the Hudson River glistens in the late afternoon sun. We're snacking on a comfy cushion of grass, soaking rays.

"What a memorable climb! It really takes my mind off crap. Thanks for bringing me here."

Woody says "An adventurous climb boils things down to the basics, giving perspective, and making me more capable to tackle the lunacy in the office. You handled yourself well today."

"My first 5.8. Of course, you led all the hard pitches."

"No biggy, I've done it before. Next time, you'll be able to lead the final crux."

I reach for my water bottle and take a swig. "Do climbing grades consider the approach? You know, the wilderness aspect of it? That should be part of the rating, don't ya think?"

Woody turns to me, "Yes and no. European alpine climbs have such a system. But no one usually bothers. Most American climbers focus on the technical merit of the climb itself, not where it's located."

"Seems lame," I reply. "Anyone can climb 5.10. But can they do it miles from nowhere?"

Woody chuckles. "I agree but the world is hung up on the difficulty of the climb, not the slog to get there."

Speaking of a slog, it's time to rappel. Drat.

A rock climber's toolbox. From left to right: slings with carabiners, rack with protection, rope, harness with a chalk bag. June 1987.

Descending to the *Diagonal* ledge, it dawns on me this is more intense than Roger's Rock. Luckily I went with the flow and rappelled without thinking.

Back on the talus, it's getting dark with no sign of Jim and JC; we can only assume they're still on the wall. Tosh is wailing up a storm, with lots of yapping and barking. Entering the clearing, it's not a pretty sight. Thank God our tent is safe. The other one is in shreds.

JC tied the poor dog to a tree to go climbing. I imagine rabbits, skunks, or even a bear wandering nearby caused him to rampage the tent, gashing huge holes in the sides.

After enduring my penance last weekend, I agree with Tosh. I'd be pissed off being left alone all day.

~

I'M on the sharp end, shaking out my arms, standing with my toes wedged into a teeny horizontal crack on *Pete's Farewell*[4].

Eric and I left the Barn for the day in mid-July, ready to bag yet another classic 5.7 route at Pitchoff Chimney Cliff, nestled in Cascade Pass, twenty miles east of Lake Placid.

Thirty feet from the belay, I stuff a bomber Hex into the overhanging roof of the right-facing dihedral, where two walls intersect at ninety degrees. *Hex* is short for Hexcentric; its five-sided design wedges tighter under load. Rigged correctly, it can hold a pickup truck.

Physics is at work, but I need to be careful. A force from the wrong direction could pull it out, which would be bad. Tugging on the sling, making sure it's solid.

Eric is already bored, shifting his stance to look at the lake below, the sun glinting off the green birch leaves, wondering when I'm going to climb. He can't contain himself and belts out, "Fire or retire, Flinny."

"Fire" is climber slang, meaning to get moving, to take action. Alternatively, the climber may retire, take a step back, and surrender. Fish or cut bait. *Just do it.*

The move over the roof is seriously exposed. I make the mistake of peering down; one hundred feet below lurk ravenous rocks. If I peel off this ledge, I'll dangle like a trout. If the Hex fails to hold, the boulders await. Rattled, I retire and step back onto the ledge.

Reviewing my plan for the fifth time, focusing on the Hex keeps my mind occupied. Once the pro is set, it's just the rock and me; no other distractions and all the necessary safety measures are in place.

Hardly much of a ledge, its roof forces my body to arch back in a tenuous balance. I look over to Eric and shrug. "Sorry. I need to hang out for a minute or eighty." Yeah, I'm scared.

"Man, you're off route. You're supposed to follow the diagonal crack to avoid that roof."

"This line looks much more fun," I yell back.

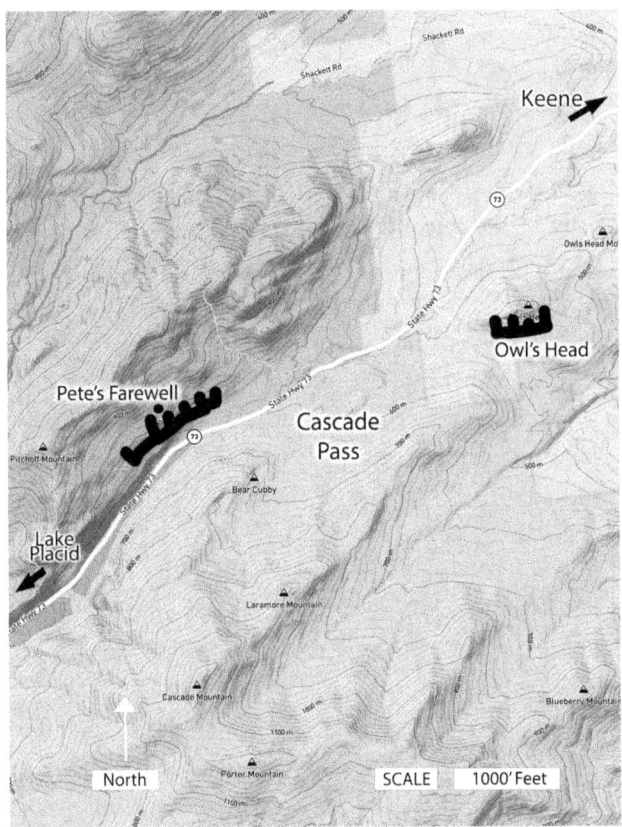

Cascade Pass is nestled between Keene and Lake Placid in the Adirondacks of New York. Climbing walls noted by black lines.

"Lovely," Eric replies. "I'm glad you want to lead it, but stop dawdling. It's cooking out here in the sun."

"Got it." Reaching into my pocket, I pull out a mangled Hershey's bar and rip the tin foil with my teeth to wolf down the yummy candy. There's nothing better than a blast of chocolate to get the mojo going.

It's a clever prop to focus my mind and ignore the fear. I shake and chalk my sweaty hands, yelling, "Here goes, time to fire!"

With my right side against the wall, my left foot snug on the opposite roof lip, I place my right hand high into the crack to form a fist. As my hand slides, my skin begins to tear. My fist bulges, instinctively squeezing tighter to force a hand jam.

Keeping my heels down avoids over-extending my calve muscles. Standing too long on tippy-toes can cause sewing-machine leg, and the resulting jiggle would toss me off the crux.

Push off my right foot and shoot my left hand over the Hex, pulling over the roof. A grin forms, blood cooling, and I'm firmly in control. The climb retires this time.

Swimming in the refreshingly cool lake is our reward after the final pitch and feeding the last black flies of the season. Cascade Pass connects Lake Placid with Keene, a twisty mountain road through the wilderness.

Climbs on the side of Pitchoff Mountain are located near the road, a two-minute stroll down to the lake. Sometimes the pass is heinous, blasted by wind, but today the sky is spectacular, and the July temperature a marvelous eighty degrees.

"So how's life in the computer mapping world?" I ask, my mouth dribbling lake water.

Eric floats on his back nearby. "The job is cool but the military aspect is a bit troubling. My coworkers are focused on raising their families or watching football, you know the drill. It's great to go climbing and get a break from it all."

"Guess we better keep at it before we settle down. Not sure I'm ready to spend my weekends schlepping youngsters to soccer practice."

He spouts water as if a whale. "Yikes, what a thought. Speaking of kids, do you think we can hit the Mountaineer before it closes? I could use another locking carabiner."

Swimming back to the beach, I say "Love a clever ploy to justify a stop at our big-boy toy store."

The Maverick trundles down the winding road into Keene and Keene Valley, home to a mountain playground in the High Peaks region.

It joins other meccas of the climbing world, such as North Conway in New Hampshire's White Mountains or the Gunks outside New Paltz. We pull into the parking lot of the Mountaineer, the carburetor knocking as the engine turns off.

Jamie on the *Pete's Farewell* crux variation, Pitchoff Chimney Cliff, Adirondacks. Note the large Hex in the crack. Photo by Rich Leswing in 1982 from the Jamie Cunningham collection.

The store is wedged between Route 73 and the AuSable River. The modern saltbox roof design sheds the winter snow, and the covered porch is welcome when it pours rain.

Gear stores draw climbers like bears to honey, and this one is packed with the best: backpacks, tents, boots, snacks, clothing, skis, and especially climbing hardware.

Carabiners are critical to climbing. Their oval shape with a gated hinge connect rope, pro, and harnesses.

Eric beelines to the back of the store in search of carabiners. The workhorse of the climber, oval-shaped with a spring-loaded gate, the carabiner is critical to the safety system. These snap links connect slings, ropes, pro, harnesses; everything. You can't go climbing without dozens—never enough gear.

"Hey, Dave, how are you?" Tim asks when I approach the counter.

"Doing great. Eric and I had a blast on Pitchoff. You climbing much?"

"Less than I should. Overworked with these two jobs." It's tough to make a decent living in the North Country. The cash and convenience of the big city versus the stress-free lifestyle of Mother Nature.

"Ouch, mixed blessings, huh?"

Tim's broad shoulders, metal glasses, and cropped black beard give him a mountain-man appeal, a Keene Valley version of a rugged explorer. He's an excellent resource for weather, black fly sightings, and climbing. I met him last fall after finishing the Chapel Pond slabs.

"Are you working these days?" he asks.

"Yeah, I moved to Rochester for a mapping job. It's a bit old school and the pay stinks."

Tim's smile breaks through his beard. "And a bit far from Keene Valley, I bet." He nods to someone behind me.

I turn my head and notice a man leaving the office at the rear of the store. Looking back to Tim, "You got that right. The drive's a bear for the serious weekend warrior."

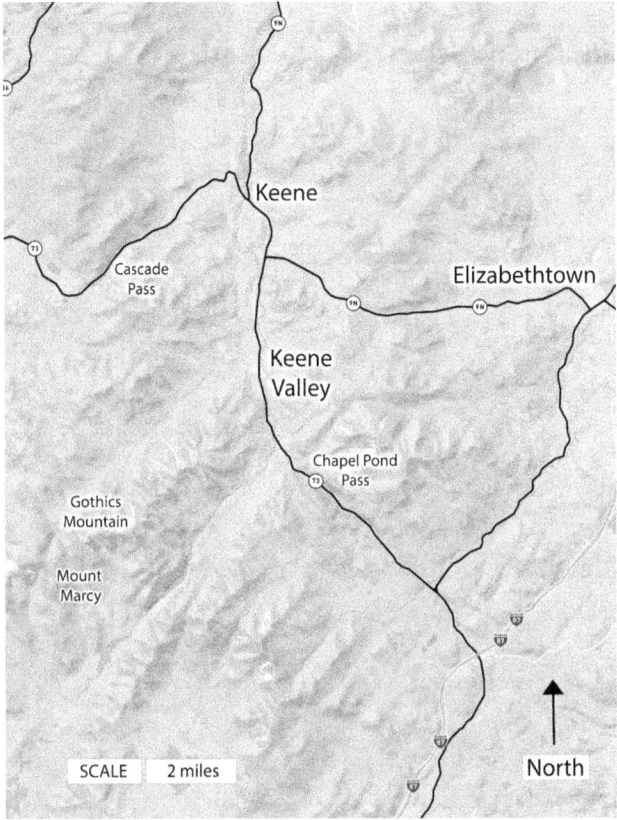

Keene Valley is smack dab in the High Peaks region of
the Adirondacks, two hours north of Albany, New York.

Tim scoots around the counter, standing behind the cash register.
"This is Jim. He manages the store here."

Jim walks over and extends his hand in welcome. Ageless, with a
long shaggy brown beard and silver-rimmed glasses, he must be
Gandalf's brother.

Shaking his hand, warmed by his smile, I instantly feel special. His
demeanor personifies the Mountaineer.

I introduce myself and tell him this is the best climbing store
around. "I'm sure you hear that a lot."

"People are always happy to visit, except when it rains. How's the
climbing?"

"Really awesome. We had a great time on *Pete's Farewell*. Keene Valley is a spectacular place. How's business?"

"Funny you should ask. Our sales are excellent since it's busier than usual. Talking with Tim about getting additional help, he mentioned you might be interested. Would you like a job here?" Jim opens his hands in a welcoming way.

It's one of those moments when time slows to a crawl. The stairs creak under a customer's weight, and sumo flies, trapped in the fishing rods, buzz around. The rustling of a child playing in a tent and the *cha-ching* from the register as Tim completes a sale.

My heartbeat accelerates, my lungs take in more oxygen, and my mind races, finally connecting with my voice.

"Wow. Ah, um, what do you have in mind?"

"We need full-time coverage during the weekends. Tim mentioned you ran the Syracuse Outing Club. I assume you are familiar with outdoor equipment?"

"Oh, definitely. I'm a climbing leader and the departing president. Are you serious about this?"

"Oh, yes, I am. Are you in?" he asks, his big, bearded grin and gleaming eyes charismatic. Meanwhile, my head is nodding, bobbing for apples, my brain scrambling. Jim knows he has me, a fish caught on the hook.

Eric comes to my rescue. Stomping up to join us, he gives me a light punch in the shoulder. "Flinny, you have the chance to work in this amazing store? It's the holy grail for climbers. Dump that lousy job in Ra-cha-cha."

Tim adds, "Oh, yeah. I should mention that we have a vacancy in the Red House across the bridge. We need a roommate. How awesome is that? A job and a room."

My mind spins like a floppy disk in a computer. Four dollars an hour making maps seven hours away—the same money here, living in magical Keene Valley instead of gritty Rochester. My mind fires.

"I'd love to work here. Thank you." I shake Jim's hand to seal the deal, ending my shortest job interview ever.

~

The Mountaineer in Keene Valley after a snowstorm.
The covered porch leads to the entrance in the center
of the building. Photo by The Mountaineer in 2005.

"You should have stayed at the mapping company," Dad says as we sit around the dinner table.

I prepped for this grilling on the drive down, knowing I'd survived them in the past. Dad has to say his piece. Arguing or snide comments tend to prolong things.

"Dad, the economy is a wreck, and minimum wage in the city barely covers the rent. I tried, but there's no way to get a raise. I'd rather live somewhere enjoyable."

Mom smiles as she passes me the potatoes, knowing I need more. "You sound happy in Keene Valley. I'm grateful you're able to support yourself." She's been doing well since this round of chemo is over. Almost back to her cheerful self.

Scooping half the bowl, I plunk mashed potatoes onto my plate.

"Exactly. I'm ahead of the game. It's the same money and a short drive to climbing." I conveniently fail to mention the 40-percent discount. "But you're right about my college degree. I have a plan if you want to hear it," pointing to the gravy boat.

"I bet I know," Lissa says. "You're looking for a sugar momma so you can climb all day." She teases me with the boat, pulling it back as I reach for it.

I sigh. "No, that's not the plan, but it's a good one."

"Katy, oh Katy, do you have any money?" Lissa croons as she hands me the gravy. Never gonna happen the way I'm going.

My brother, Andy, five years younger, chimes in, "That's not David's style, pining for some girl. You've got something creative cooking." Lissa nicknamed our brother *Bear* thanks to his love for hibernating and sleeping late in the morning. A car could crash into his bedroom, and he'd sleep through it. "Let's see, selling climbing maps, that would work."

I finish my dinner and sit back. "Close, my smart brother dear. I'm starting a magazine for adventure lovers. I'm calling it the *Adirondack Alpine Journal.*"

Silence flows across the table as Dad processes my news. Mom nods. "Writing about climbing in the mountains. Maybe when I read it, I'll understand why you love it. Very creative."

Mom always wanted to be an artist. Instead, she worked for DuPont to support Grandma, but she paints when she can. She's on board with my plan, I can tell.

"I know it sounds crazy," I continue, "but it gives me something to do instead of watching TV. There's a niche for it. Along with writing articles and drawing maps, I'll develop the photos. My neighbor agreed to fly me in his plane to take some pics. It makes tons of sense."

There, I knew I had him. Dad loves his camera. He handed his darkroom down to me, and I've been processing film since high school. He has thousands of African photos in the living room. He can't argue with me on this.

He sighs. "Well, at least you're trying to be productive. Wish you'd get a real job."

I think I've sold him. Pushing back from the table, I collect the plates. Even editors must do the dishes.

~

LED ZEPPELIN'S "HEARTBREAKER" washes over me as I open the Red House door to the kitchen. Ken is here; his brown Toyota Corolla wagon is parked next to my Ford Maverick.

The pantry is stocked with peanut butter and ramen noodles, while the fridge is crammed with jelly, beer, and milk. My three housemates are all climbers: Jamie, Bob, and Tim. Bob's room is off the kitchen near the tiny living room, often filled with rogues like Ken crashing for the night.

My first time baking cookies in the kitchen gave me pause. I opened the oven to make sure it was clean, and lo and behold, found a television stashed inside. Jamie decided the empty oven would be an excellent place to keep the TV after failing to get a signal. With a chuckle, I withdrew the television and placed it on the fridge. Glad I checked.

Bob, a chef at the Lake Placid Club, wouldn't dream of cooking for us. He's clean-shaven and trim, very different from SUOC Bob. Upstairs, Tim's large room has the best view, and Jamie's is to the left of the small bathroom. Outside my closet-sized room at the top of the stairs is the office of the *Adirondack Alpine Journal*.

I have a light table—light bulbs under glass allow me to see photo negatives easily and trace lines on vellum taped to the surface—covered with photos, half-written articles, and my typewriter. The turntable hangs from the ceiling to prevent record skips.

Since the music is coming from upstairs, I snag a Molson Golden from the fridge and dash up to see what's happening.

The rear of the Red House. The kitchen entrance is to the right, near Jamie's VW Rabbit. Photo by Jamie Cunningham, Summer 1982.

"Flinn, man! You're back," Jamie says, a beer waving in his hand as he prances around the room to the beat.

Ken grins at me. "Flinny, glad you made it in time. We're brewing up an adventure." Ken lives two hours south in Albany, our very own road warrior.

"Sweet," I reply, barely able to hear him over the music.

Tim is lounging in the editor's chair, and Bob sits on the edge of the couch. I know these two are holding back their delight, whatever the plan is.

I turn to the road warrior. "Okay, Ken, I see that glimmer in your eye. What crazy idea have you and Jamie devised?"

"We're going to solo the slabs and spend the night up on Bob's Knob. Let's roll!"

Ken jumps up from the couch and bolts down the creaking stairs. The other lads follow his lead, scattering to gather their stuff.

I ponder the wisdom of climbing a thousand-foot slab without ropes. Changing the record to the Allman Brothers' "One Way Out," I pivot to my closet and collect a sleeping bag, foam pad, and headlamp.

The floor bounces up and down to the rhythm of the music.

In the kitchen, we mash as many beer cans as possible into our packs with a few token bagels. Soon we're outside, piling into Jamie's Volkswagen Rabbit and my Maverick. The Red House is all fired up for climbing in the dark.

It's a gorgeous summer evening in August as we cinch the waist belts of our packs. Climbing shoes are on, and it feels odd without the jingling of harnesses, carabiners, and pro.

Ken goes first, and shortly the entire gang is climbing. The moon gives off enough light that we can see without headlamps. Reaching the first ledge, the Washbowl cliffs across the valley are awash with ripples of yellow and streaks of gold.

Bob rests with me, waiting for Tim as Ken and Jamie ascend the slab. I can hear them taunting each other as they scurry on.

Tromping around when the sun goes down is part of the outdoor experience, but this is my first time climbing at night. "It's kinda surreal out here in the dark," I say. "Are you scared, Bob? I'm feeling a little antsy."

The *Regular Route* on the Chapel Pond slabs with
Bob's Knob nestled on top. The road is two hundred
feet from the bottom, July 1987.

"I try not to think such thoughts; I don't want to freak out. Just going with the flow. Hey, there! You made it."

Tim joins us on the ledge. "Ah, what a fine night for a Bob's Knob bivouac! Where are the other two lads? Oh, wait, I can hear them."

The reason for the hollering becomes evident as headlamps switch on and light beams dance around; Ken and Jamie search for the route. "Glad we let the Bitch-and-Moan Brothers go first."

Bob refers to Jamie and Ken as the Bitch-and-Moan Brothers when they begin to moan, boast, or complain. We love their motivation but need to razz them to tamp down their boisterous energy. We follow the climber's code to lovingly tease our friends since humor takes the edge off a scary situation. I chuckle at the rants floating down from above.

"Well, laddies," I say, "there's no time like the present and less so for dawdling."

We follow the *Regular Route*[5], which is tricky with my full backpack. Using the extra weight to mold my feet into the rock, I'm close, 150 feet from the top of Bob's Knob.

My right leg extends onto the moonlit face, my left shoe wedged in a shallow crack, my belly straddling a slight bulge. When I push off with my left foot, the lichen under my right gives way with a sudden ripping sound.

Adrenaline flows, and my hands scramble for holds as my foot peels out. I face-plant squarely onto the slab, 600 feet off the deck, smashed like a bug on the rock. Fear scuds through me, and I imagine crashing into Bob and Tim, a cartwheeling cartoon character careening down the slab. Things I think of as butterflies bounce around my stomach.

My body responds by turning off my brain and using my sore left knee. Gingerly extending my right foot, I transfer my weight carefully to avoid the lichen. Standing, I regain my balance and scurry up to join the lads, fear whisked away by the action.

We crack beers and settle in for a most excellent bivouac on a memorable summer night.

"Look at the moonlight on the Washbowl Cliffs," I say to the others. "I can make out *Hesitation*, my favorite line."

"It's stunning," Tim agrees, crushing his empty beer can with his foot. "Hey, Jamie, why don't you and Ken dash over and solo it? We can start fires and send smoke signals to each other."

Ken takes the bait. "A fine idea. But hell with *Hesitation*, that's for wimps. I'm for flashing *Drop Fly or Die*. But Jamie, the loser, won't do it."

"Bah, you jest, bonehead," Jamie replies. "You've never done that climb. You would peel off and bounce down the talus slope, leaving a yard sale of beers."

"Heck no! I'm a better climber than you. I can do it blindfolded." Ken stands up and starts swaying, a cobra entrancing his prey. "Big chicken, you'll never go."

Jamie jumps to his feet. "Who are you calling chicken? You're a snake, talking big; you'll never leave this sweet bivy. Sit down and pop another beer."

Tim pipes in, hoping to stir the pot. "Don't goad him. Ken's trying to relax from a long week. No need to prove anything."

"Jamieie-poo won't go," Ken chants. "Too scared for an old geezer."

Tim's teeth shine white in the moonlight as he opens a fresh beer. Bob chuckles, focusing his camera on the yellow colors washing the cliffs across the valley.

Here we go again. Will the Bitch-and-Moan Brothers launch on yet another wild adventure? Watching television the North Country way, a genuine Red House classic in the making.

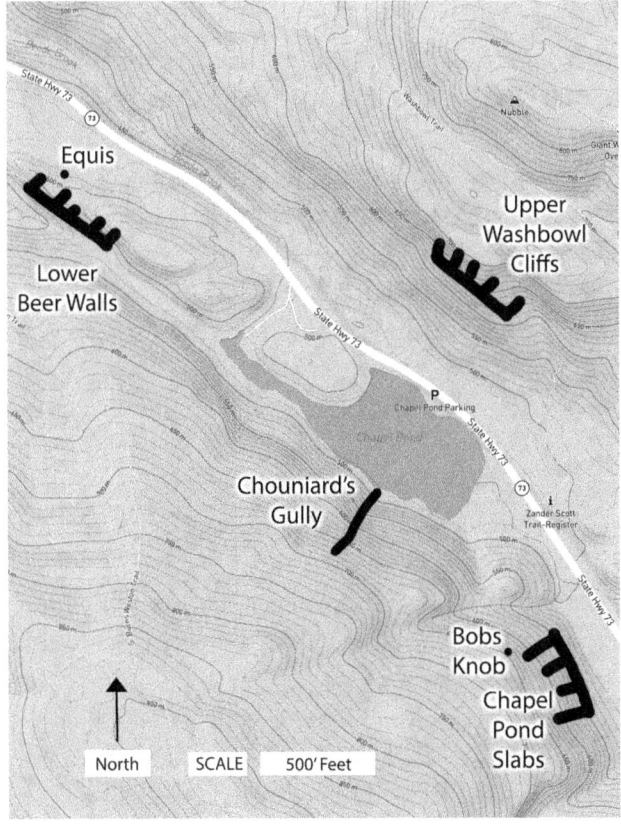

Chapel Pond Pass in the Adirondacks is host to famous climbing, indicated in thick lines.

THE NIGHT IS CALM, the street quiet as a mouse with no one around. Midweek is wonderful as the traffic to Lake Placid mellows. Outside the Village Grocery, I drop my quarters into the pay phone. I hear a voice whisper, "Hello?"

"Hi, Mom, it's David calling to say hi."

"Nice of you to call. I'm a bit tired right now. Lissa is here, and your father is at church." Mom doesn't sound good.

I think fast. "Mom, I saw the most amazing thing while walking in the backyard. Stumbled upon a quaint deer family, a momma, and two fawns. They weren't scared of me at all. Finished their snack and dashed off into the brush."

"Oh, that's nice," Mom says softly. I can tell she's in pain. She moves the phone away, and I hear her speak to my sister. "Here's Lissa. I need to lie down. I love you."

"Bye, Mom, take care. I love you too." Not good.

My sister gets on. "Mom's not doing well. It's been a long couple of days. I'm worried for her."

Turning away from the lamplight, drops of rain start to fall. Of course, I forgot my Gore-Tex. "Should I come home? I can drive down after work tomorrow."

"She's better than she has been. Call and talk to Pop tomorrow. I should go."

I hear the concern in her voice. "Good night, sister dear." Hang up the phone as the drizzle increases, soaking my head. Crossing the street, I'm splashed by some clown in a rush to get to Lake Placid.

It's warm and raining a few days later. Too wet for climbing, hiking a fail with nary a view due to the cloud cover. My shift at the Mountaineer starts in three hours.

Sipping coffee on the Red House porch, cars whizz by, crossing the bridge over Johns Brook. Its super-strong metal girders support the road ten feet off the brook, thirty feet long. An idea percolates in my brain; I turn with conviction to grab some gear.

Changing into wool pants and a rain parka, I wiggle into my

harness, rummaging for slings, carabiners, and two etriers (the French word for *ladder*).

Jamie stumbles down the stairs. "What's up, Flinny? All decked out for climbing?"

"I'm going to practice aid on the bridge." Using pro to hold my weight is called "aid climbing."

Back in the 1940s, all difficult sections were climbed using slings of nylon ladders, attached by carabiners to a piton hammered into a crack. Today, it's frowned upon but sometimes necessary.

"You're nuts," Jamie mutters on his way in search of coffee.

Fifteen minutes later, I'm hanging in the etriers under the bridge, practicing my big-wall aid climbing and thrashing around for a while, getting the hang of it.

Belay on, dangling like a mzungu.

Jamie on *Roaring Brook Falls*, Keene Valley, February 1980

CRUX

OCTOBER 1983 – APRIL 1984

"The Grateful Dead are coming to Lake Placid." Chatting with Carol, using the phone at the Mountaineer, saving a trek to the Valley Grocery pay phone. "Hope you can come, being it's a Monday night show." I met her last week when she stopped by the store. My fingers are crossed, fiddling with a carabiner.

"Let me check my calendar. Looks good; I don't have classes early in the week. It would be great to see the band. And you, of course."

"Excellent. Can you come Sunday?" Without any customers, the building is as silent as a mouse. Jim left an hour ago, and I'm holding down the fort.

"Hmm, I should be able to stay late on Tuesday. Can I let you know for sure next week?"

"Certainly. I hope we can squeeze in a hike up Baxter. I'll call you next Sunday to check in. Can't wait to see you. Bye!"

And hug you. I place the phone down gently and let my breath out. Outside, the sun is about to drop below the High Peaks. Time to blast outta here.

Lock the front door and glide down the porch, almost tripping over the iron boot scraper—perfect for muddy or snow-clogged hiking boots. The crushed stone in the parking lot crunches as I float into the Maverick. Gazing over the steering wheel at the Ausable River ten feet away, I pound the dash like a drum, belting out, "Yes, yes, yes!"

Driving past the intersection to Etown—Red House slang for Elizabethtown—The Rolling Stone's "Miss You" starts playing on the cassette deck.

I'm a turtle sticking my neck out, hoping to actualize a real relationship. When Tim's girlfriend and Carol visited the shop a week ago, time stopped, and the angels paused. Singing along with Mick Jagger at the top of my lungs, I'm thrilled that Carol is coming to see me.

Pulling into the Owl's Head[1] trailhead, I park next to Jamie's Rabbit and Ken's Toyota. Other people get together at bars or tennis games, but my friends prefer to bond on wild adventures. Running the quarter mile to the base of the crag, I discover a Red House siege underway with top ropes rigged and the lads crawling around.

Owl's Head is yet another gem in the area, with short climbs and beautiful views of the Great Range. I amble over to Bob who belays Ken.

He's the quiet one of the Red House. Newer to climbing, introspective, and stoic in the face of adversity. Bob introduced me to a local treasure, the Keene Valley Library. A fountain of knowledge on mountaineering books, he's a shoo-in for the Journal's book review editor.

"Watch, Ken; he's going barefoot," Bob replies. Most normal people use climbing shoes, but sure enough, Ken's feet are jammed in the crack as he hoots with displeasure.

"Got me? This is killing my toes. Oh, fook!" And he pops off, swinging from the rope as Bob holds him tight. "Let me down; to hell with this. Double hell to Jamie for sandbagging me."

"What's the matter, Kennie-poo, feeties too soft to climb like a real man?" Jamie yells from the other rope, also climbing barefoot.

"Screw you," Ken bellows as Bob lowers him to the ground next to me. Not leaving the belay, he sits down and laces his climbing shoes.

"Having a tough day?" I lean over and punch his arm as a sign of affection. "You going to climb or dangle around? I want a try before the sun sets. No more bitching and moaning."

"Back off, Flinny. Be helpful and take some pics. The ladies are clamoring for some good shots." Ken is dreaming. No way girls are in his life. He's too wild.

"Get cracking, Romeo," I answer. "Climb on." Chuckling, I turn back to Bob. "Has he been cranky all afternoon?"

Bob tightens the rope slack in the belay. "Nope, he's mad about being suckered into Jamie's barefoot thing. Ken's dialed in, going for the crux."

"Ah yes, the crux is the biscuit." The most challenging part of a route.

Bob resets his hands, keeping watch as a good belayer should. "Yep, every climb has a beginning, end, and a crux." The point of no return that defines success or failure. Ken is poised on the edge, where the handholds are thin and footholds the size of a pebble.

"You're waxing philosophic today." I reach into my pack for the camera. "There're many stages to a climb. Let's not forget about the approach, summit, and rappel."

"True! But not today. That's why I love top roping. Scooch around the back and hang a rope. A much simpler way to push my limits without all the hassle. Just me and the rock."

"It also avoids the potential of a long fall on the sharp end." Usually, the first climber, dragging the rope, takes all the risk—the danger of cratering to the ground if the system fails.

Bob nods. "Lead climbing is tricky, and soloing is super crazy. But the crux stays the same. It's up to us to overcome our mental traps and push on through. The climb is simply there."

"Potent stuff, Bob. You should write an article for the Journal. It needs deeper thoughts than the usual 'I was there' climbing story."

Ken moves onto a small ledge, shaking out his hands. I take a picture, hoping for a before and after shot if he falls. "He's about to go for it."

"Yup. Got ya', Ken. Crush it." Bob holds the rope, eyes focused.

Grumbling noises echo around the amphitheater as Ken mutters under his breath. Framing the shot, I nearly drop the camera with a snort. Four feet away, casual as can be, Tim sits on a ledge looking bored as Ken mumbles to himself, totally gripped.

I'm amused by how Ken is laboring on the crux while Tim relaxes casually. It's climbers' humor, juxtaposing badass intentions with the slouch of Why Bother?

Capturing the shot, I turn to Bob. "All we need is Jamie's boom box blasting out Hendrix to complete the craziness."

"Better to play the Grateful Dead. More appropriate." Bob pulls in more slack.

"Can't wait for the show." And to see Carol.

"This will be my first Dead concert." Bob keeps his eyes on Ken as he scoots past the crux, leaving Tim to his ledge of boredom.

"My first one, too," I say. "Saw lots of good bands in Syracuse: The Who, The Stones, Frank Zappa, and Little Feat. But this concert will be the best since Carol is coming."

I'm all dreamy, remembering the last time I saw her, with blonde shoulder-length hair, green eyes, and a mischievous smile as she waved goodbye.

"You haven't mentioned her before. Where did you meet her?"

"She's from Plattsburgh. She stopped in the Mountaineer last week. She's super busy working on her Master's. Can't believe she's going to come." Don't mention her lithe, fit body and the sharp, witty mind that leaves me in the mental dust.

"You warned her about the Red House, right? You should buy some real food before she gets here."

"Hmm, never thought about it. She handles the Plattsburgh parties; I think she'll be okay."

Bob gives me a Spock-raised eyebrow. "You better stash some toilet paper in your room."

I do live in a glorified frat house. Better get the vacuum out.

"Score!" Ken shouts. "Off belay. Beat you, Jamie, you wimp." Ken's arms are outstretched as he twirls in a victory dance, tangled in the rope.

Bob waits patiently and drops the belay when Ken stops his gyrations and unties from the rope.

"You're still a lunkhead." Jamie's voice sounds muffled. "Try the climb with a real handicap."

Ken on the crux, Tim chilling above at Owl's Head,
Cascade Pass, Adirondacks, October 1983.

Bob and I turn to see Jamie upside down, climbing up backward, feet first. The Bitch-and-Moan Brothers are fully unleashed. What is Carol going to think?

THE CROWD MILLS around the entrance as rain splatters, soaking our cotton clothes. Ken had to work in Albany, leaving the four of us. And no Carol.

When I called her yesterday to check in, she became evasive, saying stuff had come up, keeping her in Plattsburgh. Bummer. But she'll come this Saturday. Better late than never.

The doors open to our sigh of relief, and we flow onto the floor with the rest of the horde. Anticipating the best view, we find a spot near the back.

Before I know it, someone hands me a joint. Glancing at Tim, he shrugs, so I pass it on to the girl behind me. The lights dim, the chords of "Sugaree" jump out of the speakers, lights from a spaceship blaze down, and the show is underway.

There's plenty of room for dancing without chairs on the floor. Tons of people are decked out in tie-dye shirts and other hippie wear. Many lurch around in headbands and bare feet, their spacey eyes signaling me they're on acid. We sway to "Terrapin Station."

"Love the crowd," I shout over the music to Tim. "Folks are so happy. That's why they call it Lake Acid. How ya' doing?"

"Great. I love to dance. This is my third show." In the Dead world, it's respectable to be a groupie, traveling from city to city with the band. Anyone attending over twenty shows gets massive credibility at parties. "I love this song."

Everyone is having fun. You can tell the locals by their flannel shirts and hiking boots. Entering the arena, Tim noticed extra tickets on the steps, free for anyone to snag. This only happens in Lake Placid; Dead tickets are usually a hot commodity.

We're dancing in the venue built for the 1980 Winter Olympics, the same arena where the "Miracle on Ice" happened, the US hockey team winning gold. Everyone's a winner tonight.

Whisked into a human chain as the chords for "The Wheel" begin. The crowd skips along while the light show flashes, intoxicating and dazzling. We dance around the entire floor with a thousand people in tow, forming a human wheel. Above us, Jamie joins a congo line in the upper decks going the opposite way, the locals alongside the hippies.

Poof, the lights come on, trapping us like deer in headlights. Hard to believe it's over as we shuffle out like herded cattle from the arena. I drive us back to the Red House; everyone settles down and drifts off to bed. Alone.

~

I CAN'T BELIEVE IT. She's here. The house is empty, the lads out on a glorious Saturday morning. Totally worth taking the day off. I clasp Carol's hand and escort her upstairs. The office sits quietly, the sun glinting off the turntable hanging nearby. We pad into the closet, my hobbit hole.

"There you are." Carol lies on her tummy, eyes tracking me as I return from the john.

"Hey, honey, wanna back rub?" I don't give her much choice, straddling her cute buns. Slowly kneading her back, starting with the heels of my hands and transitioning to my fingers in a tapping pattern.

"Oh, this is good. Don't stop," she purrs.

"I won't." Bending over as my fingers work up her neck, I kiss her cheek. Her eye flashes open as a smile forms on her lips.

The best thing about the closet is that it's cozy.

~

BAXTER MOUNTAIN OFFERS a blueberry-bush-lined micro-hike minutes from the Red House. It's too late in the season to gobble the fruit, but the forest is still green and lush; fall is waiting to pounce. We sit on the summit overlooking Mount Marcy to the right, Dix to the left, and the Great Range in the middle. Stunning. Like Carol.

"This has been fun. I'm glad I came." She shuffles her feet.

"Me too. It's wonderful to be with you." We hold hands, our lunch of cheese, salami, and apples demolished.

Carol lets go and wraps her arms around her knees. "About that. My life is getting more complicated, David. You're far away. I've applied to Boston University for my Ph.D. We have a lot in common, but I'm not sure the long-distance will work for me."

Clouds form to block the sun, and I shiver with chills. What? This is getting heavy quickly. Didn't we just meet?

"Ah, I see. Isn't it the wrong time to apply to school?" All I can do is stall.

"My professor encouraged me since he knows the chairperson. My research should make it easy to get in. It's something I've always wanted to do."

This doesn't sound indecisive. "I can respect a calling. It's why I came to Keene Valley. When will you find out?"

"I should hear back soon, perhaps at the end of the month. I'm sorry if this is sudden."

The clouds have thickened and ruined our sun-worshipping. "It's getting late. Let's head back." My dream of an alpine girl stays on top of Baxter as we jump rocks on the way down.

"No stepping on the dirt," I say. "Last one touching stone wins." When in a funk, it's time to spice it up with a game, a trail version of hopscotch.

At the Red House, Carol packs her bag in the car and puts on flops. Her blonde hair rustles in the wind as we embrace, her body warm and snuggly. At last, she steps back and opens the door.

"I'll let you know as soon as I find out. Thank you for a great time. I'll never forget it."

Blowing kisses as she backs out onto Route 73, I wave as her car chugs down the road. Rain starts splattering. Sitting on the porch, staring at the bushes, sadly realizing I've been dumped. Wonder if I'll ever see her again.

～

THE SUN PEEKS through the trees as we scootle along the approach to the Beer Walls. Discovered last year, the two crags are 150 feet high, littered with one- or two-pitch climbs, and fifteen minutes from the Red House.

The Maverick and Rabbit are parked across from the Spiders Web, another dramatically picturesque cliff near the road. The quarter-mile hike scales a tiny ridge filled with young birch, spruce, maple, and hemlock.

The Lower Beer Walls in Chapel Pond Pass of the Adirondacks. *Equis* is hidden by the tree branch on the left, *The Sword* is just visible. Photo by How Hulher, March 2019.

Jamie stops at the crossroads where the climbers' paths split left and right to the top of each crag. "Ah, what a glorious fall morning. Check out the patterns on the ground."

The dappled sun creates flickering shafts of light on the forest floor. "Whoa, trippy, nature's Dead show," I say. "Which wall today? I vote for Lower."

Catching up, Bob says, "I love this approach; not even working up a sweat. Easy-peasy. Where are we going?" He's dressed in a button-down blue shirt, khakis, and trim hiking boots. You'd think he's heading to the office.

Jamie settles his pack, harness cluttered with pro and slings, which generates a soft jingling of wind chimes. "Lower it is. Remember, be kind to the trees on the way down. The increased foot traffic is eroding the soil."

As we continue south into the sun, the trail drops steeply into a gully filled with baby hemlocks. Swinging from tree to tree, pretending to be Tarzan, we come to the bottom of the sixty-foot descent.

Turning right past the classic *Fast and Furious*, we enter the Lower Beer Wall sanctuary, a collection of twenty routes. Trundling past

Draught Dodger, *Rockaholic*, and *The Sword*, Jamie stops. "What about this one?"

"Ah, look at that flake," I say. "Super. I'm game to lead it." The flake, a thin slab of rock detached from the main face, reminds me of an elephant ear.

"It's called *Equis*[2]," Jamie says. "I did the first ascent this spring. A bit gnarly and thinly protected, but it's a pleasing little line." He drops his pack near the birch tree at the base.

"Excellent, I'm psyched. Thanks for letting me go first. Gotta be back at the Mountaineer by noon."

He settles on a boulder and lies back. "You'll do fine. Is this your first 5.8 lead?"

"Yeah. I've done a bunch of 5.7s, but this will be my first hard climb. Not sure it'll go, but might as well try." And not think about the crux.

"Ah, young Skywalker, there is no try. Only do."

I can't help but smile as he sounds like Yoda speaking in a Scottish accent.

Being Tuesday, the crag is quiet without weekend warriors swarming the place. I sling my pack to the ground, pulling out my new Firés (pronounced *fee-rays*), all the rage due to their grippy, sticky soles.

My toes begin their usual complaint as I wedge my feet into the cramped climbing shoes. On goes the harness, the tinkling of a carabiner against the figure-eight belay device, followed by my Grateful Dead chalk bag.

Tying the rope into the harness, uneasiness worms in my stomach. It always happens when anticipating something new, the uncertainty seeping through my body, ready to hatch and take wing in my mind.

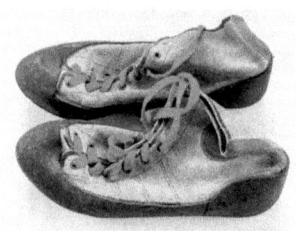

Firé climbing shoes by Boreal from the early 1980s.

To combat the bugger, I breathe deeply, focusing on my equipment to conquer the fear.

"You can do it, Flinny," Jamie chirps as he notices my apprehension. "No nasty weather or bugs to mess with your concentration. Rack up!"

Jamie at Mount Jo in the Adirondacks., Spring 1978.
Photo from the Jamie Cunningham collection.

Jamie's full of life, driven to climb, but remarkably compassionate, the Red House version of Hamish MacInnes, the famous Scottish climber, the father of international mountain rescue.

He runs a climbing school and uncovered many routes on the Beer Walls. It's a tough life, but he's determined to make a living doing what he enjoys. Because of the recession, he's struggled to find a job using his Forest Management degree. He figured, "Why not start a guide service?"

Jamie's patient teaching style is usually accompanied by a Scottish brogue thrown in for fun. He channels Hamish as his hero, ready to launch into sustained monologues about the glory of climbing in "full conditions," Scottish slang for lousy weather.

I reply timidly, "No sweat. I've been trained by the best. Bob, are you ready with the belay?"

"Absolutely. Nothing better than a bomber birch," he replies, setting the belay anchor around the eight-inch tree with a sling.

Bob was raised outside of Albany, two hours south. After years of being trapped in the Air Force, he escaped to Keene Valley and got sucked into the climbing world after renting a cheap room in the Red House.

He reminds me of Galen Rowell, a dapper photographer who is drawn to the artistic dimensions of climbing. Bob is fantastic, supportive, and caring, never uttering a harsh word.

The final ritual begins with the Sorting of the Rack. I organize my pro, metal devices of all shapes and sizes used in cracks as anchors. Each of the twenty pieces has loops with wire or nylon, similar to a fishing lure. The collection of pro on the rack has a riot of colors, easy to distinguish one from the other, but also for fun. Style does matter.

Bob notices me futzing around. "Yo, Flinny, you can do this. You did great on *The Sword* the other day. You'll be fine."

"Thanks for the support. Gotta boost the ol' confidence." My palms are sweaty. I wipe them on my shirt before stuffing them in the chalk bag. Smacking my palms together raises a puff of white.

"Relax," Jamie adds. "Most of the route is easy. Place solid pro, rest, and focus on the birch. The crux is on the flake."

Craning my neck, I mentally take note of the birch tree. To combat this whoosh of anxiety, it's time to delve down, breathe deeply, and trust my body to act. I can do it. Time to stop fear in its tracks. "Excellent intel. Okay, lads, time to move."

Bob belays me to the lower ramp, where I reach a sloping ledge, placing a stellar Hex. Clipping in with a sigh of relief, now protected from a nasty fall. It's one of the reasons I love climbing, engineering my pro in the name of safety.

"Flinny, the spiders are spinning cobwebs. Off to the flake you go!" Jamie encourages me, hoping his humor helps me relax.

Easy climbing below the crux, the vertical right-facing flake looks like Dumbo's ear. Comprised of two chunks of rock, stacked like layers of Pringles potato chips, the flake rounds right for ten feet, then doubles back to the left another twenty feet to the tree. Settling in to place a wired Stopper, I check the time. My sense of duty starts to nag, urging action instead of dawdling. I don't want to be late for work.

Climbing protection from the 1980s. Starting from the left: figure-eight belay device and carabiner, Wild Country Rocks, Lowe Tri-Cam, Chouinard Hexentrics, Wild Country Friends.

Hanging out next to the Stopper, the severe exposure to the flake grips my mind. The more I hesitate, the more nausea unwinds inside. Paralysis builds as the fear grows, and assurance in my ability wanes.

I let go of the pro and the carabiner clinks against the rock. Peering into the flake, feet awkwardly balanced, the left arm bent instead of straight. My tummy grumbles; the caterpillars are quaking in their cocoons.

The flake requires a funky move before continuing to the bomber birch. My left foot starts to jiggle, caught up in sewing-machine leg, calf bobbling up and down as it strains to hold.

"Come on, man; you can do it!" Bob shouts from below. "You might wanna place some pro!"

"I'm on it." Wheezing and struggling to breathe as my brain abandons my body, my lack of confidence blossoms. I step into Dumbo's ear, thrashing in a failed attempt to insert a *Friend*. Jamie let me borrow his most coveted piece, designed to insert quickly into a waiting crack.

Ten feet above the Stopper, exposed to a nasty fall, the lack of oxygen burns muscle, my body contorted on the crux. Gripped as fear courses through me, trust in my ability is shot. I go to that ugly place, calculating the twenty-foot fall—splat city kitty.

Bob yells, "When in doubt, run it out!" as encouragement. Gotta do something. Fast. Back down to place gear or dash for the birch? What to do? Clenching my right fist in the widening crack, I shake out my fried left arm. Lock my fingers and move my left foot into the crack—time to run it out.

As my arm strength fails, I try to visualize success, reaching the tree, when suddenly my right-hand pops free. The caterpillars hatch abruptly and the butterflies are poised to fly.

My left hand tries to keep its grasp on the flake, but I swing out, a barn door opening. The shelter of the birch tree fades as my foot rips from the crack, and I pitch backward.

Bob and Jamie yell as I dangle from the rope after falling twenty feet, saved by the Stopper. Hanging free of the wall, spinning slowly, Bob lowers me forty feet to the ground. All is quiet but the creaking of the rope.

"Dave, that was intense." Jamie hugs me. "You made it a bit too quick, but at least you didn't crater."

I shake my head. "So close. Just a tad longer, I would have made it." Slowly untying from the rope, my poor left ankle yelps in pain, torqued when I peeled off the flake. "My first long leader fall. Lucky that Stopper held."

"Dude, you should go back and try again," Jamie says. "It's better to return to the scene of the crime. Fear of falling can linger with you."

Sitting in the dirt, shaking my head. My ankle pulses with pain. The butterflies turn into wasps as I realize I'll be late for work.

STILL HOBBLING AROUND two weeks after the fall, I've had plenty of time to recall my mistakes. It's a bummer that things with Carol went south; I thought she was the one. Compounded by spacing out when it mattered most on *Equis*. I need to know what I want and take it. Enough woolgathering; it's time to rally.

Channeling my angst into creative energy, I focus on the Journal. After yapping for months about publishing, it's time to buckle down and get her done.

Bob is rigging the belay at Owl's Head in Cascade Pass,
Adirondacks, October 1983.

The articles cover climbing, backcountry skiing, and hiking. Magazines such as *National Geographic*, *Outside*, and *Mountain* are great, but they rarely cover Adirondack outdoor adventure.

This first edition will have book reviews, how-to guides, and hand-drawn maps of the area. Need to grab content from Jamie and Bob to round it out.

Pondering about waxing philosophical and writing about my fall. Climbers are expected to show strength, never give up, and continually strive for success. Do folks want to learn from my mistakes? Nah, no one wants to read about losers. The Red House gang shrugs it off; big falls are part of the game.

The door slams and Bob yells from downstairs. "Flinny, get down here. The sun is gorgeous; time to play Frisbee. Stop moping."

Good idea.

The backyard of the Red House is my favorite. One hundred yards away, the Ausable River bubbles as it flows north to Lake Champlain.

Bob tosses the Frisbee, and I lunge as it careens over my head, diving into the grass jungle.

The two-foot tall wavy green stalks whisper to me as I stumble. Waddling over to where it landed—a few snarls, then a triumphant grin —and thank the grass for returning it.

I zip the disc back to Bob. "It's time for a beer. Enough of this."

"Okay, Sir Gimpasaurus, I'll snag the libations." Bob heads into the kitchen while I gratefully sit in the beach chair, welcoming the sun's warmth. My ankle still aches.

"Ah, thank you." I take the proffered bottle. The river gurgles as the slight wind rustles the grass. It doesn't get better than this.

But I'm still glum. "You know, I freaked out when it mattered most. Certainly, my downfall."

Bob takes a swig and snorts. "You're still obsessing? We all make mistakes. Think how you'd feel if you'd cratered. Gads, get over it. You should focus your addled brain on that girl Carol instead of moaning." He reaches over and gives me a light punch.

"I'm trying. Processing my screwup helps to avoid the next one. Should have focused harder on the crux."

"Or down climbed to place pro. Remember, young Skywalker, let the Force flow within you. Believe in yourself."

"Right, that would have been better. Faith in my ability."

Bob clinks my beer. "Start by letting it go and call Carol. Don't Bitch-and-Moan. I avoid the sharp end. That's how I manage my fear." Bob smiles and sits back, soaking in the glorious rays.

The door slams and Tim strolls over. Wearing a flannel shirt underneath his fuzzy jacket, he's our Marlboro mountain man, without the cigarettes.

"Tim! Great to see you. You look exhausted. Cop a squat." I free the extra chair from my propped-up leg. "How's the house?"

He sits in the empty seat, tilts back on the rear legs, and cracks a bottle of water. "Coming along. The second floor is framed, and tomorrow the roof goes on. We hope to finish before the first snow. Should take a few weeks."

Since I started at the Mountaineer, Tim works full-time as a designer for a local builder.

Tim after ice climbing at the North Face of Pitchoff in
Cascade Pass, Adirondacks, December 1983.

He loves to pound nails, is great at drawing plans, and does it all to
punch the clock. He's doing well using his college skills, but North
Country pay is barely better than minimum wage. But he'd never
consider moving to the city to make more.

"Listen to this. Remember the rainy day at the Dead show? I had
lunch with the foreman at the Noonmark Diner today."

Tim takes a sip. "He claims a Deadhead entered the laundry and
tossed her dress into the dryer. While waiting for it to finish, the girl
danced around buck-naked to some internal tune."

Bob spits out his beer. "You gotta be kidding me. Too funny."

"No wonder the locals are talking about this weeks later," I add.

Tim smiles. "Wish I could have seen it." His face forms a frown
suddenly.

"You look sad, matey," Bob says. "Relax, it'll snow, and you'll be
happy."

Tim pulls a postcard from his jacket pocket. "I stopped at the post office and grabbed the mail. This is for you."

He hands me the card slowly. As I take it, he says, "Sorry, man, hate to be the messenger."

It's from Carol. My heart bounces as I skim the note. She's leaving Plattsburgh shortly and starting school at Boston University in January. Hopes I'm well. Good luck climbing, signed Carol. No "miss you" or "can't wait to see you soon." Guess she meant it—a cloud scuds by, blocking the sun. The breeze rustling the grass blows leaves at my feet.

~

THE FOLLOWING SATURDAY MORNING, my housemates are busy, and I'm hanging with Ken. There's not much else to do in Keene Valley but head into the woods. My ankle is stiff, but I relish some exercise.

Bored with Chapel Pond Pass, we trundle over to Poke-O-Moonshine, another Adirondack classic, its name adapted from the Algonquin language. Our eyes are on *Gamesmanship*, one of the top 5.8 climbs.

The approach is straightforward, a half mile to the base, and we follow the long rock wall, searching for the route. The tiny photo in the guidebook doesn't cut it. I wish we had checked with Jamie.

"What do you think, Ken? Keep going?"

"This line appears to be *Freedom Flight*."

"Wow, that looks fun. What's the grade of this one?" I point to our right. Birch trees wave in the sunlight, peering over the top of the crag.

"*Summer Solstice*. That looks wild—a bit much at 5.11. Crap, you're right, Flinny. On we go."

We keep looking, popping into a sun-dappled clearing to discover belay spots for many climbs. We drop packs at the base of what we think is *Gamesmanship*[3] as Ken reviews the scant details in Mellor's book. That's the challenge with guidebooks. They often provide just enough information to confuse you.

Camping out on a boulder, I wait for Ken. Thank goodness he loves figuring out routes so I can just relax and follow his lead.

Ken on the first ascent of *Look, Roll, and Fire* at Hurricane Crags,
Adirondacks. Photo by Jamie Cunningham, April 1984.

He graduated from Union College in Electrical Engineering and has a great job at General Electric. He's chosen the weekend warrior life, working in the city during the week and driving to Keene Valley on weekends. Ken's highly motivated, passionate about the outdoors, and full of energy. I love his spark and nothing gets him down.

After my fall, I'm melancholy about leading, happy to follow. Moping about Carol, a double whammy to the ol' confidence. I play with a maple leaf, slowly stripping the blade from the stem.

"Okay, Flinny, enough putzing around; I'm climbing this sucker." At long last, he's getting pumped up.

Ken struggles on the first pitch, grunting, with a few hollers for good measure. I'm using a bomber birch belay, gazing around, enjoying the chirp of swallows and the chatter of a jay.

No Zen Belay today; I'm attentive but bored. Luckily, he doesn't fall, but time crawls. He yells off belay, and I get ready, tying the laces on my Firés.

The rope rises, tightening, encouraging me to climb. I follow the line of pro as the crack swallows my feet. Soon it widens six inches, forcing me to step left on the face, my right foot wedged in the crack.

I'm not too fond of these moves, steep walls with tenuous holds. My sore ankle whines its displeasure, adding to my funk. The crack thins drastically to nothing.

My fingers root for a better grip but my right-hand slips. Focused but not freaked, I step down to rest. If you call a foot crammed into a mouse hole a rest. Instead of getting all in a lather, I look carefully for holds.

Place my left foot high, reaching past the diminishing crack to where it widens. Right foot on a nubbin on the face. I got this crux. It's a chess game, a sequence of moves that must be done quickly.

No problem. Visualize and let the Force flow through me.

Clambering to the belay, hands tinged pink; blood mingled with chalk. "Man, that pitch is a brute. Great lead, matey. You are styling to crank that without a fall. Next time I should tape my knuckles." Ken hands me a sling to clip into. "Thanks. Off belay."

He starts organizing the rope. "My arms are fried. This next pitch looks gnarly and intimidating. Not sure it's in the cards for us today."

Sitting in the harness, legs out straight to keep my balance, I ponder the crack. A vast, towering roof lurks overhead, forbidding. "Yow. We must be out of shape. Thought it would be easier."

A rappel ring makes it easier to retrieve the rope by minimizing friction. Photo by Omega Pacific.

"Probably another guidebook sandbag. Let's bail."

Ken modifies the belay for rappelling while I untie from the rope and thread it through the waiting rappel ring. It's attached to a bomber piton; we don't think twice about it.

Thank goodness the locals left it for us to use. It would suck to leave pro as booty for the next climber. The rappel is easy, and I pull the rope when two climbers arrive. And we chat about how gnarly it seems.

Climbers on *Summer Solstice* at Poke-O-Moonshine,
Adirondacks, October 1983. The route suffered a
massive rockfall in 1998 and is no longer climbable.

You dolts, they tell us, this is *Fastest Gun*, a hard 5.10. *Gamesman-ship* is back around the bend. Humbled but impressed that we didn't thrash on the bugger, we scamper off, letting the hardcore lads go for it.

This time we find the apparent start to *Gamesmanship*. Shrugging, we look at each other and drop our packs, figuring we'll do the first pitch in the remaining light—time to patch up our pride.

THE ROCK-CLIMBING season winds down as the snow falls in early November. I hope to publish the first edition of my magazine before Christmas. An eight-page, glorified newsletter for seventy-five cents.

Typing on my old typewriter in three-and-a-half-inch columns, the articles come to life. Bob finishes his book review, and Jamie adds a rock-climbing story. Using a cartography pen, I draw the graphics, maps, and logo on vellum. The light table makes tracing easier.

The choice of a printer is simple; Denton Publications is the closest. They take my precious layouts and run the presses, generating two hundred copies, folded and stapled. As I drive to Etown, the roads are clear; my anticipation is high.

I love the feel of its quality paper in my hands. It's my subtle inner desire for fame, to be a 5.10 publisher, read by all the heroes and dirt-bags in the outdoor adventure world. A dream for almost a year, and I'm grateful it's done. Creation is powerful, pushing through obstacles to make it happen—an architect of words in the woods.

A proud parent, I realize the hard part is about to begin. Producing is fun, but selling is hard. Wrapping dozens of packages, I mail them to outdoor stores in the Northeast, hoping they'll put them out for sale. Thankfully, Jim at the Mountaineer takes a bunch, and now I'm at the Valley Grocery trying to hawk some issues.

"I don't know if we could sell such a thing here," Mrs. Hall says in her local drawl. She's the iconic North Country woman, stoic and warm but with no desire to enter the woods. It surprises me that people live here and never voyage into the wilderness.

"Please, Mrs. Hall, it's a product of Keene Valley. For the adventurous souls that come into your store."

"I don't know if this is a good idea," she counters. She wears flats for comfort, her dress hidden under her white grocer's smock, its telltale smudges indicating hard work.

I cave. "How about if you don't pay for them yet? I'll collect later if they sell."

"Okay, sonny, we can try that." She cracks a happy smile as she places the journal on the newsstand. Chalk up another success in selling the North Country way.

"Thanks again, Mrs. Hall. I'll be back when the next issue is ready."

Leaving the store, the door bangs softly, and I walk over to the telephone two feet away. Using the calling card Dad gave me a few months ago, dialing Carol's number. A woman answers, and I introduce myself. Carol moved out and left for Boston last week. Sorry, she didn't leave a number. I thank her quietly, leaning against the wall, staring out into the somber gray of winter.

Shaking off the sad news, I trudge through a snowbank to the post office. Reaching into the Journal's box, pulling out crammed letters and bills, I notice a postcard from Seattle. My SUOC friend Jim wrote to thank me for the magazine and to invite me to climb Mount Rainier in June. Rainier! Now that's a real mountain. Thankfully, I see his phone number scribbled at the bottom.

Carol forgotten, I cross the street, walking north back to the Red House, a couple of blocks away. Keene Valley is a magical village with sidewalks on both sides, still slushy from the recent snow. Cars zoom by in their haste to Lake Placid. I'm glad they're rushing away from my happy place, leaving it all to me.

If I'm going to Seattle, I need to get another job. The Mountaineer is unable to provide me with additional hours. I can certainly hitch out west to save the airfare, but still need more cash. A climber's quandary: how to pay for all the fun?

I float past the houses along the way and land on the front porch, barging into the living room. "Jamie! It's time for an adventure."

He looks up from *The Fox of Glencoe* by Hamish MacInnes and answers with a yawn, "Hoo boy, you're all fired up. Gotta admit I appreciate the spirit."

Still about an inch off the floor, I can't contain myself. "I'm going to Rainier. I just got a postcard. Time for some serious training."

"New York mountains aren't quite the same, laddie. Won't help you learn about crevasses or avalanches."

I spin around. "Yeah, but we need to start somewhere. Wanna go tomorrow?"

Jamie frowns. "I've got ice climbing clients coming up from Albany, so I'm out. What's your plan?"

"Ski over Avalanche Pass and solo *The Trap Dike*[4]. Think it'll go?"

"Of course, it will. With all the snow, it should be more of a waddle than a climb. What about Bob or Tim?"

"You were my last hope, Obi-wan J-o-mi. Han Soloing, I go!"

~

THE ALARM BUZZES, forcing a yawn followed by a stretch to motivate for the cold January day: polypropylene, wool pants, and sweater. Abandoning the closet, I creep downstairs for breakfast and stuff my harness, slings, carabiners, Snarg ice pitons, axes, and crampons into my pack. The Gore-Tex parka, fuzzy jacket, and water follow. Don't forget the headlamp.

A few weeks ago, Tim mentioned a mystical group of mad-dogs called the Ski to Die Club that roam the steep open slides of the Adirondack backcountry. These snow warriors have been climbing and skiing down incredible routes on Mount Marcy, Giant, and other High Peaks. Inspired by these folks, I prefer Ski to Climb. Sure, I'll ski down, but on the trail where it's safer.

Just in case I don't return, I take a moment to scribble a hasty note on a napkin telling the lads my planned route. Grab my pack and jump into the Maverick for a drive through Cascade Pass to the historic Adirondack Loj.

Slide into my leather cross-country ski boots in the deserted parking lot; the rustle of trees interrupts the winter silence. The trailhead register has a recently scribbled name, and I follow his tracks up the trail.

Snow falls quietly from the trees, plopping into the fresh powder. My skis glide smoothly on the 2.5-mile flat trail to Marcy Dam.

I push on, crisscrossing ice-glazed Marcy Brook, dodging trees and rocks, grateful for my skis. It would be insane to post-hole in the two feet of snow, boots plunging deep with each step. Not to mention the huge energy drain.

Soon the path steepens, heading to Avalanche Pass, and I begin to thrash, ski wax useless on the grade. Talk about burning calories.

Fortunately, I'm prepared and take a break to add climbing skins to the skis. My synthetic copies of Eskimo seal skin will provide enough traction to enable me to enjoy the ascent. As an added treat, the spruces near the trail waft a strong Christmas Tree fragrance.

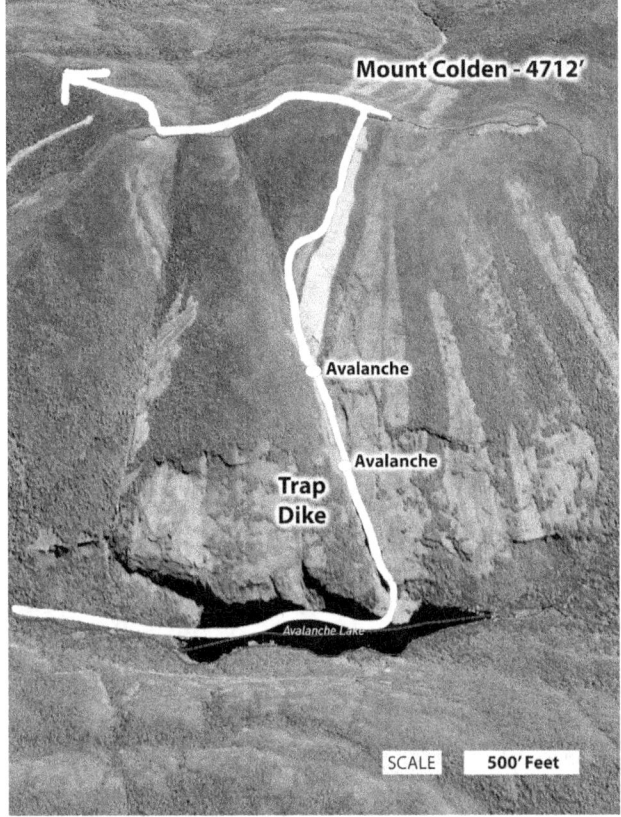

Looking east to *The Trap Dike* on Mount Colden,
Avalanche Pass, Adirondacks.

The formula for a safe and successful outing requires a mix of capability, conditions, and solid teamwork. Changing these variables can either stack or deplete the deck in my favor. Going alone could result in a 52-card pickup disaster.

Chugging to the top, I'm thrilled my ankle is fully healed. The last two months of ice climbing have built my strength and confidence.

Predicting the weather is another challenge. Rain, storms, and temperature fluctuations can drastically alter the scenario. The forecast could be perfect one day and a nightmare the next. Fortunately, today's weather is classic winter.

A thread of worry forms in the back of my mind, questioning the wisdom of going solo five miles from the road in the middle of winter.

I'd rather be with my friends for safety, but when the conditions are ripe, it's time to motivate and take the risk.

My skis halt when the woods thin and the wind spins snow devils around me. The sky is gloomy gray as I approach Avalanche Lake from the narrow confines of the pass, yet patches of blue beckon.

The frozen lake appears in front of me, as the wind blows constantly in my face. Minutes later, the snow-covered talus slope at the base of the Dike appears on the left. I stomp a flat space on a fluffy mound with my skis.

The transition to vertical begins, and I shed skis for crampons. Wolf down a PB&J sandwich and fig newtons, strap on the harness, and slide the ice hammer into its holster. Skis and adjustable poles are strapped to the pack. After a slug of water, slide the ice axe leash over my Dachstein mitten, and it's time to roll.

The sides of the Dike tower over me. Huge boulders lodge in its walls, precariously perched to thunder down at the slightest noise. Thank goodness for my trusty Joe Brown climbing helmet.

Enclosed in the steep gully, wading through deep snow, I clamber over a fun bulge that requires both ice tools for security—no time for a fall, tumbling down, crashing into a heap, miles from the road. *Stop thinking dire thoughts.* Plant, step, plant, step, reaching a snow basin to rest.

Smack dab in the middle of the climb, the walls narrow to fifteen feet wide. My skis restrict easy movement; I slowly turn and face down the dike. Avalanche Lake is a postcard scene, with the gray stone contrasting with the gleaming white, and my ski tracks are the sole indication of life.

Wading through the snow is tricky as the ski tails bump the backs of my calves. Not much of an ice climb, I grumble silently. Can almost swim in this stuff.

Whomp. A loud noise echoes throughout the dike.

Snow begins to slide, forcing me back against the wall. A roaring whitewater river, the rumble grows louder as it rushes by, waves complete with snow, chunks of frozen bergs rising to the bubbly surface. Thankfully, I'm wedged in the eddy, a haven. Or so I believe.

Looking into *The Trap Dike* on Mount Colden.
Avalanches commonly form in the channel in high
snow years. Photo by Carol Hatch, January 2022.

The snow pushes against my legs, trying to pry me loose. As it moves faster, I instinctively grab the closest secure thing, a slender birch sapling, pulling me close to the wall.

An avalanche! I've read about them in books. It's hard to process the reality of what's happening. Sweat drips down my back. Twenty seconds ooze by, and finally, the angry hissing snow slows to a halt.

Wiggling out from the pack, whacking my skis against the wall, I root for the water bottle to take a drink, munching chocolate, figuring out what to do next.

Am I shaken up? Yup. Will I make it? Absolutely. After pondering the options, it's simple: climb up or thrash down. The avalanche path is two steps away, and my eyes swivel back and forth, looking both ways to cross the freeway at rush hour. Shit.

Sweat chills the body, growing tired of mental shenanigans. Cavers go down; climbers go up. Seeing the exit of the dike ahead, I slowly tread snow as water, my left hand on the wall keeping my balance, the right holding the axe, its shaft pointed straight down as if it were a ski pole.

Wallowing to the top of another bulge, and sure enough, *whoom-pooof* echoes in the dike, and more snow shears off.

Thank God I'm out of the way, and the bus-sized slide thunders past, generating another flurry from my belly. This avalanche stuff is getting old.

Nearing the top, I dash over short ten-foot headwalls of ice, praising the Charlet Moser hammer for its security when ice shatters under my crampons.

Adrenaline pushes me up the final slog to the spruce and fir trees on the summit ridge. I'm tired but happy to have made it to the trail. The constant need to be on guard makes soloing exhausting.

It's time to reap the reward of the vista that flashes in the wind-swirled snow. The stunted trees at the top are encased in ice rime.

The wind fills the path with snow as dusk and cold descend. Standing on the top as the wind gusts, I deserve to dawdle and gawk after the avalanche drama. Across the pass, the ice on Algonquin glimmers between the snow squalls.

Dusk descends, hastening me to head back, stumbling, sliding, struggling with tired limbs. Finding a break in the wind, I sit on my pack to shed the crampons, helmet, and harness. After wolfing some Toblerone chocolate and water, I pull out my skis and, with a schuss and a boom, slide down the bobsled track of a trail.

Exhilarated after channeling my version of a Ski to Die Club adventure; headlamp on, stars out, crossing Marcy Dam, skis hissing. The wind drops, and the icy brook gurgles as I plod on.

Avalanche Pass is aptly named, and my fear residue schusses away, but the tipping point of its crux humbles me before it goes. Maybe all this climbing and skiing is about testing my survival skills. A way to cope in case things turn bad in the real world, knowing I can overcome adversity. The mountain tossed its worst, but I prevailed.

IN JANUARY, I begin waiting tables at the Holiday Inn in Lake Placid two evenings a week, where I can clear $100 a night if it's busy. Last Sunday, I had a huge order on my shoulder when the tray slipped down my back and crashed to the floor. The cook was steamed but didn't throw his spatula at me. Humbling for sure.

A few months later, Mountaineer Jim's in the office doing boss man stuff, leaving me to lounge out front, waiting for customers. Usually, a bunch of ice climbers are thawing out next to the fire. The store attracts outdoor adventurers with perks not found at other shops. It's the subtle things that add spice to life.

Flipping through the latest issue of *Mountain* magazine, I enjoy the quiet solace of reading by the wood stove until boredom sinks in.

Walking to the counter, I use the phone to call home. Dad sounds the same, telling me Easter prep is in full swing. Asking about Mom, she jumps on the other extension, saying she's tired but hanging in there. Spring is busy season at the office, she explains, with lots of houses coming on the market.

"Glad you guys have a lot going on. I'm finishing up issue two of the AAJ. Going hog wild with real pictures, glossy paper, a much nicer product."

"That's great, Dave," Dad says. "How's the job?"

"It's going okay. I enjoy helping people, but the magazine makes life interesting. How are Bear and Lissa?"

"Andy's at LaSalle, and Lissa's working at the seal sanctuary in the Bronx."

My brother is going to a military academy; bless his soul. Lissa's saving harbor seals at a small aquarium. I don't tell my folks about the avalanches on *The Trap Dike*. They've no concept of what climbing is about. I'm not trying to hide things, but too much information can be bad.

Hearing the tramp of footsteps, a man walks into the store. I quickly say goodbye to Mom and Dad.

"Hello, my name's David, and welcome to the Mountaineer. How are you today?"

"Huh? Oh, hi. I'm good." He barges past the counter and heads to the climbing section in the back of the store.

As the dude reaches up to rub the toys, another creak on the porch precedes the door opening. I gaze into the eyes of the most striking woman I've seen all winter.

"Ah, hullo. Welcome to the, uh, Mountaineer. Let me know if you —you need any help with anything." Cat got my tongue.

"Hey, honey, come over here," the man yells. "Check these babies out."

She cracks a small smile and walks over to the climbing section. I could have sworn she rolled her eyes.

Jim walks out of the office carrying a box of new gadgets for sale. As he joins me at the counter, he looks over at Beauty holding a cashmere wool sweater. He turns back to me; we both shrug.

After Beauty uses the bathroom, they take off in a shiny BMW without buying anything. I lounge back against the counter. "What the hell's a gorgeous woman doing with such a tool?"

Jim sighs and leans next to me, crossing his arms in his professor pose. "All I can say is he has some hidden talent or tons of money. But why do you care? I saw you with that blonde girl last fall."

Stiffening, I look down at the floor. "Ah, I haven't heard from her. She moved to Boston. Don't know what went wrong."

Jim's silent for a bit. "Climbers are a wild breed, David. Most women don't understand what drives us. They love the energy and intensity, but that cools when they realize we may never alter our priorities in life. They can feel they're always second to our love for climbing."

His eyes are compassionate, and I'm grateful for someone who can describe my feelings.

"Thanks, Jim. That helps. I hope to meet a girl that wants to tromp around in the woods."

"If you find one, marry her. Take my word on it." Jim taps me on the shoulder and walks back to the office.

Mountaineer Jim styling on *Pitchoff Right* in Cascade
Pass, Adirondacks, January 1984.

The door squeaks open, and Tim marches in. "Yo, Dave, working hard?"

"It's exhausting batting away imaginary customers. I finished vacuuming hours ago. Since you're here, let's pick out dinner for our trip tomorrow." I beckon, walking to the freeze-dried food section.

Tim's eyes brighten as he grabs a Mountain House package. "I want stroganoff."

"Sounds good to me. Look, scrambled eggs and bacon for breakfast! Let's splurge."

Tim gives a thumbs-up as he places the packages on the counter. "I need to snag some more granola bars."

Coming from the backpack section, Jim sees our food choices on the counter. "An outing in the works? What's the plan?"

Tim shakes his hand. "Going for *The North Face of Gothics*[5]. Flinny and I decided it was time to fire before winter melts away." Not to mention it's the most famous ice climb in the Adirondacks.

"And a decent training run for Rainier," I add. "Figure it's a good

145

place to test my bivy sack and new boots."

Jim chuckles. "That's for sure. Gothics is a great line. Regardless of the snow level, the ice should be nice. Hey, one tip." He taps the egg package. "Take a little butter with you. These will taste a lot better."

"Any other thoughts?" I ask.

"Lighter is righter, except when you need it." Jim smiles, his teeth showing through his wizard's beard. "Hey, it's really slow tonight; why don't you head out, and I'll see you Tuesday."

"Sweet! Let me settle the bill."

"Nah, don't worry about it; climb safely. Can't wait to hear about the trip."

Tim and I bolt out of the store before he changes his mind.

The Red House is quiet, and nary a snore rumbles from the lads as I lie in my closet, a shaft of light streaming in the window. While the heat blows its glorious gift on my feet, I'm thinking of Carol and what could have been.

Similar to the crux on a climb, I need to want her, visualize being together, to prove it. Fire or retire. Oh well, I chose to retire. Tears start to flow as sadness overtakes me. Gentle, soothing, a few sobs, muffled by the heater. Accepting the results of my hesitation is hard. Wiping my face on the pillow, I roll over to watch the trees sway in the moonlight.

It's the crack-o-noon when we stuff our packs into the Maverick and drive the mile to the Garden trailhead. With marginal snow in the woods, we leave our skis behind, hiking in our climbing boots. Tim hedges his bet and carries snowshoes while I scoff at the idea.

The 3.5-mile trail leads southwest along John's Brook into the heart of the High Peaks. The brook is named after John Gibbs, who lived near the Red House in the 1700s.

The snow crunches underfoot as we stroll along, and I ask Tim how his new Gregory backpack is settling in.

"Fits great, much better than that geezer of yours. Hey, here's a trail junction. Should we cross and take the south trail? Nope, it looks less traveled; let's stay on this one."

"Love the idea of an easy trail," I say, keeping up the pace. "Glad I ditched the heavy Eureka tent. Lighter is righter."

"We're alpinists. Why bother with a tent when we can sleep under the stars?"

Tim cranks into high gear and motors up the trail. An hour later, I find him at the Orebed Brook trail junction, munching on a granola bar, looking quite pleased with himself.

"Glad I have snowshoes," he says. "It's gonna be fun watching you struggle when we leave the trail." Tim knows I don't have any, but believes that I should have borrowed Jamie's. Having the right equipment at the right time is vital to the climbing game. Many hours before a trip are spent deliberating on the optimal tool for the job.

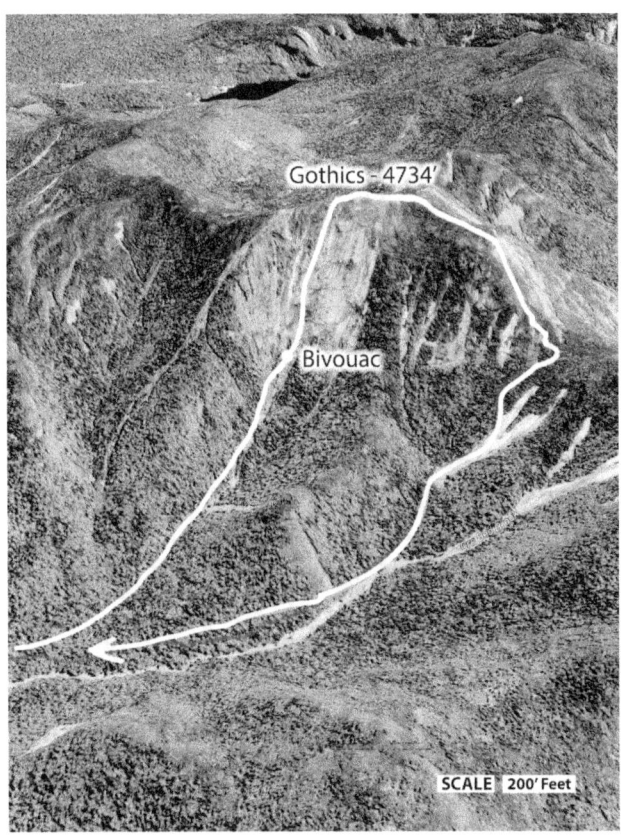

Looking to the northeast, the *North Face of Gothics* is
the classic ice climb in the Adirondacks.

Ignoring the snide comment, I glance at the map. "We have another half mile until we branch left and bushwhack to the North Face."

"Let's roll. The sun is behind the ridge, and I'd like to settle in before dark."

Trudging a bit further, we reach the Orebed lean-to. The Adirondacks have dozens of these three-sided log shelters scattered about. This one is devoid of humans, but mice are sure to thrive underneath. Yuck.

We avoid the dank and musty shelter, opting for a bivy under the stars. Soon after passing the lean-to, the trail veers right, and the brook continues straight. Leaving the path, I plow ahead while Tim plops off his pack to lace on his snowshoes.

It's a standard winter afternoon, thirty degrees, the sky gray. The snow changes from crispy and crunchy to fluffy and deep off the trail. I navigate around shrubs and hummocks peaked with snow, lumber up a mound, and with a *fwoomp*, slide back down between two boulders.

The pricker bushes close in. A few whacks with the ice axe proves useless as thorns catch my gloves and wool pants. Gasping to heave oxygen into my lungs, searching for a better path, trapped in a sea of mounds, prickers, and slush. Stopping to rest, my left boot is submerged in an ice-rimmed puddle.

Frustrated, I'm fully ensnarled in an Adirondack winter thrash.

A small storm cloud of angst brews, thoughts turning inward, away from the fantastic wintery scenery and the wind rustling through the junipers. Step, crash, stumble, gasp, rest. The cycle repeats for too long, each boot plunging down into the muck.

Finally, seeing Gothics through the trees, I'm energized. Post-holing onward, as darkness descends, I break into the clearing below the ominous face of the mountain. Tim is waiting as I raise my arms in celebration: the thrash is over for this mzungu.

Snowflakes puff into the air as my pack thumps down in the snow, two feet deep at the base of Gothic's slide. Sitting down, brushing twigs and snow from my pants, I sigh as dusk pools around, stars twinkling, the night settling in with a whisper. Snowshoes would have been great.

Tim roots around, pulling his headlamp out of the pack. The start of the climb is a snowball's throw away, but having a flat platform will be better for our bivy sacks—nylon overcoats for sleeping bags.

Tim getting ready to leave our bivouac under *The North Face of Gothics*, Adirondacks, April 1984.

My new Marmot down bag is rated for -5 degrees, and the bivy sack should add a few more, but the foam pad is key to insulating my body from the cold snow beneath. Without it, I'd freeze to death, the ground sucking away my heat while sleeping, never to wake again.

Tim unpacks and tamps out an igloo shelf. Handing me the quart-sized metal fuel bottle, I lay down the foam pad in the camp kitchen.

After pumping pressure into the bottle and lighting the gas, the new MSR WhisperLite stove purrs while I fill the two-quart aluminum pot with snow. True alpinists frown on stoves, but I couldn't imagine getting up in the morning without hot coffee.

When the pot top starts to rattle, I pour the boiling water into the stroganoff foil pouch. Its glorious fragrance wafts in the steam.

Since freeze-dried dinners take ten minutes to hydrate, I place the sealed bag on my pad to let it cook. My thick wooly Dachstein mittens soak in the pot's warmth as Tim adds more snow for after-dinner tea.

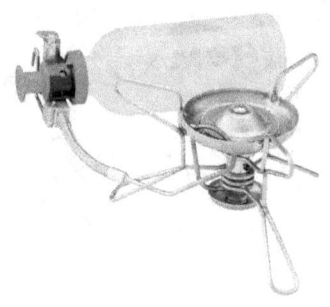

The MSR WhisperLite is a multi-fuel stove, perfect for melting snow. Photo by MSR.

Our bowls are quickly emptied and rinsed with warm water.

It's getting colder, and we prep for bed, careful not to guzzle too much. Rousting in the middle of the night to pee is no fun; too easy to fall butt-naked into the snow.

Relaxing and sipping tea, I wiggle my toes in the sleeping bag's warmth. "You seem a bit distracted, what's up?"

Tim places his cup on his snow shelf and nuzzles deeper into his bag. "Just wondering if the building trade is for me. Frustrating dealing with all the issues."

"The rest of us get by with minimum wage jobs. The economy sucks but living in the city, yuck. What else would you do? "

"That's what troubles me. The tradeoff of making good money or living in Keene Valley."

"You could move back to Albany and do the road warrior thing like Ken."

"There is that option," Tim replies.

I decide to turn things around to a more lively topic, "Hey, have you ever climbed a big mountain in Europe or the Rockies?"

"Nah. I've been stuck here most of my life. Looking forward to bagging a real hill. Thinking about Mexico. Not too far away, not too cold."

"I can't believe I'm going to Rainier. Always read stories, but I never thought it would happen to me. Hope I don't freak out or fall into a crevasse."

Tim turns over, taking off his glasses. "Ah, you'll do fine if you get some rest tonight. Time to go sleepie and stop the talkie."

With help from my headlamp, I pluck out my contacts and stuff the case in my sleeping bag. Judging from the deep breathing, Tim's already zonked out.

He's so lucky to have a girlfriend. She comes to visit occasionally and somehow tolerates the Red House frat-boy lifestyle. She's adventurous and loves the outdoors. Yeah, she melts all the climbers' hearts. I can't complain, she introduced me to Carol. Ken's got the job but Tim's got the girl.

Stars twinkle overhead in the clear night sky, looking fuzzy without contacts. Pushing my boot liners aside, socks still on, long underwear coiled in a ball at my feet. It's funny, but sleeping naked is toasty. Plus, I like the feel of down against my skin.

My stomach stirs at the memories of my flail on Equis. I'm back on the crux, gripped, hesitating, waiting to fall.

Stop it. No need to go there. That was months ago. Remembering Bob's cry of "Run it out!" helps crush the pesky negative thoughts. Reliving mistakes gets old, especially at four in the morning.

Dawn paints the wispy clouds orange in the clear sky. Gloriously warm, breath steaming, I ponder my dilemma. Coffee requires hot water, but the stove is three feet away. Didn't think this through last night. Oh, well, time to fire.

Unzip my warm cocoon and wiggle into polypropylene long undies, pants, and down jacket, all while trying to avoid knocking frost from the bivy bag onto my naked skin. Finally, roll over to put my eyeballs in; the contact lens game is more challenging without a mirror.

Thankfully, the lighter works and sparks the pressurized white gas as it should, and the WhisperLite hums along while I add fresh coffee to the drip funnel. Purists bring freeze-dried, but nothing beats real coffee in the morning.

"Wake up, you big slug, looking all cute and comfy in your bag. It's a fine morning, sky clear, the sun is lighting up Big Slide."

Tim starts to rustle as I head over to the stove, adding more snow for the scrambled eggs. Along with butter, of course. Gazing at the 900-foot slide of snow, ice, and rock, I'm not looking forward to climbing this sucker lugging a pack. The plan is to take a direct line up the face due to the thin-ice conditions and maximize snow mounds as rest stops.

Dawdling time over, we don our packs and go for it. Climbing over the fifteen-foot headwall gets the blood flowing; a hundred feet later, it's time for a break.

"Awesome view," Tim says, mashing a platform for his feet, gazing at the vista. "Look how the sun glints off the ice on Basin."

"Stupendous! What a great climb. Thank goodness for these snow ledges. A lot less scary and airy."

"Well, don't get too hasty." Tim turns and points. "Look what comes next." The face looms above as I take a sip from his proffered water bottle, soaking in the exposure.

"Okay then. He who hesitates is lost, right?"

Tim grins. "Toast, you mean. He who hesitates is toast."

Due to the steepness, I pivot and place my crampon front points straight into the ice. Forcing the unease down, burning off hesitation with a vengeance, knowing now's not the time to delay.

Sprinting ninety feet, I forget to breathe but find a tiny mound of snow to stop and rest. Placing the ice tools with a *thwack*, clipping my harness into the leashes provide the facade of a belay. Taking pictures, off to my right, Basin and Marcy peak over the top of Gothics. Tim is fifteen feet to my left, focused, and not gripped.

Without a rope, I'm on my own. Four hundred feet from the bottom, the exposure yawns and vertigo builds. Close my eyes, and breathe in and out to slow my beating heart. The mind starts to relax as the body takes over. With no way to rappel or bail, it's time to toss doubt and run it out.

The North Face of Gothics has a sixty-degree angle, similar to the streets of San Francisco. The ice is reasonable for climbing but is spotted with verglas, a thin sheen of alpine ice barely an inch thick. When the snow melts, it trickles down the rock, and frigid temperatures cause it to transform. Without continuous running water, ice can be thin and brittle.

Luckily, the snow hides the ice. Out of sight, out of mind. Baby alder saplings line the edges of the slide, promising some sort of anchor if things turn desperate.

Climbing another hundred feet before stopping again, clipping into my two ice axes for security. Snap goes the camera.

Tim using his front points on *The North Face of Gothics*, Adirondacks, April 1984.

Mount Marcy to my right is glorious. Waving to Tim, I point the way out, making sure not to look down. This climb is one big crux.

Exhilarated, I find myself on the sunken snow path to the summit. Tim is with me, steam blooming from his breath as we soak in the view. The beautiful sunny day has turned gloomy as clouds move in with a vengeance, the wind blowing snow devil wisps along the exposed ridge.

"We topped out just in time." I point. "The clouds are filling in, and snow is coming. We should bail and head down the Orebed Trail."

We've already crushed the hard part, soloing *The North Face of Gothics* in true alpine style. No need to over-achieve; we're already heroes.

The vista southwest to Saddleback and Marcy is stellar as I take some snaps with my Olympus XA camera. The snow barrels in from the north, and Giant is already hidden by the incoming storm.

The famous Gothics cables are buried under drifts of snow and ice. They help hikers navigate the steep section but are useless to us now. Basin pops in and out of view as the snow continues to intensify. We're happy to trample along in crampons with the trail icy and exposed. I can't see much below; the tree line is barely visible, forcing me to stop before a steep section.

Tim joins me, his hood up, exposing an ice-covered beard and stoic smile. Tired but not wanting to let on, I give him a thumbs-up and continue down. I'm facing out, using French technique, pushing my weight down into the ten crampon points. Descending thirty feet, the grade steepens, and a sudden gust threatens to knock me off. Hands windmilling, I almost pitch forward down the slope.

Resisting panic, squatting to lower my center of gravity, I jam the ice axe spike into the ice behind me. Saddled with my backpack, staring at the icy rocks fifty feet below, frozen in a crux of my own making.

It's an unnatural position, leaning backward, processing my options. The boulders look hungry, ready to feast as snow gusts do their best to knock me down. Time slows.

All numb inside, my mind disconnects from the reality of my potential energy. *Oh shit, hope it's not time to join Ed.* Plummeting would be a horrifying way to go.

The butterflies are buzzing as Tim comes close. "Dave! Stay there," I hear him yell through the wind. Thunking his ice tools next to me, he reaches out with his left hand and grabs my pack. "Quick! Pivot onto your front points. I've got you."

Moisten my lips, then take a breath. Slowly straightening my knees, Tim's hand keeps me in balance. Grabbing my ice axe, I swing the tip into a heavenly pocket of ice with a satisfying *whack*, almost giggling at the absurdity of it. I let the butterflies free and fire.

I'm on *The North Face of Gothics*, with Mount Marcy
in the distance, April 1984. Photo by Tim Broader.

Shifting my weight as both hands hold the ice axe, I spin my left foot
and follow with the right to the front points. "Total kudos, Tim," I
gasp. Safer, back in action, rescued by my very own superhero.

"No sweat. You would have made it. I helped speed you up. Glad
you didn't peel off and crater. Here comes the snow."

A slog always takes the fun out of a grand day out. It's the price a
climber must pay. Plodding along, my near fall is almost forgotten
during the long, cold descent. I'm dreaming of the Star Trek ability to
beam myself to the Red House. Or a wingsuit that badasses use to fly
down, avoiding the lengthy hike.

"I'm done with these crampons," I tell Tim. "Enough stomping around like the Pillsbury Dough Boy. Love the security, but they sure are slow."

He smiles. "I don't mind moving slowly and safely. Not hasty as someone who has to be all fancy on steep ice."

One crampon is off before I realize he's teasing me. I'm sure to never live this down. "At least I avoided going to splat city. Appreciate your hand back there."

"No problem. Finish your candy bar, and let's get out of here. It's a long way down."

Tim's demeanor is stoic and more cautious than my more impulsive spirit. He's a great person to have around when things get dicey. Probably because he was on the long-distance track team in college.

It takes us half an hour to make it off the ridge, snow dancing with the whoosh of the wind. Dusk follows, leaving us in full conditions. Cold, tired, can't see more than twenty feet. The Orebed Brook gurgles, happy in its descent down to the lean-to, past my thrash in the woods from yesterday.

My toes are bearable, but my fingers are cold, so I make a fist inside the mitten to warm them. The snow crunches under my boots—plod, stomp, and step. Lucky that the trail is firm, keeping Tim's snowshoes on his pack. I vow to bring a cassette player on the next trip to make the slog go faster.

The four miles to the Maverick allow me to reflect on the winter. Memories of Ed flit through my mind; I can't believe it's been over a year already.

So much has happened. Graduation, Rochester, and now living in Keene Valley. Soloing hard climbs, dancing out of avalanches, ankle healed, the fears toast. Carol didn't happen, but I might see her in the future. No need to shut that door. Faith in myself, learning to trust my instincts. Ready for the big adventure out west.

DRAGGING myself out of bed and creeping down the stairs, I tiptoe past a late-night visitor snoozing in the living room.

The Red House became a crash-pad for climbers.
Thus, we needed rules, March 1984.

Climbing rope, slings, and random bits of clothing adorn the furniture, drying out from yesterday's adventures. The climbing posters look down on the slumbering one. Another bum crashed at the Red House. Fortunately for Sleeping Beauty, the kitchen door is closed as the necessary coffee brews a complement to my bowl of Cheerios.

Ken's Toyota in the driveway identifies the road warrior. I consider cranking up the tape player with a reasonable Hendrix good-morning anthem. Tim staggers into the kitchen.

"Morning, Timmer," chirping with a caffeine-induced smile. "Coffee?" I pour a cup of joe to awaken his body and mind.

"Uhmpph. Yeah, sure, thanks." He reaches for the mug, sitting down in a chair.

Noticing his work clothes, I point out that it's the weekend.

A snore wafts in from the living room.

"Need to finish a drawing," Tim says. "My boss wants to show the customer on Monday. Fricking Ken with all that racket."

"I should pour coffee on his pillow. Oh, wait, then he'd wake up. Jamie's still down as well."

"Ugghhhh." Tim takes a big sip.

After a few minutes, the caffeine will soak in, he'll perk up, and witty Tim will return and tease me till bedtime. Before that can happen, he makes his escape out the door and leaves me to Ken.

I creep back upstairs to work on the next edition of the Journal. The quiet ends as the Bitch-and-Moan Brothers start banging around. It always happens when they're together. Jamie and Ken transform, similar to Jekyll and Hyde. Our very own dynamic duo. I head downstairs to the kitchen to prevent a cooking disaster, anticipating a wild venture brewing.

"Flinny! Make some pancakes," Jamie orders. "We need fuel." He cranks the tape player, blasting out the Stones' "Start Me Up."

I nudge him out of the way and take over. He's a great climber but a so-so cook. Pouring in the milk, I ask what their plan is. "Must be something, or you'd still be sleeping."

"There's a spectacular roof in Cascade Pass I saw the other day with my clients. I call it *Jaws*⁶. I know it'll go, but this slug is not feeling well."

"What's happening, matey?" I nudge Ken's shoulder, and he groans. His head rests on the kitchen table, nestled in his arms, hands wrapped around the coffee mug.

"The wimp's feeling lousy," Jamie says. "Maybe it was last night's tequila shots."

It's no fun when Ken's not on his game—placing the cakes on the table, plunking down some real maple syrup. "Have at 'em. Sit up, laddie. You're taking up the entire table with your moaning."

The song changes to "Satisfaction." In between pancake bites, Jamie sings along with the Stones, dancing in the tiny kitchen. Syrup spills on the table.

Jamie on *Jaws* in Cascade Pass. Photo from the
Jamie Cunningham collection, February 2, 1984.

Hours later, after we return from climbing *Jaws*, Ken is still toast,
now snoring on the couch. Who needs television? No matter that Ken's
sick with the flu, the Bitch-and-Moan Brothers always entertain. Going
to miss these yahoos when I bail and hitch to Seattle.

159

Mount Adams from the summit of Mount Rainier, June 1984

SUMMIT

June – July 1984

S ummer is in full swing as I drive two hours south from Keene Valley to visit my folks. The rain is holding off as wispy low clouds scud by, Star Destroyers parallel to the Adirondack Northway. Mom's doing as well as anyone after months of chemotherapy. Her wavy brown hair has long been gone, as the chemicals have attacked the disease and her body. Since having a mastectomy twelve years ago, each year has been a blessing, and she never complains about her bad luck.

A honk jostles my wandering mind, prompting me to accelerate and return the Maverick to freeway speed. Raindrops urge me to turn on the wipers; the *fwop fwop fwop* is hypnotic as the miles flit by. A year ago, Mom's initial arthritis diagnosis turned out to be the blasted cancer. It's been festering in her bones for years and coursing through her body. I hope she gets to hug her grandchildren someday. Please, God, give her that much joy. It's raining cats and dogs when I pull into the driveway.

She smiles when I clamber onto her antique bed. The rain drumming on the roof complements the hissing radiators as they warm the room, and open curtains welcome the gray light. Wallowing cozy on the soft down comforter, I roll over to give her a big hug.

"You look good, Mom. Glad to see you again." Kissing her left cheek draws another smile, her face drawn, not as cheery as usual.

Her blue eyes sparkle in contrast to the pink cap snuggled on her head. "Did the rain make your drive difficult?"

There goes Mom, constantly worrying about others. I update her on the crazy things I've been doing and go light on the details, especially the near-epic avalanche. Gothics is a good story with a friendly, safe ending. It's doubtful she understands my climbing, but as a mom, she knows I'm fired up and full of life.

I plunk the latest *Adirondack Alpine Journal* on her lap. "Here you go, issue three hot off the press. I mailed twenty packages to outdoor stores yesterday. Now time to relax."

Mom starts flipping through the twenty-four pages. "This is looking snazzy. Beefy. Anything interesting for me to read?"

I know she's teasing. "Chock-full of climbing stories and guidebook information. Perfect nighttime reading."

"It's lovely, David. I'm proud of you." She places the Journal on her side table.

Reaching back to fluff the pillow, I look into her eyes. "Mom, I'm thinking about another adventure. Not sure if I should go, but wanted to talk to you about it."

"What crazy escapade have you dreamed up this time?"

"My good friend Jim moved to Seattle last year. He asked me to climb Mount Rainier with him."

"Why do you need to go way out there? The Adirondacks have big mountains." She sounds curious, not concerned—the grandfather clock in the hallway bongs three o'clock.

"This is my chance to try something big. Sure, it's risky, but doing the same old thing gets boring. Remember when you got that nasty tapeworm after I was born? You almost died. We should have bailed out of Africa. Why did you want to stay?"

Her eyes glow with the memories. "It was so exciting helping the people. I felt we were destined to be there. It was the best time of my life." Mom married Dad to move to Uganda, a far cry from life on her family farm.

"You instilled in me a thirst for adventure. Summiting the third-highest mountain in America would be amazing. It's my opportunity to play the climbing game at another level. I need to push myself. Safely, of course."

"How long do you think you'll be?"

"About a month. The Mountaineer needs me back in August. I don't need to wait tables at the Holiday Inn anymore." Feeling guilty, "I don't want to be a dirtbag and abandon you."

"Davidite, I licked cancer years ago, and this is yet another round. I feel good and will be here for a long time. The month will fly by. You'd be bored sitting around here, driving your father crazy." She reaches out and holds my hand.

"At least I'm good at pestering. I won't go if you think it's a bad idea."

"A bad idea? Being happy and living life is what God wants, and you do that in spades."

"Speaking of spades, let's play Crazy Eights." Reaching for the deck on the night table, I shuffle and deal. Mom closes her eyes, clenching her teeth for a moment, smiling weakly as she picks up her cards.

JUNE SUNLIGHT DAPPLES through the maple trees while waiting for a ride north out of the Adirondacks. Lightening my load, I shipped a box to Seattle last week. I'm still feeling guilty leaving Mom and Dad.

A gnawing notion runs through my mind as cars pass by. It's possible I'm neglecting my duty to leverage my college degree. Three years ago, after my first hitchhike, I horrified my parents when I considered quitting to become a helicopter mechanic. Bet they wonder what I'm going to come up with this time.

I've worked hard to save money. Traveling by thumb saves six hundred dollars in airfare—over two months of work. They weren't thrilled with me hitching, but they don't have any spare cash; with two kids in college, money doesn't grow on trees. Mom's working through her cancer pain to sell real estate for a reason.

My woolgathering is interrupted by a sweet ride to Cornwall, right over the Canadian border. Strolling across the bridge into Ontario, I head north to Ottawa to join the Trans-Canadian Highway. A hop over to Stittsville, followed by a ride with a young couple to Cobden. Bearing pizza and beer, a total savior ride that beats PB&J any day. Outside metropolitan Pembroke, dusk falls as I climb a fence to an open field next to the Ottawa River, 180 miles north of Keene Valley.

As the sun sets over the river, I find a flat spot to rig the Sierra Designs tent Tim lent me and contemplate the urban geography of the two countries. American towns are older and seem to be laid out haphazardly. Canada feels more organized with homes built on a grid. Brushing my teeth before crawling in, hypothesizing that older towns appear to have less city planning, wondering about the meaning of all this. Guess I was paying attention in geography class after all.

Dawn yawns, and cars hiss by. Rain sprinkles on the tent as the mosquitos bump and buzz. Tim needs to know this sucker rocks. I doze in my cocoon until it's time to rise and head out into the bugs.

A few hours later, pacing back and forth on the outskirts of Deep River, I'm still cursing the dastardly little pests. My hitchhiking theory is simple: since the Trans-Canadian Highway is the sole east-west road through Canada's huge swamp, snagging a ride should be easy. Spacing out as rain splatters on my head.

I miss the Red House already. My friends, the customers at the Mountaineer, and even the rogues who crashed for the weekend. They were incredulous that our State Police neighbor dropped off a Mott's beer ball for us to finish. "No way, the cops bring you beer?"

What? A Volvo stops, and we're off to North Bay. I'm lucky this somber quiet mom is going to the far side of town; no walking this time. A few minutes later, a young feller in a BMW 2002 fires me out to Sturgeon Falls. While I wait in the intermittent rain, the Gore-Tex jacket keeps me dry, maintaining my optimism.

Some weirdo picks me up and takes me for a spin, hoping for excitement. Caution screams in my veins as I calmly cajole the clown to drop me back at the edge of town. Perhaps other hitchhikers are searching for sex, but I'm looking for speedy rides to Vancouver.

Another short lift into downtown Sudbury requires a three-mile walk to the edge of town. There are too many distractions in cities, with vehicles buzzing around everywhere. In the center of a town, I never get a lift. It's all about optimizing my starting point when it comes to hitching. A long highway entrance ramp is best, with plenty of room for a car to pull over. The wide-open road broadcasts my Western intention.

Reviewing my trusty road atlas, I wonder if it's time to ditch Canada and head into Michigan after 250 miles of slow progress. The drizzle winds down when two cousins from Stuttgart stop and pull over. With their minimal English and my useless German, it's hard to have the usual chitchat.

After a few hours of watching endless trees zoom by, the cousins indicate they are going to Calgary, and I'm welcome to stay with them. My jaw drops, processing this boon.

Lounging in the back seat, I transition to a mellow traveling pace. My usual hitching tempo runs fast, *go-go-go* coursing through my veins. The rush to catch miles after a long wait for a ride. Worrying when the next ride will come. The horror of getting stuck in the middle of nowhere or trapped in an urban hell. I'm thrilled to hang out for the 1600 miles to Calgary, let the car do all the work, and relish being the third wheel.

The Sierra Designs Divine Light tent and the Marmot Mountain Works sleeping bag are made from Goretex. Note the brown Pontiac in the background with one of the German lads in June 1984.

Driving a brown Pontiac Ventura west, the lads are traveling Canada for free. They had the clever idea to hook up with a transport company that needed drivers. I jot this tidbit in my journal for next year, a more stress-free strategy versus the adventurous hitch.

Thinking of writing brings me to the next issue of the magazine. While articles are critical, hand-drawn maps are the most fun. I'm considering a two-page spread showing the crags in Chapel Pond. It's excellent that Keene Valley climbers are providing articles. A hitching narrative might not work, but one about Rainier could.

Heading north out of Sault Ste. Marie, we stop and crash in someone's yard. When the morning dawns clear and cold, I pull out my pile jacket. At least the bugs are hiding.

Finally, the lads motivate and we drive to Thunder Bay, six hundred miles away. The roadside is littered with desolate pinkish granite outcrops with spruce, aspen, and birch boreal forest, barely ten feet high. I bet the winter must suck up here.

Lake Superior is undoubtedly superior, at least on the Canadian side. The rolling hills are pocked with ponds, loaded with muskellunge and northern pike, festering with black flies and skeeters. Each town has a pulp mill and not much else—just this two-lane road in the middle of nowhere.

Thunder Bay, perched on Lake Superior's western side, is the home of vicious summer thunderstorms. Paper mills abound, with the big port stocked full of grain elevators. Wheat, barley, and corn are hauled by rail from Manitoba, Alberta, and Saskatchewan and shipped worldwide via the St. Lawrence Seaway.

Snoozing in the back, I'm jolted awake as the lads suddenly turn south, leaving the highway. Hampered by language obstacles, it takes me half an hour to grok they are visiting family friends. My panic attack ebbs as we pull into a dirt driveway in front of a quaint farmhouse. Relieved they aren't going to kill and stuff me in a barn.

Day turns into night, crammed full of sausages and beer. Oblivious to the chatter of the four Germans, I learn to appreciate the experience of never knowing what may happen next.

In Manitoba, the Trans-Canada becomes an actual highway instead of the trashed excuse of a road in Ontario.

My German lads, their family friend, and I after snacking on sausage
and beer. Thunder Bay, Ontario in June 1984.

Another four hundred miles to Winnipeg, about halfway across the
country. It's the junction of the Assiniboine and Red Rivers, a big deal
back in the day for the Hudson Bay Company's fur trade.

Walking around the city center doesn't do much for me since
nothing is open. The information yahoo at the border raved about
downtown, but he must be thinking of Ottawa.

The lads stick out as Europeans due to their canvas shoulder bags.
With their love of beer and sausage, they probably don't understand the
phrase *vegetarian*. They head over to the German Club while I bail and
wander back to the hostel and update my travel journal. This is yet
another city. Boring.

Cruising across Saskatchewan's plains, past farms that raise cattle or
crops depending on the season and water availability. Tractors, cows,
pickup trucks, rain, grass, dogs, dust, and gas stations.

After 350 miles, we slink into a campground east of Regina and
head into town to find a bar. They call them licensed beverage rooms in
Canada. Weird. The barmaid looks straight into my eyes as I sit, asking

for my order. She returns with the beer and a change machine slung around her waist. Definitely not in Kansas anymore.

We've been hoping to go swimming somewhere. Good luck. All the lakes are shallow and foaming with sodium sulfate—white precipitation —along their edges. Fat chance you'll find me in there.

Two days later, we reach Medicine Hat in Alberta. This fantastic ride ends as the most excellent lads drop me off at an entrance ramp south to the States.

～

THE AFTERNOON SUN glistens off a spectacular, massive rock perched on the Blackfeet Indian Reservation near Glacier National Park. Chief Mountain is sacred for vision quests where boys become men. The peak thrusts out of the earth, drawing attention from miles away. It's majestic, Montana's version of Wyoming's Devil's Tower.

Trapped in my own mzungu quest, waiting for a ride back to Canada, in awe of the green prairie spreading for miles, disrupted by the black asphalt road. A stem from the sweetgrass clump near my pack is better than chewing tobacco to pass the time.

Assessing the flat summit of the mountain: its sedimentary layers aren't safe for rock climbing. Scuffing my boots in the dirt, continuing another round of pacing, and praying for traffic. Cars whizz by, ignoring my outstretched thumb beseeching a ride.

I'm in the throes of a full-blown Zen Belay when a dark red Cadillac screeches to a halt. Stunned by my luck, I toss the sweetgrass, grab my pack, and hustle to the car. The front passenger door opens, and a hand beckons me inside. Three Blackfeet are packed like sardines in the back seat. No room there. My mind races, processing options.

Wait for another ride to the border or jump in with the five Blackfeet? I lived on the Crow Reservation two years ago when working fire patrol for the Bureau of Indian Affairs. Decision made, I stuff my pack on the front seat floor and squeeze into the car.

Confirming a drive north to the Canadian border, the charming fellow next to me chats about the Reservation and how he went to college and returned to help his people.

Chief Mountain from my hitching spot near the Canadian Border in
Glacier National Park, Montana, June 1984.

He does all the talking while the others sit quietly, grinning.
Charming asks a few innocent questions. Living with the Crow taught
me that showing respect is vital, especially from a white boy.

Finishing my spiel, Charming's hand creeps up my thigh, slowly
making its way near my crotch, gripping tightly. Butterflies burst in my
tummy as hitchhiking horror stories crash down, and I wonder how this
is going to end.

While sitting with Mom two weeks ago, I dismissed any possibility
of danger on this trip. I'm terrified of what the cops will tell her when
they find my dead body.

My brain kicks into full gear, alarm bells clanging, stuck in a car
with the hand of a giant on my thigh, cruising down an empty road
ten miles from the border. Freaking out is not an option, despite the
gyrations going on in my stomach. Placing my hand next to his, I
quietly ask if he will be so kind as to let go. Charming pretends

nothing is happening and keeps chatting about the tribe's oil money windfall.

Pushing against his hand, bug-eyes whirling in my head, somehow, I inhale. Charming removes his hand as he finishes the story. Turning to the driver and the others in the back, he speaks in Blackfeet. My sweaty palms begin to cool as I look straight ahead, barely breathing. The border is my best shot. Don't want the car to stop since I have no chance against five of them.

Charming starts talking again, smiling like an eagle about to dismember his prey, fingers clenching my knee while I gulp for air. Keep calm, stay cool, steady now. Unfolding my moist palm over his hand, I stroke his skin, feeling the rough surface worn from the sun. Smelling my sweat and looking straight into his eyes, I remove my hand. His grip loosens as the car pulls up to the border.

I grab my things and shove them out the open door, mumbling a thank you. As the red Cadillac pulls away, my pack falls into the dust. For five minutes, I praise God repeatedly until the bright sun emerges from behind the clouds. Charming must have been toying with me, trying to make the white boy cry. Everyone has a game to play. Walking to the border, I've never been happier to see a Canadian Mountie.

YOU CAN'T BEAT a night under the stars next to the stunning Prince of Wales Hotel in Waterton Lakes. Strolling the majestic halls searching for a bathroom, I decide it's too luxurious for stinky ol' me.

After a jaunt around the lake, I hitch north to the Icefields Parkway, the most beautiful fjord in North America. Scoured by glaciers, the mountains soar nine thousand feet above the road, capped by Mount Robson. The horizontal sedimentary nature of the rock means it's safer to climb in winter. Ice and snow provide a great glue to keep the abundant loose rock tamed. Very different from the solid granite of the Adirondacks.

After pillaging an excellent map from a helpful ranger, I scamper up the moraine northwest of Mount Athabasca to clear the fear of the Blackfeet incident. Being an extrovert, I'm energized when interacting with people. Bonding with nature also draws out my spirit, the mountains' stoic strength dare me to connect. Relationship obstacles abound, whether mortal or encased in stone.

The trail is formed of loose shale, and the summit approach is steep. It's crisp and cold, with clouds whizzing over Mount Kitchener to the north. Avoiding a rockslide and the approaching nasty weather, I hang out on a pleasant ridge at 9500 feet, letting the altitude burn out the remaining fear residue.

Running and jumping down the slope, I link sweet telemark turns in the imaginary snow. The Blackfeet drama ebbs away with the activity. Abandoning humanity for the wild enables nature to soak into my pores, cleansing my soul. After gathering my stashed pack and refilling the water bottles, I return to the road.

Hours pass reading, writing, waiting, walking, and cursing. While family-filled cars cruise by without stopping, at least the scenery is fantastic.

Thinking about that ranger, she seemed nice. I wonder if I'll ever meet a mountain girl. Someone who likes to hike around in the woods. Heck, they don't have to climb, even though that would be amazing. Oh well, at least I have the Red House lads and my SUOC family.

At long last, a Toyota pickup pulls over, and I climb into the back, munching on a grapefruit. The big sky of the west is terrific. The vast distance creates horizontal vertigo, unfolding as I bounce along the road —time to relax and enjoy it.

"Hı, Dad, I'm calling from the Icefields Parkway in British Columbia."

"I was there back in the forties with cousin Cholley driving all over the US and Canada," Dad reminisces. "We walked on the glaciers near Banff. Certainly an interesting experience. Not fond of the cold, though."

Guilt gnaws at me as I ask how Mom's doing.

"She's chipper. Still coming down to the table for meals and eating well. Loves reading from her pile of books."

"How about the *New York Times* crossword puzzle?"

"She plows through it every Sunday after church."

Cool. Life seems normal. "Can I speak to her?"

"Of course. Before I go, your Aunt Julie is in the hospital for breast cancer surgery."

"Oh my gosh, that's terrible. I loved riding around in Uncle's combine during corn harvest." Hope farm chemicals aren't the cause of these cancers. Or something genetic. Worried for my sister.

"Here she is," Dad says goodbye and hands the phone over.

"Hi, Mom; I've been thinking about you. I'm in British Columbia, and you'll be glad to know I had a wonderful ride with these two lads from Germany."

There's no way I'm going to mention my Blackfeet buddies.

STANDING on the Continental Divide in the middle of nowhere, chewing tobacco, waving at couples passing by in their Winnebagos, and avoiding boredom by reading *The Golden Soak* standing up. A car comes, and out goes my hand. Nothing. Here comes a big truck. What the hell? I thumb the sucker. Holy cow! It stops. After climbing in, the driver asks me where I'm going. He smiles and declares, "Let's go to Vancouver!" He wants to drive all night, and that's okay with me. We smoke butts and shoot the ol' BS, passing the miles away.

I make the 10 a.m. ferry from Vancouver to Sidney. Standing in line to board, I'm yammering with an older lady about the lack of buses due to the labor strike. Noticing a young woman behind me, I ask whether she's heading somewhere special.

Her dimples frame her cute smile. "Nope, just heading home."

"This sure is a superb boat." I think, *Why would she talk to me?* Followed by, *I'm a smelly hitchhiker.*

"I can tell you're not from around here. We call them ferries. Where ya' from, eh?" she asks in her Canadian drawl.

Luckily, my body takes over and calms those dang tummy rumblings. I look into her eyes and say, "Keene Valley. A magical town nestled in the Adirondack mountains. It's comparable to BC, without the glorious ocean."

On the Continental Divide watching Winnebagos pass by, June 1984.

"Ah, the States. Have you been here before?"

"Oh, yes, I love British Columbia. I traveled here two years ago. Vancouver Island is stellar, but the San Juan Islands are pretty sweet too." Surely my local knowledge will impress her.

"Ha! You haven't seen the coast we have right here, have ya?"

As we walk into the main cabin, the miracle continues, and we sit down next to each other, just like it's supposed to happen.

Her eyes glow golden green, surrounded by her luscious brown hair. Her teeth flash white when she smiles, and I love her accent—my skin tingles, electric with the possibility. Suddenly, a loud *ahhhhwooogaaah* causes me to stiffen as a voice over the crackling loudspeaker says the ferry is about to dock. Drivers, please return to your cars.

I look at her with puppy-dog eyes and ask, "Do you know where we could have a snack and continue chatting?" My mind does a backflip as it waits for her answer.

"Come on, grab your kit. I know just the place."

Sidney is a cute town four miles from the Vancouver ferry. We drop my junk at the Princess Marguerite Ferry Terminal and start our date with a tour of the Sidney Museum.

Angie mentions over lunch that she lives on a 40-foot sloop. She pays close attention as I briefly describe my life to her. I like her gaze. She takes the seat next to me before lunch arrives. Perhaps it's not the wisest move but I've learned from hitchhiking to pivot on a dime and seize the opportunity when it presents itself. Go for it.

As we stroll back from lunch, holding hands, Angie's gorgeous eyes sparkle in the sunlight. "Would it be okay to come back to your place and meet your folks?" I ask. "It would be great to see your sailboat." Holding my breath as the waves lap against the boats in the marina.

"I'm not sure now is the best time. Dad won't approve of me showing up with some boy in tow. I need to talk to them first."

"Got it. Jim will be happy I'm not delaying the trip to Rainier."

"Can you come back after your climb? That way, I can ease my folks into things." Angie stops walking and drapes her hands over my shoulders.

"Ten days, then."

Our goodbye kiss is long and deep. The ferry honks its departure horn, and I scurry aboard. The four-hour ride flits by as I float in my seat, giddy from meeting Angie, hoping it won't fizzle as it did with Carol. As the ferry bashes into a big wave, my worries wash away. I love Canada, chock-full of ferry rides and amazing girls.

IT'S a fabulous June day when Jim and I visit the University of Washington outdoor climbing wall[1] smack dab in the middle of Seattle. Earlier, we rescued my kit from UPS, and now it's time to train. My toes unleash a cascade of complaints as I wedge them into the Firés.

"These danged shoes work great, but I swear they're too small."

Jim chuckles. "Yeah, the price to pay for excellence. I know it's weird climbing on concrete, but there's no need to think about routes, grades, and ropes. Focus on the climb and have fun."

He places his foot on the artificial climbing wall, tongue clenched in his teeth, and levitates with precision, effortlessly. Hope I look as relaxed and skilled. Finding a starting spot, my body takes over, leaving doubt behind.

Jim bouldering on the University of Washington
climbing wall, Seattle, Washington, June 1984.

Twenty minutes later, my arms are trashed—pumped from too much finger-work on the wall—I chill out as Jim finishes his workout. He joins me as we change our shoes.

"So, what do you think?" He rubs chalk from his hands on a towel.

"It is a bit weird but most awesome. Remember the mausoleums in Oakwood Cemetery?" It was a SUOC thing to take a break from classes and head to the graveyard for practice. We figured the dead wouldn't mind.

Sitting in the grass, his handsome six-foot frame is topped with brown hair and a bushy mustache that all the girls love. But his demeanor means a lot to me—kind, caring, and one helluva good climber.

"Those good ol' days back in Syracuse." Jim brightens. "Remember that day on Wallface when Tosh trashed our tent? That was classic."

Chuckling, "I'm glad you thought it was funny. At least you guys climbed *No Man's A Pilot*. Something good came out of that adventure."

"It was a fun climb and I do miss the Adirondacks. But oh, the big sky out here is stupendous. The Cascades are stocked with stunning alpine terrain, and Alaska's dramatic peaks are nearby. Everything is on a grander scale."

I put my Firés away. "I'm not sure I could move so far away from my friends and family."

Jim's smile fades. "After graduating, I needed to move. Sad memories, but now, it's time for dinner. Let's roll."

Don't want to pry so I follow his lead and pack up my kit. We snag some groceries and head back to his apartment.

Lounging on the couch while he cooks, I notice a thick book with a brown cover, the title *Cascade Alpine Guide* embossed in silver.

"That's the bible around here," Jim yells over his stir-fry creation. "Fred Beckey climbed hundreds of routes in the Cascades. He grew up here and published three volumes. You should read the chapter on Rainier before we go."

"It sure is meaty, definitely an armchair book. Who would carry this sucker on a climb?"

"Most routes are high up in the mountains, over ten thousand feet, unlike the short crags in the Adirondacks."

Flipping through the pages, "Is Rainier like Mount Washington?" I don't want to be a total rookie, a dead weight for Jim to haul around.

"Similar. Out here the long approaches and altitude are the real deal. Also, the glaciers and rock fall. Bergschrunds and crevasses, big holes in the snow. Dinner's ready."

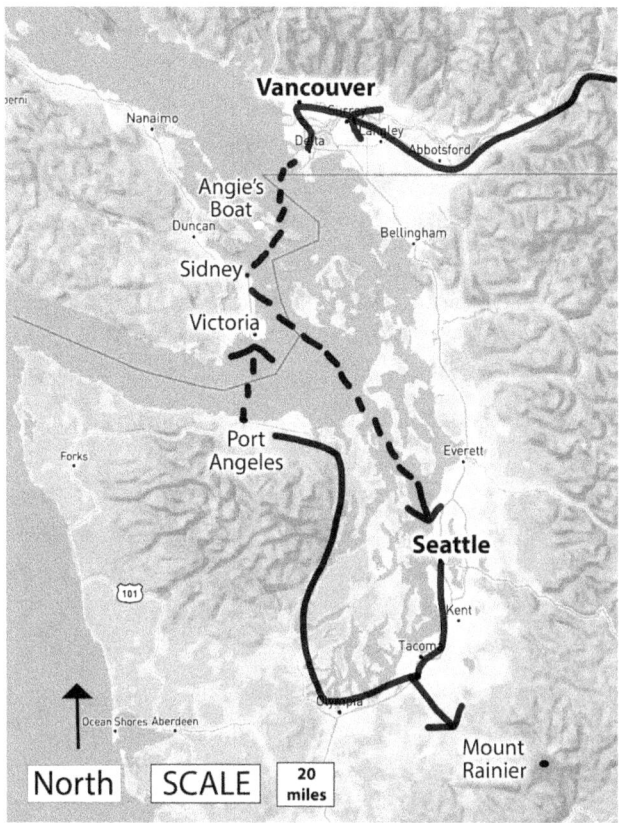

Mount Rainier dominates the Seattle skyline. I also
visited Vancouver, Sidney, Victoria, and Port Angeles
hitch-hiking in June 1984.

After demolishing the yummy concoction, I vigorously clean the
dishes, my body is buzzing with anticipation. After a beer, road fatigue
catches up with me and I curl up on the couch.

When Jim leaves for work in the morning, I play tourist downtown,
starting with the Space Needle. Stepping out of the elevator and taking
in the big-sky panorama, I walk the perimeter of the building, two football fields high.

Above the sprawling city, a massive, snow-capped peak juts up from
the ground. My focus is drawn to the volcano, and I hardly notice the
buildings. Mount Rainier is breathtaking. The clear blue sky and bril-

177

liant sun illuminate the glaciers and ridges over 50 miles distant. Hard to believe I'm going up there.

Sitting outside the natural history museum an hour later, munching on a falafel and reading Beckey's book. Supposedly now is the ideal time to avoid glacial disasters. Winter ended in April, and the hill has had months to bake in the sun. Not sure why people rag on Seattle. The weather here is incredible.

It bugs me that many of the book's route specifics are sparse. *"Go up the goat trail to the base. Climb loose rock until it clears, and head for the summit. Three hours."* Useless. I can deal with terse prose when it's backed up with maps or photos. It could be the geographer in me with high standards.

Friday morning dawns clear, writing postcards to my family and the Red House gang. Call home that evening and check in. Mom's doing well, although she whispers into the phone. Dad sounds perky. Before I jump off the phone, Andy's voice comes on the line.

"Yo, brother, what's happening?"

"Bearso! You're home from Rochester!" Andy's going to the Rochester Institute of Technology in upstate New York. He's the math whizz of the family.

He replies, "Yeah, wrapped up my finals and blew outta there. Trying to land a summer job here at home. What are you up to?"

I fill him in on the hitchhike and the upcoming climb. He's amused about my Angie escapade.

"Just be safe out there. I don't want to lose you to some crevasse or avalanche." Bear is the best brother, kind and relaxed. One of those people who everybody enjoys being around. He surfs the tide of life and always catches the best wave.

"Later, dude. See you when I get back." Hanging up the phone, the pang in my stomach reminds me I miss him. I miss everyone. Waxing melancholy, futzing around with my gear one last time before heading back to the living room. Prep work and planning help me control my universe. Having my ducks in a row calms my jitters.

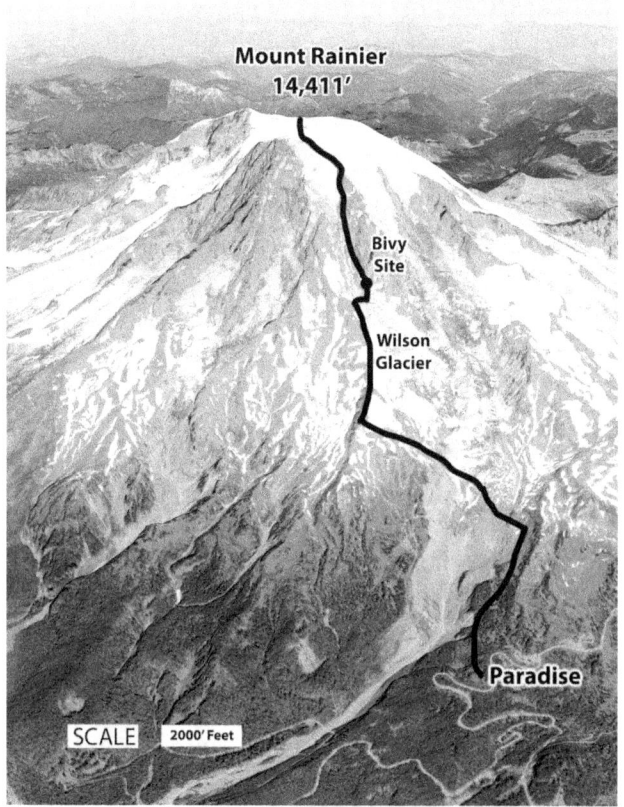

Looking east to Mount Rainier and the *Fuhrer Finger*.

I can see why Jim likes it here. Seattle's not bad for a city. With tons of majestic climbing, bigger than life, it makes the Adirondacks look like kindergarten. And scads of humongous mountains to explore, acres of alpine terrain, treeless and wild.

Tossing in my bed, on the verge of sleep, I recall my Gothics solo climb with Tim, but this time I see myself fall, cartwheeling down the ice face, cratering into the snow with a huge thump.

Sitting up in a cold sweat, my vision fades with Mom trudging up the trail dressed in black.

DRIVING UP TO PARADISE, Jim's Volvo rocks "Truckin'" from the Grateful Dead, cranked up over the rumbling from the busted muffler. The station wagon with New York plates chugs up the hill to the parking lot. Mount Rainier is majestic, its 14,411 feet soaring over everything in sight.

"Wow, it's staggering; hard to believe it's real."

Jim turns the car off, smiling. "You get used to it. I can't wait to be on top."

"It's a big mountain, the training climb for Mount Everest. Think we can do it?"

"No problem. Who cares that most people don't; no reason we can't huff up this hill."

Jim and I bounce out of the car and start packing. Bad news: the bulb on my JustRite headlamp broke last night. Good news: I won't have to carry the four-battery beast.

We're going alpine style with a sleeping bag, bivy sack, foam pad, two liters of water, and gobs of granola bars. Don't forget the glacier glasses. Leaving behind camping gear, we hope to climb faster without carrying too much junk.

Paradise is a fitting word, with the bluebird sky and white snow in contrast to the cloudy and bug-infested Adirondacks. After registering at the ranger station, we follow a guided team of eight from The Mountaineers.

Passing a few stragglers from the Seattle-based climbing club, I overhear a girl bitching about her soggy leather boots. Plastic ones have become a thing, and my discount from the Mountaineer bagged me a stellar pair of Koflach Ultras, perfect for the wet snow.

Noticing their huge packs, Jim belts out, "Lighter is righter," in a crazy jingle.

After a mile of passing tiny shrubs along the path, it dawns on me they're the tops of submerged trees. There must be ten feet of snow beneath me; no need for skis or snowshoes.

While most people hike onward to Camp Muir and its cushy cabin, we're going on a real climb and branch left to the Wilson Glacier.

The weight of the pack settles on my shoulders. We've been hiking for hours, passing the last spruce trees on Rainier's slopes. It's all rock, ice, and snow from here. The steady uphill plod saps the last of my breakfast energy and my breath wheezes as the altitude increases.

The sun bakes down, intensified by the dazzling light reflected in the snow. My lips are parched, and the water bottle is almost empty. French bonbons motivate me to catch up to Jim resting on a rock.

Koflach Ultras provide a rigid footbed and a double boot for the ultimate in winter climbing.

My back lets out a sigh of relief as the pack thumps into the snow. "Thank God for a break. Did you stuff a boulder in here? So much for lighter is righter."

"I snuck a few cans of Olympia in your sleeping bag." I know he's joking; Jim would never drink Oly.

Sitting down to munch a PB&J sandwich, I tease out a few sips from my last liter of water. "What an incredible view. The ridge to the west looks like a dragon sleeping." The cloudless, brilliant blue is vibrant against the mountain vista, the white snow and gray rock sprinkled with tiny green trees.

"The vista gets even better. The big western sky is refreshing after living in the dense eastern woods for so long." Jim drains the last of his water with a frown.

I'm still soaking in the scenery. "That dragon back silhouette is fantastic. Almost imagine a girl riding it." I recently finished reading *The Dragonriders of Pern*, Anne McCaffrey's trilogy of fantasy novels. Another adventure from an imaginary world that merges with my own.

"Since you brought it up, what about that babe you met on the ferry?"

"Haven't thought about her lately." I pop the last of my sandwich into my mouth.

Jim rolls his eyes. "What else is there to life but climbing and girls?" It's easy for him. They flock to his good looks wherever we go.

"I'm a bit more cautious around women. Leery of getting hurt or let down. Sensitive."

He laughs. "Let me get this straight. You climb rocks, hitch across the country, wrestle badass Blackfeet, but hesitate to visit a girl who lives on a sailboat?"

"Now that you put it that way, it does seem silly," I mutter.

"Hoping to give you some insight. Speaking of perspective, look at Mount Adams over there." Jim points. Anything to distract me from my luck with girls is a good thing.

My tired limbs groan as we continue, passing the rest of the Mountaineers. The fun starts as we cross the Wilson Glacier, heading for the steep, narrow couloir of the *Fuhrer Finger*[2]. Two hundred feet apart, gray rock buttresses surround us on each side, the channel filled with loose talus underneath the snow. It's a humongous version of *The Trap Dike* in the Adirondacks.

"Let's rope up," Jim says. "Remember the strategy we discussed earlier?"

"Keep it tight between us, twenty meters apart. Coil the remainder over my shoulder." I hold one end of the rope and tie it to my harness with a figure-eight knot.

Jim nods. "Exactly. What happens if I slip into a crevasse?"

"I jump into self-arrest, using my ice axe to break your fall. The tough part will be pulling you out." Imagine lying face down, frantically holding onto a wood axe plunged in the snow, while your buddy dangles from a rope tied to your waist.

"Let's not worry about that part. The good news is that the glacier seems pretty chill. No one has fallen in this year; I think we'll be fine."

Jim starts, and when the rope tugs, it's my turn to follow. Hopefully, those SUOC caving trips will help if I'm sucked into an ice cave. Avoiding crevasses is easy, but it's a bit giddy to glimpse into the bottomless depths. Shivers run down my spine thinking about being surrounded by tons of ice and snow, a death trap for the unwary.

An hour later, Jim waits for me, plunked in the snow, untied from the rope. "See that last big crack down there? That's the bergschrund connecting the Wilson Glacier to the Fuhrer Finger."

"Glad to know now, after tromping over it without a clue." Ignorance is bliss.

A crevasse waits for the unwary climber on the Wilson
Glacier, Mount Rainier, June 1984.

"Yeah, falling into that monster would be nasty. It could go down
hundreds of feet. We'd be goners for sure." He turns and continues the
never-ending slog as I coil the rope.

Imagining such a whale swallowing me as a morsel for dinner makes
me queasy. Struggling to shrug off this vision, I move on. Letting
anxiety get the best of me doesn't help. As we climb, the snow softens,
like walking through mashed potatoes.

Jim points to rocks scattered in the snow at our feet. "See these suck-
ers? Where do you think they come from?"

I crane my neck, looking for the giant who flung them. "Perhaps
they were uncovered when the snow melted?"

"Close. The hot sun warms the mountain, thawing the frozen boulders so they tumble down our couloir."

"Holy guacamole. That's the rockfall danger I read about in Beckey's book."

Jim nudges one of the rocks with his boot. "Climbing the narrow chute now would be suicidal. We'll go in the wee hours of the morning, when the snow is frozen, making climbing easier, faster, and safer."

The slope steepens as we march into the Finger. After another hour, Jim is looking pleased with himself when I crest onto the snow ledge. A rock buttress towers over us, forming a comforting shelter from the steep couloir. The sun beams down, glittering off a tiny waterfall, fantastic for filling our empty water bottles. The thin, constant stream pours over the buttress, a natural kitchen sink just for us.

I'm parched, my two liters long gone. It's a total boon to find this unlimited water supply. Combined with the stunning view, it's a perfect camp. A mile below us, The Mountaineers rig their tents and fire their stoves.

After our sandwich supper, it's useless trying to sleep with the sun glaring in my eyes.

"This place reminds me of Mount Washington," I say. "Lots more snow, though." Of course, that brings back mixed memories. "Hard to believe it's been eighteen months since losing Ed."

Jim says "That must have really sucked. I've never lost anyone climbing."

"My one regret is not going to his funeral. I don't know why I didn't. Maybe I was confused or didn't think it was important at the time."

"I remember the memorial service you had for him in Syracuse. Don't beat yourself up." Jim replies.

"Yeah, I rallied later and did the right things, but I would have liked to tell his family I'm sorry."

Jim says, "No worries. It's good never to forget. Let's try to get some shuteye. It's an early start."

Mt. Adams twinkles golden as we settle into our sleeping bags, each to his thoughts. I've been through several epics, but nothing as horrible as that New Year's Eve on Mount Washington.

Jim soaking rays at our bivy in the *Fuhrer Finger*
couloir on Mount Rainier, June 1984.

The best way to remember Ed is to keep him close, treasure his sacrifice, and know my limits.

The sun glows as it sets over the dragon backs beneath us, the sky clear. I'm settling in, hoping to sleep, covering my eyes with the balaclava to stop the bright sun, grunting in frustration, turning over, and trying to get comfortable. I hope to meet dragon-girl Angie in my dreams.

"DAVE, IT'S TIME," Jim calls out. The sky is pitch black; stars glisten, the still air chilly, no sign of the moon. It's one in the morning, and after crunching granola bars, we rope up. The Mountaineers below are already on the move, hours behind us. Jim takes the lead and heads out.

I'm perched at the edge of the couloir, darkness daunting, feeding the rope. The slushy snow of yesterday is now hard-packed and crunchy Styrofoam. When the line tightens, I follow with the ice axe shaft-first into the slope for balance.

Jim's headlamp creates a Pink Floyd light show as he scouts the couloir. Turning to rest, facing outwards, exposure yawns beneath me. A twinge of vertigo causes a settling of my feet, ensuring that the crampons bite into the snow.

In the still quiet, the Milky Way glows, and the rock buttresses reach out in a cold embrace. The beauty of the scene takes the edge off my fear. Faith in my climbing gives me the boost of confidence needed in the couloir, avoiding thoughts of falling, a runaway sled into the hungry bergschrund below.

The rope tugs firmly, bringing me back. There's beauty and joy in being a small creature stuck on the side of this big hill.

Blasted by the intense wind, Jim hunkered down in the summit caldera on Mount Rainier, June 1984.

I've overcome the lack of light, not letting it intimidate me. It helps to concentrate on the outline of Jim's zigzag footprints up the steep slope. Popping out of the notch, he belays me near a rock outcropping on the summit ridge. Startled by the sudden intense wind, I miss the quiet cocoon silence of the couloir and zip my parka shut.

The wonder of being high on the mountain under a clear midnight-blue sky keeps me distracted, with no need to chat. Mount Adams glistens in the alpenglow, our reward for hours of climbing.

As another blast of wind breaks the stillness, it's time to get cracking, chewing on French bonbons for energy.

We head to the summit, the treadmill slope much more manageable, with no threat of slipping. Buffeted by sustained gusts with jet-engine force, we lean into the headwind to avoid getting blown off. Maybe it's time for the rope.

Exhaustion dampens my drive. Thankfully, Jim keeps chugging, mentally dragging me up. The altitude is the real deal; my head is dizzy, and my breath ragged.

Jim takes a snap of me below the summit of Mount
Rainier, June 1984.

The pack grows heavy; I resist the urge to toss it away. The Cascades spread below me in all their glory, but my mind travels inward, barely noticing the sunrise.

Suddenly, Jim stands, ice axe raised high, lashed by the spindrift. My mind wakes, and my mouth forms a huge grin. Made it! With winds gusting up to eighty mph, we jump into the summit caldera to avoid the blast.

"We knocked the bastard off! Congrats!" Jim gives me a huge hug that shatters the ice encasing my balaclava.

"Where's the calm and serenity quoted in the books?" I wonder. It's funny how fatigue vanishes when the body realizes it's done its job.

Jim turns to look over the rim of the summit. "Must be armchair mountaineers writing that drivel." Swirling snow devils hide the view. Inside the caldera, it's a cave. No view or sun to soak in, just a dark, dank place to wolf down chocolate. Since all there is to do is freeze, we opt to bail.

More oxygen energizes us with each downhill stride. The wind mellows, making the descent easy. The view of Mount Adams is stunning; I can pick out the ridges covered in white as the volcano thrusts out of the landscape 120 miles away. Below us, clouds fill the valley, hiding the glaciers. The sun is glorious, highlighting the smile plastered on my face.

Our efforts are rewarded as we trek down in quiet calm, soaking in the vista. Navigating the dangerous terrain has been tricky, but technically easy. The altitude is the crux and endurance is the key.

As we pass the ascending Mountaineers at the top of the Fuhrer Finger, I'm thrilled about our success, but the steep drop into the couloir sobers me.

Not to mention the dreaded rockfall and the potential to be caught in the Giant shooting gallery. In theory, since it's nine in the morning, that shouldn't be a problem. Jim declares the best part of the climb is the glissade. Whatever that is.

There's nothing better than learning a new trick when it matters the most. Off with the crampons and rope. Jim talks me through the process. Two thousand feet to the glacier, glissading is not that different from tobogganing, albeit with a few twists.

Sitting down, the ice axe shaft held by my side acts as a rudder, using my body as a sled, pushing off, sliding faster and faster, a runaway freight train.

Halfway down, traveling too fast, starting to freak out. I force the ice axe into the snow as a brake, flipping over on my stomach. The self-arrest method works, bringing me to a standstill after sliding two hundred feet.

After the terrifying roller coaster ride, my heart is racing with adrenaline. Glad I didn't ricochet off the couloir walls. I celebrate bagging my first mountaineering summit with a triumphant yelp, thrusting my arms into the air.

I CALL home from Jim's apartment, and Sister Dear answers. "Hey, David, glad you called." Her voice sounds tired.

"Hi, Lissa, whatcha doing home?"

"Dad asked me to. My internship was over, and he needs help with Mom."

This doesn't sound good.

"How is she?" I ask softly.

"Resting a lot since she's in pain. More than before. I hold her hand and sit with her, but she's not talking much."

"Shit. Can I speak to her?" Maybe it's time to stop playing mzungu and head home.

"She's napping, but you can talk to Dad, hold on."

My euphoria after reaching the summit of Rainier sails out the window. Without mentioning the climb to Dad, I ask about coming home. Mom's hanging in there. but it would be great if I return soon. He's on the fence but leaving it up to me.

Placing the phone on its hook, I sit back in the chair; the ceiling fan slowly spins, cooling the room. Unsettled, I head into the kitchen.

"So, what's up?" Jim finishes up another creation on the stove.

"I gotta roll. Mom's not doing well." The counter is littered with dishes, beckoning me to clean them.

"Bummer. Cancer's a nasty thing to deal with."

"Yeah, for all of us, especially Mom."

"Going to see Sailboat Sally?" He grins, handing me a bowl of another scrumptious stir-fry.

"Yeah, gave her a jingle before calling Dad. For at least one night. If I don't go, I'll never know if she's the one."

"Glad to see you have the right priority. Climbing, girl, then family."

"Not sure that's the correct order. But heading out tomorrow is the plan. I really appreciate all you've done for me. The hospitality, the ride, and definitely for leading the climb."

Jim smiles. "No sweat. We had a great week. Good luck getting home. I hope your mother gets better."

Jolted by the news about Mom, anxiety mixes with the traveling blood coursing through my veins.

⁓

THE THIRTY-FIVE-FOOT SLOOP cuts a mean line across the Strait of Georgia. Angie's dad recommends weaving around Galiano Island to avoid cruising into the shipping lanes. It's big water out here. I'm happy the islands are nearby.

"Any orcas around?" I ask Angie. She holds the tiller sitting next to me. Her folks relax in the front of the cockpit, giving us some theoretical privacy in the six-foot space.

"Heck yeah. But we'd have to go south to get closer to Victoria. Salmon and seals, their food, cluster there. Tough to do today. It's late, and the wind is shifting on us."

"Not sure I want to see one up close anyway."

She laughs. "We could always rent kayaks."

I shift my legs, cramped in the tiny cockpit. "No need, I'm happy in your lovely big boat. Kayaks are too small and exposed in open water."

"I'm kidding," she says. "I'm not a big fan of them either. I prefer the security of a motor when we need it. See the mainsheet telltales?"

Angie points to the small strips of fabric attached to the sail. "They're stalling. It looks as if the wind is dying. I'm going to come about and head back to port."

The wind continues to fuss as we return to the marina. Part of the sailing game is to minimize using the engine, relying on wind power as much as possible. Angie flips on the motor as we pass the breakwater, and we stow the sails. Maneuvering through the obstacle course of a harbor under sail would be nuts.

After securing the sloop, I splash out on fish and chips, soda, and chowder from the marina snack bar. We swing our legs over the water while sitting on the dock. The rising tide lightly laps against the pilings, and the sunset reflects on the clouds hovering over the Vancouver mountains to the east.

"This is a wonderful place," I say, finally putting down my chowder spoon. "I could stay here forever. I love the freedom that sailing provides you, the boat, and the wind. Worth the cramped quarters. What do you do in the winter?"

She dips a French fry in the ketchup on her plate. "In the fall, my folks go back to the house in Duncan, and I head across the strait to the university."

Angie and her Dad are in the Strait of Georgia near Victoria, British Columbia. During the summer, they call the boat home. June 1984.

Tossing my fry into the water, I wonder if a fish will snarf it. Okay, enough stalling.

Putting my plate down and hand on her knee, I tell her about Mom. "Her cancer is getting worse. I wish I could stay, get a job, or something. Maybe later, after she gets better."

"Oh, David, I'm sorry. That's what's been bothering you. What does the doctor say?"

"It's not good. She's weak from all the chemo. Nothing more to be done. I shouldn't have come out west, but it's too late for hindsight."

The sun sets behind us as we hold hands, watching the tide rise. Occasionally we toss a fry for the fish to munch, and the ripples expand to the chirping crescendo of crickets.

The bustle in the harbor starts early and rousts me from my camp in the trees on the far side of the parking lot. I traipse over the boardwalk to the sailboat and clamber into the cockpit, where the smell of fresh coffee fills the air.

"Have a treat, David." Angie's mom hugs me. "I'm sorry to hear about your mother. Cancer is horrible."

"Aww, thanks, you're very kind. She had it years ago and has been fighting back hard. This is an idyllic place, but I need to go home."

"I understand, honey. Hey Angie, David's here," she yells into the cabin.

The ladder creaks and Angie's head pops out, "Good morning!"

"Hi Angie, you look well rested." I take a massive bite of a croissant, followed by a good slurp of the delicious coffee.

She smiles, giving me a lazy punch on the shoulder. "Run into any drunks in the park last night?"

I laugh, and we banter as one big happy family until it's time to go to the ferry.

Standing on the second deck, I wave madly, blowing kisses down to Angie. The ferry departs, and she fades away in the distance. The Rolling Stones' "Angie" plays in my mind. When the klaxon horn bellows. I hold my head in my hands, heavyhearted.

Two days later, I call home from the pay phone outside a small store in Wyoming. I should be wearing cowboy boots. "I'm zooming as fast as I can," updating Dad on my progress.

He sounds harried. "Mom's not well. You need to come home."

"I'll hitch through the night," I say, watching the tumbleweeds blow by. Holy crap. This is not good.

"No, you need to come home now. I'll buy you a plane ticket out of Denver. Can you make it?"

"Let me check." Wedging the phone under my chin, rooting for my road atlas. I quickly determine it's an eight-hour hitch. "I can make it tomorrow. Let's say a 4 p.m. flight."

"I'll call American and have the ticket booked. Go to the counter with your license."

"Okay, Dad, thanks. Promise I'll make the plane. Love you." Time to fire.

Bounding up the stairs to Mom's room, climbing on the bed as I always do. Holding her cool hand, she doesn't notice me lying beside her. Lissa and Dad warned me. Sobering to a new reality, I watch her breathing. Mom stirs an hour later, opening her eyes, and we gaze at each other.

"Mom, it's great to see you. Sorry I've been gone. I had a blast, and we made it to the summit of Rainier. I met an awesome girl. Mom?"

She's not listening. The pit of my stomach lurches as I realize she doesn't recognize me.

Lying back, I notice random cracks in the ceiling. Four weeks ago, we were playing cards and chattering away as always. I had no clue things could change so quickly. Her hand is clammy; her eyes are closed again. Snuggling up to warm her, but especially to hear her breathe. Cancer sucks.

A week later, Lissa and I cruise to buy a new mattress for Mom. We banter, appreciating the mundane chore that distances us from watching her deteriorate. We pull into the driveway and start untying the mattress when Dad comes out, sobbing. He reaches to us and stammers, "S-she's gone." We form a three-way hug, crying, the wind rustling our clothes.

STANDING in the grieving line at church with my family, a zombie. The congregation is lovely, but I'm in a state of shock. My body moves on its own, spirit and mind withdrawn, barely attached to the present. Hugs and kind words don't help. Nothing against anyone; they're trying to support us. I'm glad to leave and head home.

Sipping beer and sitting by the pool with my brother Andy Bear, staring out over the pines behind the fence. It's a lovely, warm mid-July day, but neither of us feels like doing cannonballs off the diving board. The back door creaks and soft steps rustle in the grass. Lissa opens the gate and sits down with her glass of wine.

In the shade of the umbrella, we watch ripples in the pool as the vacuum cable finishes its cleaning job. After a few minutes of quiet, I take off my sunglasses and pull up to the table.

"I've been thinking that it's time to leave Keene Valley and live here with Dad. Both of you covered for me while I blasted around out west."

Lissa reaches out and touches my arm. "You're crazy doing all that hitchhiking, but I had nothing else to do. My internship wrapped up last month, making it easy for me to help Mom and Dad. Don't feel guilty. You made it back in time."

"Thanks, Lissie. Still, I've been a slacker, flitting in, sprinkling some love, then dashing off again."

Bear puts his empty glass on the table. "None of us expected it would get this bad so quickly."

"Thanks, guys. Since college starts in a few weeks, it makes sense I move home."

"You'll blast north as a weekend warrior," Bear says. "The best way to weasel out of church." He forces a smirk. His red hair sparkles in the sunset, matching Lissa's. I'm the odd duck with brown hair.

"Ah, good point. I'm going to miss the Red House. But sometimes, fun needs to chill. Family is more important."

Bear agrees. "You've had enough adventure; it's cool that you'll cover the Popster. He shouldn't be left all alone."

Andy, me, my Dad Seymour, and Lissa at her college graduation in May 1985, ten months after losing Mom. Photo from the Seymour Flinn collection.

I join Lissa near the pool. We watch water spiders sprint across the still surface, beckoning us to jump in. Dusk settles as we lounge like seals, staring at nothing; the sun sets behind the pine trees.

It's time for a life-priority reboot. Coming to grips with losing Mom, the Red House, and the Mountaineer. Luckily, I still have my family, my friends, and my Journal. And climbing like a mzungu.

Skiers on Tuckerman Ravine, Mount Washington, May 1987

VISTA

So, now I'm a stripper. Working for a tiny publishing house, I use special tape to strip film negatives into four-page sets. Each page set prints one color at a time when mounted on a drum press. Cyan comes first, followed by magenta, yellow, and finally black. After that, it's over to the binder to cut out the pages for the magazine. I fine-tune the alignment using a light table, just like I do while making maps.

It's very different from the Mountaineer, and I miss assisting customers and fiddling with equipment. But I'm home with Dad, and that's the whole point. He immerses himself in church life, and we adjust to life without Mom. It's quieter here, away from the crazy Red House parties.

The lazy August summer day draws us to the pool. Dad's not fond of the sun and sits under the umbrella. On the other hand, I soak rays in the lounge chair, drying off after a cooling swim, my book untouched. It's glorious to relax and reflect instead of pushing on to the next thing.

"How did you and Mom get to Uganda in the first place?" For all these years, I never chatted with Dad as much as I did with Mom. Today seems as good as any to begin.

"The story starts in 1949 when I graduated from Princeton and met some Chinese bishops at a workshop. Talking to my uncle, we agreed there're two ways to learn about the world: study or investigate. After poking around the church for possibilities, I accepted a two-year teaching post in a Shanghai high school."

"Wild, I never knew you lived in China." Things you find out when you ask.

"That was the plan. But Mao Zedong flexed his muscles and expelled all the foreigners from China. The church found another position for me in Liberia teaching chemistry at the Episcopal Mission."

"Wow, that must have been exciting."

"A grand adventure. Being young and clueless about race issues, I learned quickly. In Liberia, I rarely ran into hatred or bigotry. I was just another white guy there to help. Unfortunately, my inability to speak the local language limited my grasp of what was really going on."

"That had to be eye-opening. Did you go to Uganda after Liberia?"

"I returned to America in 1951 and enrolled at Virginia Seminary to become a minister. After graduating, the church sent me to St. David's Church in Delaware, your namesake. In 1959, I met Mom at a New Year's Eve party set up by close friends. We started dating and decided to go to Uganda. We married in August and set sail on the *Queen Mary*."

"Most people don't decide to leave everything and head to Africa." And people say I'm impulsive.

"Well, it did happen that way. Mom got excited when she heard about my Liberian adventure and the possibility of an upcoming stint in Uganda. She pounced on the idea, promising to marry me if we went. That motivated me to take action."

"Bet you miss her. It must be difficult remembering those times."

He nods. "It's hard since we shared so much together. Our courtship, living in Uganda, the birth of you three children, moving back to America, and finally, purchasing this house. It's overwhelming, all that we did, and now she's gone."

"What do you miss the most about her?"

Tears form in his eyes. "Her cheerful demeanor, even while suffering from cancer, she was almost too stoic, shielding her pain from us. Her bounciness and energy were wonderful. Without her, life seems dull. She was always the life of the party."

Dad starts to sob, drawing me from my sun worshipping, and we hold hands and cry together. Always supportive, Mom encouraged me to push the envelope and not take the mellow road. She's my role model mzungu, living her adventurous life.

Hanging out with Dad gives me time to focus on the Journal. Issue five should be published soon; I'm on a roll. Not much money is coming in, but getting a few subscriptions is sweet. This issue is twenty-eight pages with a bomber cover. It's looking pretty snappy.

The last two issues featured black-and-white drawings; but now, I'm switching to gray-scale photographs. Not as sophisticated as my day job, but success fosters moving up in the world. Full color would be awesome.

As I finish typing my Rainier article, Dad calls me to the phone. Eric wants to know if I'm interested in climbing this weekend. After a couple of months at home, my brain kicks into mountain mode as we haggle out the details. I advocate for a real trip, not some car-camping drinking fest. Time to get cracking and do something big—Wallface. It beckons climbers like moths to a campfire; the attraction is deep and primal.

Driving northwest, anticipating the transition from the city to the Adirondack forest. I haven't climbed with Gaston and Eric since working at the Mountaineer. We're up for the challenge where boldness and eagles dare, answering the call to *No Man's a Pilot*[1].

The warm August night is filled with the croak of frogs and wafting earthy smells that soothe my suburban pulse. Backpack stuffing begins with the tent, sleeping bag, rope, climbing rack, first-aid kit, helmet, food, stove, and as much beer as possible. As usual, Gaston opts for Juicy Juice.

"Who's idea was this?" My back whimpers at the thought of carrying such a beast. "Oh, wait. It was mine."

"The remoteness and the lure of the big wall are hard to resist," Eric says. "Any lazy climber can flash Pitchoff or the Chapel Pond slabs."

"Yeah, it sounds great when slugging beers at the pub. Hauling all this junk, you'd think we're on an Everest expedition."

Eric takes such discussions seriously. "Climbing is why we do this, adding spice to an otherwise boring life. Playing a complex game, solving puzzles, and growing spiritually. Now, where is that fuel bottle?"

"Deep thoughts," Gaston agrees, rooting in the trunk and pulling out the white gas for the stove. "While other people are drawn to motocross or knitting, these trips make city life bearable. Climbing helps me cope with the real world."

"That's true," I agree. "Marla once inferred that climbing is life in a nutshell. Live to climb and climb to live."

"Perhaps," Eric adds, "we love the risky part of it."

Gaston chuckles as he closes the trunk. "You guys are overanalyzing it. We have a blast doing crazy stuff on rocks."

He's right. Tromping in the dark to a big wall is nuts to many. But it's good to be out again. The last three months have been intense, horrible, actually. Rushing home from Wyoming to hug Mom in her final weeks, followed by the zombie aftermath. It's great going mzungu, fueled by the thrill of adventure, hanging out with friends, and pushing limits. Climbing fulfills a passion that keeps my lights on.

Headlamp ready, I ask Gaston if he's got enough Juicy Juice.

"Absolutely. Can't stand beer; I prefer a more refined libation." Gaston doesn't need alcohol to loosen up. Boisterousness runs in the family. His two grandmothers still play pool at the local Polish pub, not a dull crowd. "Let's rock." He stomps past the trailhead sign-in roster. It's dark, making it hard to see his hot-pink tights, designed to shock mosquitoes into total disarray.

"After you, *mon ami*," I say, sagging under the weight of my pack.

The weather is warm, bugs buzzing in a cloud of wings. We arrive at Calamity Brook after an hour of hiking uphill, leaving the skeeters far behind. I drop a small tree branch into the brook, a Winnie the Pooh moment, as the water chortles and gushes under my feet on the wooden bridge. The moon shadows glitter in the river eddies. I want to lie down and sleep right here. The thought swirls away as the current takes the Poohstick.

"Full steam ahead," Eric says, crossing to the other side, setting a solid pace as the mosquitoes start to triangulate.

After twenty minutes of hiking, he declares, "This is the wrong way."

"Never!" Gaston exclaims.

No Man's a Pilot on Wallface. The Diving Board is found at the top of the highlighted line. Photo by adirontreks.blogspot.com.

I happily heave the pack to the ground. "Let's look at the map. I don't think we should have crossed the bridge." Sure enough, we missed the yellow trail markers to Indian Pass and are heading east to Mount Marcy via the red trail.

"Flinny, you bonehead." Eric implies it's my fault by looking at the map. His chuckle fades as he and Gaston turn around, heading back the way we came. Hoisting my moose, I hurry to catch up.

Heavy packs in the dark bode well for stubbing toes, bashing knees, or whacking skulls on low-hanging branches. Thanks to our trusty headlamps, we return to the Indian Pass trail.

Focused on getting to camp, we crank the remaining miles in silence. It's almost midnight when the dirt trail turns steep with boulders. The herd path veers to the left, which leads to the climbers' campsite.

Gaston arrives first and scavenges the wood necessary for a campfire. The place looks identical to when I was here with Woody, Seattle Jim, and Tosh three years ago.

Emptying my pack, a 32oz can of Juicy Juice rolls out. Gaston reaches for it with a massive grin on his face. "Thanks. Gaston appreciates your help."

A little miffed, I shuffle to the creek to cache some beers in the cool water. Returning to the tent, I say, "You're a brat, sandbagging me with that monster can in my pack." Climbers love to joke with their partners, tricking them into carrying an imaginary bag of sand to slow them down. I let it go.

Shortly, drinks are readied, and the fire crackles as it should. I ask Eric about his big adventure. Earlier this summer, he flew to India to climb with two SUOCers. The perks of having a real job.

"A fabulous time, that's for sure. Hot as hades in Delhi. And the smells! I almost passed out in the airport, waiting for Bunji. Finally, he showed up to whisk us away into more chaos. Have you ever experienced the Third World?"

Bunji's family lives near Delhi. Since no one in SUOC can pronounce his name correctly, we call him Bunji, the closest approximation in English.

"Since leaving Africa as a wee lad, I've been stuck on this continent." And I thought hitching to Mount Rainier was a real excursion.

"It's intense. All the heat, hovels, people, poverty, flies, filth, lepers, beggars, cows, tea stalls, buses, bicycles, and motorized rickshaws. I was glad to get out of Delhi and up to the mountains. But then it got weirder. Traveling by bus, we survived the suicidal roads thanks to our amazing Sikh driver. No guardrails on the winding curves with one-thousand-foot cliffs. The raging river would have swallowed us if we careened off. The best part was the rest stops and getting a cup of chai."

"Did you ever make it to the mountains?" Gaston asks, impatient to get to the meat.

"Ah, Shivling! I'd never seen a picture of the peak, but Bunji promised it would be great. When I learned Shiva is the god of destruction, I became concerned. We were hanging out at basecamp when the mountain forced its way out of the monsoon clouds. Magical. Things turned for the worse as avalanches sheared off the sucker all day. We punted that bad boy and took off for Kedar Dome. More mellow, with no Shivling avalanches. Still a bear, over twenty-two-thousand feet high. I sucked wind for oxygen big time. Psyched to have made it."

I say, "What an amazing climb! And the country with all its weirdness. Which did you prefer?"

"That's a tough one. Slogging up the mountain, it could have been anywhere. Don't get me wrong; the views are stunning. But the buses, poverty, all the rest blew my mind."

"Ah, the approach is better than the summit." Gaston rose to add more wood to the fire.

"And what an approach. You guys must go someday." Eric finishes his beer.

"I need to visit Africa first," I say. "Back to the Uganda homeland. But yeah, India, Nepal, the Himalayas."

After visiting the bathroom bush and while Eric grabs another beer, Gaston asks how I'm doing after losing Mom.

"It's been pretty hard. She had cancer when I was twelve but she always toughed it out." Tears start to build but a swig from my beer distracts me. "She was the one who gave me the right nudges in life." My rock.

Gaston comments. "That's rough. My family has been lucky so far. How's your Dad?"

"He puts on a good show. The church keeps him busy, but he's still crushed. I can't believe it's been two months already. Glad I'm staying home to keep him company. It's funny. After the intensity leading up to her death, now life floats along, drifting in the current. I'm glad to be back in the woods."

Eric agrees "Sounds like he's hanging in there."

Time to move to happier topics, or I'll start dropping tears. "How are your folks doing, Eric?"

"Loving that we kids moved out, freeing them from parenting to go canoeing. They're heading to the Boundary Waters next month."

"Do they still travel at night hoping to dodge bad weather?" I let out a loud yawn.

Eric laughs. "Yeah, it's their ritual to outwit the ol' Adirondack clouds by sneaking up on the mountain. They believe a morning start causes the weather gods to crank up the rain machine."

"Tomorrow will tell if the strategy works."

We sleep cowboy style, under the stars, with our tent designated as the closet. Looking at the stars and pondering Eric's trip to India, I wonder if I have the courage to tackle such an adventure. Maybe it's time to visualize the possibility. The moon is faint in the western sky as my eyelids close, too tired to worry about the big climb tomorrow.

～

"ANYONE AWAKE TO LIGHT THE STOVE?" Eric asks from his comfy spot.

My eyes flutter as Gaston snores. "I'm on it."

Beginning the morning routine, my toes cringe at leaving the warm, snuggly sleeping bag. After snagging the food bag hanging from a tree, I start the stove, welcoming its purr as the water boils.

Using a plastic cone and paper towels, I plop in the grounds to brew coffee. I'm slightly jealous of Eric's rich experiences, honed by his canoe-crazed parents. He grew up with a paddle in his hand, running white-water rapids in the spring and going on canoe trips in the summer. I wish my folks had taken me camping.

A breakfast of oatmeal and granola bars gets us ready to roll at a reasonable hour. No crack-of-noon start for us. Straight up the talus fields to the climb, our daypacks light, climbing gear spread out amongst the three of us.

No Man's a Pilot is a four-pitch climb; the first two pitches are mellow up to the *Diagonal* ramp. From there, two hard pitches to the infamous Diving Board. Last night, we pondered soloing to the ramp, but today, after the beers have worn off, better senses prevail and keep us roped.

"Belay on, climb away!" Eric leans back against the birch tree, rubbing his bushy, long beard.

"Climbing!" My rack jingles—the lead climber's toolbox—since it's crammed with carabiners, Hexes, Stoppers, and Friends. Wedged into cracks, the temporary anchors will keep us safe—no desire to repeat last year's plunge on *Equis*.

I'm psyched to be here with no one else around but a few hungry bugs. Whistling, I futz around with a Hex. The sun warms the granite; my fingers brush lichen from handholds. The isolation of Wallface keeps the routes natural—shrubbery in all the wrong places and loose rock galore. Part of the climbing game requires avoiding obstacles without removing them, minimizing our impact on the wilderness. Leave No Trace is the name of the game.

The last time I lead climbed was before Rainier. The knack returns quickly, helped by the easy pitch. I don't need the rope, but it makes the outing safer. Settling into a nice, comfortable belay, I retrieve the other lads. Eric takes the lead on the second pitch as the sun climbs higher.

Luckily for us, his theory of sneaking up on the mountain rings true. The sky is pristine and the morning sun sparkles off the tiny crystals embedded in the wall.

Eric vanishes behind a rock and Gaston snaps pictures, his pink neon tights glowing in the sun. Twenty minutes later, Eric yells he's off belay and ready for Gaston to climb. Now I'm alone, relishing the moment, watching a squirrel munch an acorn three feet away.

The vista unfolds as I climb onto the thirty-foot-wide *Diagonal* shelf while Eric reels me in.

The Diagonal on Wallface in the Adirondacks follows the climber in the photo, *No Man's A Pilot*, goes straight up the left wall in the foreground. Photo by Kevin Heckeler, July 2011.

The easy part over, we face two hard pitches in a funky chimney to the Diving Board. Since the guidebook raves about it, we're compelled by the eight-hundred-foot exposure. It's as good a reason as any to climb this bugger.

"Is my belay on, young Flinny? Gaston is ready to roll and flash this lovely chimney. My glowing pink tights will show the way." His handkerchief price tag flutters in the wind as he turns to face the wall.

"Belay on, climb when ready," I reply.

Eric closes his eyes, soaking rays on the *Diagonal*, waiting his turn. With two on the rope, one of us is always hanging out. Gaston reaches into the chimney and gets going. I smirk as his rants float down the rope. But my gloating wears off once I realize Gaston's thrashing means it must be hard. Finally, he yells that he's off belay, and it's my turn.

The chimney is cramped, eighteen inches wide, and chock-full of loose rock and awkward blocks. When starting a new pitch, we need to create our safety system of temporary anchors. As the second climber following Gaston, it's my job to remove the pieces.

First, I wiggle the Hex by pulling up and down on its loop, freeing it from the crack. I carefully drape the sling over my shoulder and then unclip the piece from the rope. Voila, I've "cleaned" the pro, and it's ready for use on the next pitch.

Careful to avoid bashing my head against the blocks, I hang on with my left arm and look down over my right shoulder for a foothold. Vertigo swells as emptiness yawns, threatening to pitch me backward to crater on *Diagonal* and wake Eric from his nap.

The rope tightens, jostling my mind from its trap, beckoning me to move. The chimney is a ship's ladder; the blocks act as rungs. Once this concept clicks in, it takes me no time to reach Gaston.

"Off belay. Great lead, matey," I say.

"Welcome to my awesome high school physics project." He proudly indicates the three-anchor belay with his free hand.

I look around for a comfortable spot to stand. "It's going to be cramped when Eric gets here. Glad it didn't rain last night. This chimney would become a waterfall. Did you notice the moss?"

Gaston uses the rope attached to my harness to belay Eric. "I'm sure you'll have fun on the next pitch. Crossing my fingers for a few frogs lurking in the cracks."

Great. Frogs. Moss. Chimneys. As Eric climbs, I contemplate my upcoming lead. Waiting is the worst part—too much time to think. I combat angst with my tried-and-true tactics: gabbing and futzing. Organizing my rack for the upcoming final pitch, I ask Gaston about his never-ending job search. The ploy works.

Gaston knows me. "Flinny, you can do this. Don't overthink it." He's a superb climber and a great partner. Motivated and brave, he knows how to bring out my best.

After double-checking my rack, I study the crux. It's not a good place to fall, crashing down on top of the lads. I hope that's not on their minds. At long last, Eric has the belay, and it's time to roll. My brain freezes, red warning lights flashing.

Jamie appears in my mind's eye. Sitting on a boulder, my Scottish Yoda reminds me "There is no try, only do." Shaking out my hands, I place them one at a time in my chalk bag, breathing deeply, letting my body take over.

Stemming my right foot on the wall, I stand over a bulge to place a bombproof Stopper. When I clip into it, my grimace transforms into a smile. Confidence surges as I'm back on the sharp end of the rope.

The Diving Board is stupendous, jutting out ten feet horizontally from the immense wall. Surrounded by air and supported by the chimney, it's a natural platform with massive boulders and trees 800 feet below. I imagine taking a running jump and carving a perfect dive.

Sitting with our legs dangling over the drop, we watch a hawk swoop for prey. Bantering about the climb, we munch on apples, bagels, cheddar cheese, and peanut butter. Regaling our stoic and bold venture, we are men, proud of conquering our fears, harassing each other to show our trust. It's the way climbers roll.

"Never thought I'd wiggle up a cave on a rock climb. Good job on the crux, Flinny." Gaston munches the last of his apple.

Eric hands me a piece of chocolate as a prize. "Here's to the man of the hour. Pushing the 5.9 limits."

Gaston agrees. "Many more to come. What's next, *Drop Fly or Die?*"

"While I relish the hardman cult as any studly climber should, I prefer the adventure more than the climbing. Hanging out with you guys on Wallface is perfect. No need to muscle up insane routes."

"Ah, the journey is more important than the destination." Gaston nods his head.

"Exactly. As long as it's the right adventure. You know, climbing like a mzungu."

"What the heck is a mzungu?"

"Ah, Grasshopper, a long story for another day. The short answer is to travel around the world doing wild things. It's Swahili for wanderer."

Gaston nods. "Ah, some African thing. Gotcha."

"For example," I continue, "Eric channeled his inner mzungu on the India trip. We need to live an adventurous life. It's time for me to amp things up and travel to Africa. How about you?"

"Chamonix. Gaston must go to France, of course. Then Switzerland, for sure. Arr, the Eiger. Need a job to pay for the trip."

"You and me both. Minimum wage just doesn't cut it. Hey, look at Eric; he's already sleeping. Good plan."

The perfect vista unfolds with the view south to Henderson Lake, while an eagle soars over the green carpet below. We loiter, soaking in the sun's warmth as the afternoon wanes. The fresh-smelling breeze drifts by, keeping the pesky bugs away. Closing my eyes, I imagine lying by Dad's swimming pool, with its diving board and welcoming water a few feet below, radically different from our perch on Wallface.

Clouds begin to trundle in and cut off nature's heater. The cool air stirs us into action. Gaston inspects the rap point, a friendly birch tree behind us. "This looks solid. The runner is clean and has a rappel ring."

Eric and I trust his assessment. We've rapped off scarier trees. Drawing the proverbial short straw in the rappel lottery, I go first.

"Remember, the yellow rope is the one with the knot," I say. "Don't forget to check it when you head down."

"Right, pull on my yellow rope," Gaston replies. "Now, get moving; I'm out of Juicy Juice."

I take a deep breath, step back over the edge, and out into space. There's nothing scarier than gobs of exposure as I release my weight onto the rope. Couch potatoes assume climbing is the hard part and getting down is hunky-dory, easy-peasy. Nope.

Dangling from a rope is frightening. When climbing, I have control of my destiny using my hands and feet. Launching into thin air and trusting the rappel always shakes the butterflies free.

Narrowly avoiding the loose boulders in the chimney, I continue, tugging and bouncing lightly on the ropes. Reaching the end, I place Friends to augment the existing anchor and clip in, settling into the hanging belay. Tug the rope and yell, "Off rappel," hoping Eric realizes it's his turn.

The ropes start flapping, and he makes his way over the Diving Board. Disappearing into the chimney and popping out, he lowers down next to me as I offer him a carabiner.

"Welcome to our fine hanging belay. How was your plunk over the Diving Board?"

"Awesome. A wee bit hairy but excellent. That point of no return is wild, walking off the lip into space." Eric gathers his breath.

"Aye, lad, the thrill is there, but I still hate rappelling. Tell me when you're anchored then I can signal Gaston."

"I'm good, and here're the ropes."

The vista from the top of *Diagonal* on Wallface, September 1982.

Giving a few flaps, I yell for Gaston.

Craning our necks to watch, we see him dance over the Diving Board, lever out, and stop. After a minute, Eric wonders, "What's he doing? It's dire, but he should be cool. Is he stuck?"

"I've never seen Gaston gripped. Bet he stopped to take a picture of a frog."

Finally, as he continues his descent. Eric and I chat about the disappearing sun, snug in our harnesses.

"There you are, lad," Eric says as Gaston gets close.

"Quick, give me that anchor, Flinny," Gaston yells. "The damn rope, hurry!"

"Huh? Whatcha talking about?" I ask, clipping him in.

"Phew." He sighs deeply. "The rope is cut. Terrifying! I had to keep going, praying it wouldn't break. You knuckleheads think you're marines zooming out of a helicopter."

Speechless, I collect the ropes, leaving my blue rope alone to pull on the yellow one. When processing a dire situation, it's great to have mundane work to do.

"Too bad you couldn't re-jigger the rap," I say. A cut rope is bad. Not to mention Gaston bouncing down the wall, pulling the ropes with him as he plummets eight hundred feet. A full-blown, horrifying epic.

"Impossible," he says. "I was dangling four feet below when I noticed it. Nasty."

"Ohhh, that's what you were doing up there. Wow. What a mess. Eric, can you haul on this sucker? The rope drag is heinous."

The yellow rope whips down with a few more yanks, pulling my blue rope along. Gaston points to the severe cut fifteen feet from where the two ropes are joined. My lovely blue rope—with an eleven-millimeter diameter—is sliced in half.

"Holy shit," Eric sums it up. "Holy double shit!" Seconds pass as we dangle in our hanging belay.

Untying the ropes to reset the rappel, I move the ruined end to the bottom. "Sorry, dude. I thought I took it easy but obviously screwed up. The weight of our rappelling must have sawed the rope on the edge of the Diving Board."

Eric threads the rope through the rappel ring to continue our descent. "I didn't see the rope cut, either. We should have walked down."

Gaston shakes it off. "A disaster narrowly averted. Let's get the hell out of here. Beer and Juicy Juice await."

The campfire warms our souls as we forget about the drama of the cut rope and captivate each other with thoughts of the climb and the glory of the Diving Board stuck deep into our brains.

In the morning, it's time to bug out. After hiking three miles, the trail widens to swallow a car. I'm missing Mom, and our close call with death brings back memories. I want to chat and let her into my world for a moment.

"This slog is easier without all the beer. Whatcha thinking, Flinny?" Eric asks.

"About my mom. We almost joined her up there." I navigate a tree in the trail.

With Gaston scampering ahead, Eric slows down to walk next to me. "My priest says death is part of life, but that's too abstract for me."

"Yeah. It's hard to process and make sense of things. Grateful for her ten years of life after the first round of chemo. The icing on the cancer cake of life. Still, that rope cut terrified me. Thank goodness I didn't think too much up there."

Eric steps around a mud puddle. "Freaking out would have made it worse. Falling off a cliff is a speedy way to go, but cancer's slow crawl isn't any better. All I know is that dying sucks."

"Rappelling is like sliding down a life rope: if it holds, no sweat. If the anchor fails, big crater."

"Relying on a rope is sketchy, but today, it was our only viable option." Eric holds a sapling, allowing me to pass a fallen tree without getting lashed, the fine gentleman he is.

"Yeah, Bob and Marla got lost trying to hike down." Smiling, I recall their unplanned bivy years ago. It was sad to hear that they broke up. I guess they weren't the perfect couple after all.

I continue, "It's the yin and yang of life. Shit happens whether we are ready or not. Going to die somehow, someway. Could be cancer, rappelling, or old age."

"Creating my destiny is better than leaving it to something else. Hey, look, this grind is over; the trailhead approaches."

Gaston waits near the cars. "Finally, you guys made it. Eric, open this puppy. A spare can of Juicy Juice awaits."

Toss my pack into Mom's car and gently store my muddy hiking boots. "What an amazing climb. Except for the danged rope-cut episode." My toes wink happily in their freedom.

Gaston lets out a juicy burp. "If you're not scared, it's not an adventure."

"Ain't that a fact." Eric agrees. "Let's fire, Gaston. Almost three hours to Remsen."

After giving the lads a goodbye hug, I head south, the weekend over, and back to work. I love going mzungu, hate scary rappels, and cherish my buddies.

CELEBRATING Mom's birthday is tough. I bake her favorite chocolate cake from a mix. Dad leads a somber service, reading from the Bible, and we sing a few of Mom's favorite hymns. Since her birthday is in late October, we usually decorate the house with Halloween trimmings, but we aren't into it this year. After dinner, we light fifty-three candles and use a lot of tissues. It sucks not having her here.

Monday after work, I have news for Dad over dinner. "My bud Scott called and has a job for me."

Dad sets down his fork to wipe his mouth. "What kind of job?"

"Computer mapping with a firm outside Boston. I'll be one of the first Bachelor of Arts graduates to work there."

Dad smiles. "I see. What's the next step?"

"An interview next week. I hope it's okay to take the car." Since the Maverick fell apart in Keene Valley, I've used Mom's to get around.

"Of course. I'm excited for you, David. A real job."

"It sounds great, but I'm not comfortable leaving you." Dad is the reason I bailed out of the Red House.

"It's been great having company, but you can't pass on this opportunity. Uncle Irv will be proud. I'll be over in the UK during January, anyway."

Collecting the dinner plates, I head into the kitchen. Life is getting interesting.

Leaving early, driving east, I nervously practice the presentation for a team of six engineers. I had to buy a new suit and couldn't resist pillaging Dad's Uganda tie, dark blue with colorful embroidery of the imperial crane. Gotta have a little style. While this interview crux isn't hard, there's a lot at stake. Need to present well and smile a lot.

I crush the interview and open the offer letter a few days later. Floating around the house, waiting impatiently for Dad to come home to show him the FedEx package. Luckily, the stripping boss didn't care when I told him. He's OK with me working until Christmas. A real job, at long last.

Lissa and Andy come home from school for the holidays, but it's hard to be festive. Dad's church services distract our attention and provide us with something to do. I love to belt out the hymns since they're familiar, and I'm good at singing. We're invited to Christmas parties around the parish, which are helpful as therapeutic diversions.

Andy Bear is grinding away in his Sophomore year at RIT. Too bad I bolted to Keene Valley, we could have lived together. He pivoted from Math and sold out to Computer Science. Lissa's got one more semester at Zoo Mass in Amherst. She's big into the animal rights movement. Luckily she hasn't been arrested at a protest march.

Preparing for my move, I buy a used Honda Civic since my siblings need Mom's car when they're home. Shopping for more suits, thank God for Lissa; poor Dad is clothing-clueless. Yep, joining the corporate world.

After New Year's, I'm ready to roll. Leaving Dad is hard, but it's time to start a new chapter, climbing the career ladder. The company is on Route 128, north of Boston, near New Hampshire and the White Mountains. Being a defense contractor, most of the company's cash comes from advanced research defense programs.

After three months into the new gig, I get the hint from my boss and file security-clearance paperwork. Do I have a gambling, drug dealing, or gun-running history? Bad guys could use any sketchy behavior to blackmail me into giving up secrets. Hopefully, no one in SUOC tells the government investigators too much.

The job's not glamorous. I'm a grunt translating FORTRAN computer programs, so others know what they do. Best practice says to document first, then code. Right. That never happens.

The good news is that my team manages the image-processing laboratory, and they give me a login to play with all the toys. A total boon to use high-tech computers from Symbolics, Pixar, and Floating Point Systems.

My boss introduces me to the fun of using satellite images to analyze patterns and find objects of interest that I can't tell you about. These images have multiple layers that capture different light frequencies. Using computers to visualize the data, it's incredible what you can discover. The unclassified sensors come from Landsat, a civilian satellite run by NASA.

The real deal is hidden in the SCIF, a Secure Compartment Information Facility called a *Tank*. Whatever goes into the Tank can never come out. Someday if my clearance comes in, I can work on real projects instead of playing with demo data.

Issue six of the AAJ publishes in June 1985, a few months late. Thanks to the job, I bought an Apple Macintosh. It's much easier to edit typos on a computer than with a typewriter. A printer and scanner round out the process. It's exciting to draw maps electronically instead of by hand. I strip out each page the old way, but someday it'll be possible to print directly to press negatives.

Unfortunately, driving north on Interstate 93 last week, I shifted into the Honda's fifth gear, and poof, nothing happened. Taking it to the shop, the mechanic shakes his head. Yup, the transmission is toast.

So now I've got new wheels, a spanking new maroon-red Volkswagen Jetta. Having a real job is the saving grace for getting a car loan.

During the summer, I work on issue seven, thirty-two pages, nice and beefy. Spend hours in MacPaint tweaking the maps just right. Write an article on Halley's Comet that visits the Earth next spring. Nothing to do with mountains, but too cool not to include. Another benefit of being the boss. It takes the entire fall to complete, but finally, I drive to the printer in Etown over Thanksgiving weekend. Looks fantastic.

~

WITH THE JOURNAL finished and the job under control, it's time to get back to climbing. The Red House has disbanded, but we're doing our best to keep the tradition going as full-on weekend warriors.

A parallel universe converges around Boston; amazing that the Bitch-and-Moan Brothers live nearby. General Electric transferred Ken last fall, and Jamie goes to photography school in the city.

I finally make it to Ken's Nashua, New Hampshire crash pad in late February 1986, for some ski mountaineering on Mount Washington.

"How goes the job, Flinny?" Ken burps. "Time you joined the real world, making real cash."

I laugh as he tosses the empty beer can into the trash. "I admit I enjoy making money. Miss my dad terribly, but I have to pay off my college loans. And I get to work with wicked smart MIT PhDs. Imagine me debating fractal math with these guys. Nothing like fitting hiking boots at The Mountaineer."

The pop of his next beer breaks my stride, and Ken snickers, "PhDs, bah! I fix all the disasters those smartie pants create in their labs. Hands-on engineers are the ones who make the shit work."

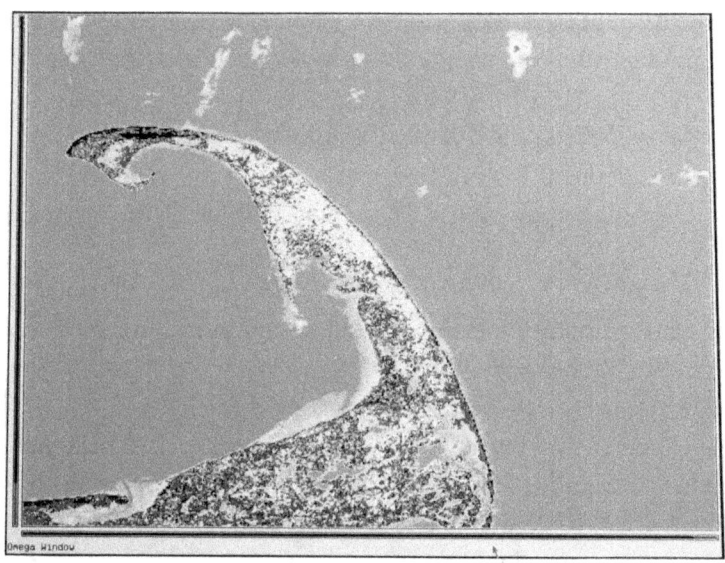

Remote sensing satellite image of Cape Cod after I played artist with the colors, created on a Symbolics LISP Machine, July 1986.

"Here's to that." I clunk my beer with his. "I'm happy to join the ranks. Imagine me, a software engineer."

Ken's sound machine kicks in with AC/DC's "Thunderstruck", and we jump up, riffing our air guitars, channeling our inner rock star.

Naturally, we get a crack-of-noon start after all the celebrating. Moving slowly, we finally rally and head north. Snow flurries make the drive a bit of a challenge, adding to our delay. Tomorrow's forecast looks good, sunshine always makes for a better vista. Ken and I crash in the Pinkham Notch parking lot since hotels are for wimps.

The slam of a nearby car door shakes me awake. Vision blurry without contacts, I note the arrival of the faint gray dawn. My sleeping bag is nice and warm, but my breath blows smoke. It's cold.

"Yo, Ken. Wake up, butthead. Let's get coffee."

Ken groans and rolls over. Looking at the remaining stars twinkling, I steel myself to do the clothing shuffle, crawling out into the grimacing cold. Leaving my stuff next to the car, I trudge over to the Joe Dodge Lodge to warm up.

The bathroom comes into focus after putting in my contacts. Hot water soothes my face, wallowing in the comfort of civilization. Ken scoots in, heads to a stall, and I skate out to wait. We stroll to the deli a few minutes later for coffee and snacks. Nope. It appears it doesn't open till ten.

"What?" Ken yells. "Closed? This is lame. Why the hell don't they have the deli open?"

"We do have my stove." Trying not to smile; I feel a rant is in the works.

"Fuck that! I want coffee. Flinny, find some. This is unacceptable." Ken starts to stamp, and I'm grateful no one else is around as he transforms into Bitch mode.

"Screw using a stove. They must have food here."

"Chill, matey. How about I ask the manager back in the dining hall? You hang out and relax." The AMC serves breakfast to paying overnight guests but not to slackers like us.

"You better. I don't want to use your stupid stove. Damn lame cramped Jetta of yours," he mutters and stomps over to the pictures of Mount Washington on the wall.

Ken with skis strapped to his pack in Huntington
Ravine, Mount Washington, February 1986.

Chuckling to myself as the bitching continues, wandering aimlessly in search of the dining hall, returning ten minutes later with coffee and doughnuts. The food and drink disappear, and, poof, Ken returns to normal.

"Let's climb this sucker," he declares as we head back to the car. "Damn dirt bag Jetta." He kicks my vehicle. "Cheapo German junk, silly DBJ. Do you have any granola bars?"

Continuing to pack my things, I finish lacing up my ski boots, and then hand him a few filled with raisins.

"It's creepy being here. I lost my friend Ed in Huntington Ravine three years ago. Slept near this spot the night before he died."

"I know, man. Losing a bud sucks. Last year a good friend got blown off Lion Head and died in the fall. Lots of folks think this place is a joke, but not me. I have huge respect."

"Why do we climb after losing friends?" I wonder.

"Heh, waxing philosophical is useless. Life is precious, and pushing limits makes it sweeter. Hell if I'm gonna let some lame-ass drunk driver take me out."

And with that, we put on our skis and head up the trail.

The snow depth is marginal, and our skis barely avoid the rocks lurking below. Fortunately, there's more coverage than when Ed died. We make it to the trail junction and boogie right.

Skiing past the Harvard Cabin, with smoke belching from its chimney, brings ominous flutters to my tummy. The outhouse, on the left, jostles my moonlight memories from that fateful night. I wonder if the climbing poster is still there.

The trail is narrow, skiing through the alders a thrash. We plan to avoid ice and climb snow with our skis strapped to our packs. Good thing Huntington Ravine has a dozen chutes to choose from.

The day turns somber as fog descends, obscuring our view. Down in the valley, the sun shines; the mist bounces and swirls around us, ghosts taunting.

"I think Pinnacle is toast," I say, stepping out of my skis. Our hope for an easy snow trek up *Pinnacle Gully* is dashed; today, it's a narrow chute perfect for ice climbing.

Ken grunts, sitting on his pack in the snow. "Should have brought the ropes. We need to find another gully with enough snow to make it an easy stomp fest."

To save weight, we left the ropes in the DBJ, hoping to solo Pinnacle and ski down *Central Gully*[2]. "Head up Central?" It looks like our best Option B.

"Yeah. I wish the sun would burn this danged fog away. What the hell."

Plodding up the gully, I follow Ken, my motivation machine. Remembering *The Trap Dike*, I ponder the possibility of avalanches. With the thin snow, it's doubtful that scene will repeat—skis on my back, ice tools in my hands, no rope, all up to me. Luckily, the ice is minimal, and my flexible boots can manage French technique.

I'm relaxing on the auto road after climbing up Mount Washington
with Wildcat Mountain behind me, February 1986.

When stopping to gain my breath, mist swirls around me. The
alpine world is quiet except for the occasional crunch of Ken's crampons above. I can't resist facing out.

The gully walls slope up and away, not suffocating like a chimney.
Down below, the sun wins the battle, slowly cooking the mist as it
angrily boils, retracting. I'm sure Ed's spirit is with me, feeling the view
wanting to burst out in all its glory.

Ken is out of sight; I hurry to catch up. At a litter of boulders, the
snow recedes to mere patches around the rocks. The gully walls collapse
into the rim of the ravine as I clump over to join Ken soaking rays.

"It's great the fog burned off," I say, sitting with him at the edge of
the Alpine Garden. "This vista is tremendous. Look at Wildcat." I point
to the east.

"Not too shabby, Flinny. Able to keep up with me. Got any snacks?"

Rifling through my pack, I find a few Slim Jims and hand one over.
In this quiet moment, I ask him if he's happy.

He shrugs a bit and looks over at me with focused eyes. "I'm getting
tired of driving all over New England for GE. Sick of being a grunt and

tweaking turbine engines in factories. Boring. Plus I really want to live in North Conway. Time to amp things up and climb 5.11."

I reply, "Cool, good idea to get the hell out of the city. Any plans?"

"Nothing yet. But for now, life is good. Saving my cash, ready to launch when the right opportunity comes."

"Speaking of possibilities, it's thin up here. I don't want to ski down this sucker. If it's this bad, Tuckerman Ravine would be nuts. I'm no disciple of the Ski to Die Club."

"You wimp. I hate it when you use logic. Where's Jamie when I need him? Don't you want to be a hero? Boast to the girls about your rad jump off the Headwall?"

I take a sip from my water bottle. "First, need to meet the honey. Second, skiing Tuck's with all this ice would be suicide."

"Yeah, I know. Damn, reality strikes again. Let's bail and ski down the Auto Road. It will be a rocket-sled ride. We'll be slugging beers at the Wildcat Tavern in no time."

Strapping on my skis, I'm thrilled we're doing something meaningful; not just sitting around watching TV. Studs who climb mountains and ski off. Anything for a beautiful vista.

LIFE GETS COMPLICATED as priorities shift, distracting me from the simple dirtbag-climbing life. Between the job and hanging out with friends, the demands of the Journal grow. Issue eight is out and looks fantastic, thanks to excellent articles donated by other climbers. But I can't count on handouts in the future. I've run into a business-model snarl.

Yep, it needs money. Thirty subscriptions and minimal sales have generated two hundred dollars so far. I've used my cash to pay the bills. It's great that the magazine is good enough to deserve investment, but this means advertising. Ugh. I love the creative part, but selling ads, nope. I would need to quit my day job and jump in with two feet. This glorified hobby brings me to a crossroads. Should I stay or should I go?

Many people at work have a Master's or Ph.D. from MIT. Swimming in a sea of degrees makes me realize I need another to fit in.

Following an impulse, I apply for a Master's in Computer Science, with classes starting in the fall. My boss convinces me that an advanced degree will boost my salary and bragging rights. The University of Lowell is nearby and offers night classes, making it easy to blend into my work schedule.

I give Dad a jingle to get his take on this. He's a big fan of education and is puzzled by my dilemma. Dad can always read between the lines. I'm worried that my job, the Journal, and school will be too much. Something must give. Guess I know the answer, but it's nice to have someone else confirm it.

"Ah, I see," Dad says after I explain the background. "Hmm. Does the magazine pay for itself?"

Good ol' Dad is getting right to the point.

I fiddle with the phone cord. "Well, no. I pay for everything. I can't keep mooching articles for free anymore. Not to mention the increasing publishing costs."

"Guess that means you'll have to drop the magazine."

"Right. It seems obvious after talking with you. Wonder why I bothered with it all this time."

"You put a lot of love into it and made something wonderful. You can always start again after finishing school. It's not forever."

I'm teary as the thought sinks in. "Yeah, I don't have to rush—I'll have time to think about it over the summer. Thanks for the chat. I appreciate it." Bummer.

After my security clearances are approved, I move from tedious documentation to actual programming. The coolest project that's not classified involves using satellite imagery to forecast the cocoa crop in Brazil. Our image-processing prowess makes it possible to infer which parts of the country will produce the best cocoa a few months before harvest.

This intel is hugely important to our esteemed customer who lives and breathes chocolate. The pictures can save the customer millions of dollars in the commodity futures market. Unfortunately, I don't win the chance to visit Brazil for the ground truth mission, validating our magic is accurate. Cuckoo for cocoa puffs.

At my annual review, I ask my boss for approval to attend a business conference this September. With bated breath, I push the trip proposal across his desk. He knows me well, and his eyebrows lift as he notes the location in Anchorage, Alaska. Launching into my sales pitch, I discuss the value of attending the ASPRS Conference (American Society for Photogrammetry and Remote Sensing), especially since I'm president of our regional chapter. After reviewing the costs, he chuckles and gives me the approval. He knows a boondoggle when he sees one.

Before we end our chat, he asks whether I can participate in a few events designed to boost corporate morale. Since folks are busy, the softball games will be pickup, and he needs to bolster the team. Of course, I agree that it's a great idea.

A few weeks later, a game pitting the engineers against the business team is planned after work. Fortunately, no one appears to be that intense, so I don't feel dorky. Glad to manage a few hits, but once, the cute first baseman tags me out before I get to the base. I stink at softball.

After the game, folks gather around the picnic tables to unwind. Huddling in our cliques, I spy the cutie with her accounting team. Grabbing a beer from the cooler nearby, I introduce myself.

"Hi, I'm David. From the remote sensing team. As you can tell, softball is not my thing."

She giggles adorably. "I'm not very good either, but it's lots of fun." Her Spanish accent is thick, but I can easily understand her. "My name is Eileen." She has glorious green eyes.

Sitting on a bench together, we chat about the usual stuff and don't notice the others giving us space. Minutes fly by, and people are packing up to go. She dusts off her jeans, and we stand together.

"Next week, I'm heading off to Alaska for a work conference," I extend my hand, "Can we have lunch when I return?"

"That would be great. It's nice to meet you." She clasps my hand and gives it an elegant shake. Smiling, Eileen heads off as I return to the bench.

She's delightful. And I think she likes me.

The rhythms of "San Jacinto" meander through my ears as I wait in Logan Airport. Soon, I'll be flying west and north to Alaska. Bouncing to the music, I can't believe I'm getting paid to see Denali. It's been years since blowing off out west to Rainier, and it's time to crank it up.

From outside my earphones, a loudspeaker announces the flight is ready. Click. My escape to the world of Peter Gabriel ends as I pack up and board. The third flight of the day takes me to Alaska. The Chugach Mountains are stock-full of peaks, snow, and tundra. Ocean to the left, mountains to the right. No roads, towns, or villages.

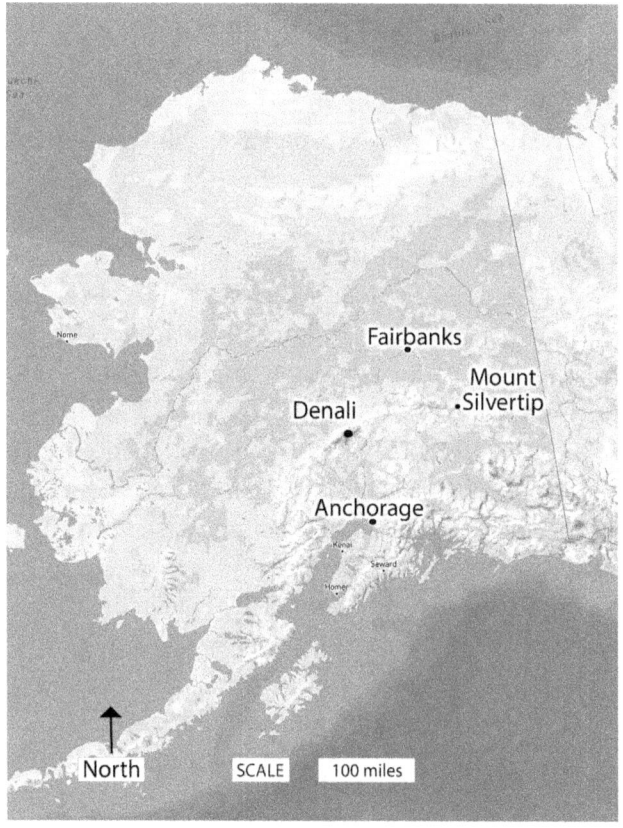

Alaska is the home of Denali. I visited Fairbanks and Anchorage on a "business trip" in September 1986.

As we near Anchorage, the mountains end abruptly, leaving a flat delta of tundra, festering—I've been told—with bugs and moose. The plain is interlaced with glacial rivers running to the ocean and birch trees glittering yellow as fall approaches, contrasting with the vast forest of black spruce.

Puddle-jumping to Fairbanks has Denali (Mount McKinley) rear up out of the plain, capping the best view of the trip.

George picks me up in his Toyota pickup. He's a friend of Ken's who crashed at the Red House a few times. It was great for him to invite me to visit.

He lives out in the bush, a little shack of a place, smack-dab in the middle of Iditarod country, where he cares for forty-five sled dogs. George takes the hardman approach to Alaska, busting his butt to make it in this harsh world.

"What a great cabin." We're hanging in his living room, sucking down beers. "How did you get the job caring for these dogs?" A few yelps barely draw our attention. I'm getting used to it.

"I left New York after graduation to escape the lunacy. Couldn't find a job once I arrived; my college diploma was useless. The Iditarod Sled Dog Race is a big deal up here. I met a musher at a bar who offered me a job. It's not a lot of money, but the rent is free."

"Winter must be intense. Are you happy here?"

"Yeah, the vibe is cool. People don't care about stupid shit like lawns, pink flamingoes, or swimming pools. No room for extravagance. Only the hardcore. Climbers, mushers, hunters, and fishermen. We love living on the edge of the wild."

I yawn, my body not yet adjusted to the time change. "At least you're making it happen. What's the plan for tomorrow?"

"Let's head up a glacier and bag a reasonable peak. It'll push us; much bigger than Mount Washington."

"Sweet. Since I climbed Rainier a few years ago, I should be ready to roll."

"Excellent. You can crash here on the couch. I need to settle the dogs for the night. See ya' in the morning."

It's eerie, but going to sleep with the sound of crooning dogs grows on me.

We pack for Mount Silvertip[3], 9400 feet high, nestled on the Castner Glacier a few hours southeast. It's an excellent introduction to Alaskan mountaineering, not as tall as the behemoth Denali. We're hiking on a glacial moraine covered with tons of tree stumps, rocks, and dirt. Since the ice constantly changes, the trail is never consistent.

Four miles later, thanks to our extreme crack-of-noon start, we find a flat spot with a tiny tarn nearby for water. After scarfing pasta, we get ready for bed. Then George tells me he's suffering from clogged sinuses, fighting a cold. Great. And we're sharing a tent.

I wake up to a groggy and congested George. After the stove starts to purr, he staggers from our gravel rock bed to quaff some coffee. "I ain't going anywhere today." he croaks.

"Crap, we should bail," I say. "No point in staying here for you to get even sicker. You up for it?"

George groans but nods his head slightly and turns to grab his stuff. Heading out, we scuffle down the glacier in our clunky Koflach plastic boots. At least we get to the truck before it rains.

The next day we cruise to Denali as good tourists should. Lucky for me, it's the only week of the year the park service admits private vehicles.

George and I on the Castner Glacier in the Delta Range, a few hours southeast of Fairbanks, Alaska. September 1986.

George still feels dodgy, and while the scenery is tremendous, the beauty gets old after an hour. But slowly, Denali's power grows on me as we swoon over a couple of grizzly bears. Past Polychrome Point, the road travels high above the glacial plain, and the vista unfolds. The poor lighting makes photography a challenge. Denali's in the clouds somewhere; I can imagine its immensity.

On my final day before leaving for Anchorage, George and I are hard at work clipping dog toenails. Like their wild ancestors, long claws are lethal when pups wrestle.

"Thanks for all the great hospitality. I appreciate it." He is good with the clippers. Five dogs done.

"No sweat. It's nice to have company. Sled dogs just snarl and bark," he chuckles. "Good, hold this sucker tight, he's a moose."

"Are you ever going back East?" I ask as the dog struggles to get free from my full-body embrace.

"Heh, I doubt it. Nothing for me there." George's tongue is clenched in his teeth as he clips the claw. "No reason to go back to the fucking city."

"So this is home now?"

"Looks like it. I need to build my life. You Red House guys are welcome anytime. There, all done."

After letting the final dog go, I ponder probing deeper but remain silent, allowing him to decide whether or not to continue.

Brushing off the dog hair from our clothes, we return the tools to the barn as dusk falls gently, the wind rustling the grass.

In the morning, George drives me to the airport. I'm grateful for the sun and blue sky, hoping for a peek at Denali. Hugging George, I wish him all the best in carving out his frontier life. Heading into the terminal, I turn to wave, but he's already gone. There goes a true mzungu.

At the ASPRS conference, I learn about new stuff in photogrammetry and mapping. My job has cutting-edge technology, but the whole defense angle troubles me. Here it's all civilian, using high-level aerial photographs for urban planning and forest fire management.

Most fascinating is the focus on surveying and flashbacks to explorers pushing limits in Alaska, full of bugs, bears, and caribou. It's good to see the balance between old-school wilderness mapping and the newfangled satellites.

Flying home takes forever. I'm still antsy, wishing for the go-go-go adrenaline of the open road, traveling unfettered. Relishing the "every day is a Saturday" lifestyle, each morning leading to the next, with no goal but more travel. Love having a job that subsidizes an adventure.

Descending into Logan Airport, a glorious vista sprawls beneath the plane: golden yellows and intense reds as the sunset lights up the maples and oak trees starting to lose their leaves.

The job has helped heal my spirit after the loss of Mom. Alaska has lit a flame in my adventure oven. Time to shift into a higher gear.

Belay on, climb when ready.

I'm rappeling in the rain on Whitehorse Ledge, New Hampshire, September 2006

Rappel

November 1986 – December 1988

I n November, life is turned upside-down by Eileen. I stopped by
her office a few weeks ago; one date led to another, and boom,
we're going out. Yep, head over heels. It's lovely to be wanted
without the usual dating games that go nowhere. It seems natural; she
and I agree, "we're doomed." It's not so much doomed as blessed.

I don't miss the woods. Usually, this time of year, I'm bitching
about the cold, rainy yuck between fall and winter. With work, school,
and the girl, everything is blissful. One morning snuggled in bed, she
asks if I'll come to Puerto Rico over New Year's. Stuck in my mind and
ignoring my heart, I tell her I'll sleep on it.

Later that morning, I drive her to the airport so she can spend
Thanksgiving with her family. After a super-duper mushy hug, she
hustles into the terminal, and I head home to see Dad.

A few days after the holiday, I visit Tim at his non-Red House
geodesic dome on a cool evening in Keene Valley. I can't hold back
gushing about Eileen. Tim chuckles, happy for me but puzzled by my
hesitation to visit her during the holidays.

"Flinny, let me get this straight. We both love traveling; it's obvious.
I'm always game to visit friends in their own country, especially when

they speak the local language. Eileen happens to be more than a friend. What the hell is your problem?"

Hands clamped around my beer, I'm dumbfounded by such clarity; my brain clunks while my heart thumps.

"You don't have a choice," he adds. "You must go. I've been dying for such an opportunity." Tim reaches over and gives me a light punch to snap me out of my funk.

He's right. It's time to wander and immerse myself in another culture. Alaska whetted my appetite, and now I'm hungry for more adventure beyond the horizontal.

Thanks to the verbal smack in the head, the next day I call Eileen to let her know. She laughs. "Now remember, this is your idea, not mine."

Besides being attractive, she's wicked smart, and I love her accent. Her green eyes glow in her golden-brown face, surrounded by silky black hair cropped at her shoulders. Her smile lights up the room, and her compact body is fit in all the right places. Yep, off to Puerto Rico I go.

Strolling off the plane the day after Christmas, I calmly search the San Juan airport for Eileen. The warm, tropical smells wafting in the open-air terminal are a welcome contrast to frigid New England. Concern mills around my insides when there's no sign of her. You'd think I'm hanging off a crux with sewing-machine leg. Of course, she bailed on me. Spanish assails my ears, adding to my uncertainty. I'm not in the comfort of my woods.

Suddenly, a mildly hysterical girl squeals my name and gives me a humongous hug. Relief floods out the anxiety, embracing her fiercely, dazed with the realization, "Jeepers, I'm here with my girlfriend." The tactile grounding of her skin makes me feel safe. This mzungu's doing a good job channeling his geeky gringo.

Slowly climbing out of my shell, we head to her apartment in South San Juan. It's awkward; everyone's quiet as we adjust. Her mom speaks Spanish, but her brother can communicate in English, so it all starts to jell. I keep my hands to myself, attempting to behave and not be overly mushy. She is alluring; I want to kiss her again.

When I unwrap my Christmas presents, I find a bathing suit and a pair of flip-flops. It's time to head to the beach near the Hilton Hotel.

Sunset in Puerto Rico, January 1987.

We jump into the tepid water, frolicking as if we're seals. While the swirls of the ocean soothe me, I begin to relax and be myself. Our term is *recursive wows*. Computer nerd-speak of the continuous mention of the word *wow*, in waves of emotional wonder. I guess this is love.

After a romantic crack-of-noon start, we drive to La Parguera, one of Puerto Rico's three bioluminescent bays. Arriving in the afternoon, we wander around and find a quaint place for dinner. I'd be doomed without my local translator; no English is spoken this far from the capital. My heroine saves me great face and orders a heaping shrimp delicacy. Need to learn Spanish.

At dusk, our guide boat chugs out into the wide bay. Thinking it's a total scam, I'm positive the captain installed underwater lights. Slowly, it dawns on me that it's true; the buggers really are generating light. The micro-organisms in the water pulse blue as we splash and swim off the guide boat. Treading water, spouting like a whale, I see a glittering glow flow out of my mouth. Using a floaty for support, our feet churn the ocean; the sea turns glorious in blue-green sparkles. This is what dreams are made of.

Afterward, the only bar in town is chock-full of pool tables and grizzled older men; it's not fit for lovers. We buy a bottle of wine and head down to the dock, hand in hand. The moon is hidden on the other side of the earth; the stars glitter in the midnight blue sky. It's the most romantic evening we can have with our clothes on.

As the week flies by, we zip around the island. Most memorable is our micro-hike to El Yunque, the rainforest. I don't remember the jungle in Uganda, so this is my first experience of lush foliage, bursting with green and home to oodles of nasty-looking insects. But the cute coqui, the native frogs, feast on the bugs while their chirping generates a soothing melody.

We flit around Old San Juan as lovebirds, sipping coffee and holding hands. Picnics fill our afternoons, lying on a beach blanket, dozing, and soaking rays. Time meanders in our tropical river, but soon, as all vacations must end, we fly back to the Boston freezer.

I SPEND lots of time with Eileen, floating along, grinding through my algorithms class and the latest work project. Over President's Day, we head up to Jackson, New Hampshire, for a cross-country ski weekend. After shopping at IME—International Mountain Equipment, the most amazing outdoor store that rivals the Mountaineer—she's all tricked out with new skis and a svelte matching outfit. Luckily, she has a blast. Given her tropical roots, I was nervous she'd reject skiing.

March blows in the snow, and my midterm takes too much time. Usually, I blaze through discrete math, but this class is a bear. Eileen is studying for an exam in finance as part of her master's program, and we don't see each other as much. I start planning a hiking trip for spring break.

The phone rings, and it's Eileen. I can tell something is wrong. She's quiet, not her usual bouncy self. Immediately concerned, I ask her what's going on. She sniffles and says she's breaking up with me. Stunned, I collapse onto my couch and almost trip on the phone cord. What? Wait, why? She says it's over, there's nothing more to say, and hangs up. Stupefied, in a zombie trance, I dial her phone, but it rings and rings.

The next evening I can't take it and drive to her apartment, waiting to confront her, hoping to understand why she doesn't love me anymore. After a few hours, I leave and head home, still wondering what the heck happened. Finally, a few days later, she comes to see me at my apartment, confirming she's moved on, with nothing left in her heart for me. It's a tough confirmation, but I get my closure.

It's early April, doom and gloom. I spend the next few weeks pining as the spring showers melt all the mountain snow and keep the rocks too wet for climbing. My boss notices me moping and tries to perk me up. Away from work, I spend a lot of time with my nose stuck in Zen Buddhism books trying to make sense of it all.

My go-to place is the local cemetery, not for the company but because it's the closest thing to a park near my apartment. The quiet gives me time to ponder why it went wrong. Wandering around the glacier of our brief relationship, I fell abruptly into a hidden crevasse.

Trapped inside, I realize that I had taken her for granted. Too self-absorbed to provide her the attention she deserved. Eileen needed more in her life than some climbing-crazed mzungu.

SNAPPING OUT OF MY FUNK, I head over to the SUOC White Water Derby in May. Since moving to Boston, I don't climb as much in the Adirondacks. Having this annual party at the Barn helps me stay connected. I stick to Class VII at the race and climb at Moxham Dome.

My friends do their best to haul me out of the crevasse. Eric and Scott now have girlfriends, Gaston finally got a real job, and everyone's saving money for big adventures. Time to coil the rope and pack the climbing shoes.

School's out for summer, and my grades are solid; I'm halfway done with the degree. The sun is shining, the crags are dry, and Ken gives me crap for being a wimp. At long last, in July, I drive up to see him.

"It's been months since she dumped you," he says. "Way too long to mope around. Time for some climbing."

Naturally, we're deep into beers, lounging around his Nashua apartment, ready to roll in the morning.

"Still trying to wrap my head around it," I say. "Guess I'm too self-involved."

"Stop your pining, Flinny. She's a princess who wants to be showered with princely lovey-dovey all day long. Heh, that's not you. You're one of us, a climbing dirtbag through and through." He crunches the can and launches it at the trash. "Another one bites the dust."

I laugh at his audacity. "You do have a point. Ol' Mountaineer Jim was right. He tried to warn me to find a mountain girl. Few women can peer into our minds and not be afraid." Lurching to my feet, I head into the kitchen.

"That's the spirit."

Snagging another beer, I notice a photo on the wall. "Dude, this pic is tremendous. Annapurna, right?"

Ken jumps up. "Yeah, the Bitch-and-Moan Brothers attacked the big hill, were blasted by a blizzard, and had to bail at twenty-three thousand feet. She's a monster; lucky we didn't die. A serious amount of bitching on that bad girl."

"What happened?" I was in Eileen la-la land when the two brothers went to Nepal.

"A moose of a storm kicked in. We arrived late in the climbing season since we couldn't hire enough porters. By the first week in December, we stumbled into basecamp. The South Face is truly massive. The storm blew us off Camp Five, three thousand feet from the summit. Very gnarly, mate."

Sinking into the couch as the Ken television show goes full-tilt. He prances around, reenacting the heinous rappels off the beast. Finally, I get an intermission when he cranks up the stereo to Deep Purple's "Strange Kind of Woman."

I feel better as I settle in for the night on the couch. Ken's great company, but I wonder if I'll ever meet someone. Drifting off, fantasizing about a nature-loving Cinderella.

Ken and I arrive at Cannon Cliff at a reasonable hour instead of our usual late start. The car door closes as we stretch our legs, peering up at New Hampshire's big wall across the interstate.

Reaching for a doughnut, I say, "Glad to see you all fired up. Happy to chill out and soak Zen belay rays." I finish my coffee and pull out my pack to start organizing.

"Heh, if you're going to be a belay monkey, you can carry my stuff. I'll take a rope and the rack. We can wear our harnesses up to the base."

"Lighter is righter," I agree, stuffing snacks and other essentials such as water and rain jackets. The second rope is slung over my shoulder, and we dash across the road to the scree slope. "Let's do *Vertigo*."

Ken chuckles. "No frigging way, you hoser. Not dragging you up that. We're going for *Moby Grape*[1]."

Looking north, Cannon Cliff dominates Franconia
Notch, New Hampshire, the biggest and baddest wall
in the East.

I'm using a Salewa Sticht plate to belay Ken from a bolt anchor on *Diagonal*, Cathedral Ledge, New Hampshire, August 1987.

Dancing up the boulders to the base of the wall, I'm lightly winded but glad to be done with the approach. Pulling gear from my pack, Ken sits down on a boulder nearby. He transforms out of Boast mode, preparing to lead, eyes serious.

He flashes Reppy's Crack in total style. Imagine a thin one-inch wide fissure that extends straight up for one hundred feet. While some folks rap off after the primo pitch, we're gung-ho for the entire route.

The granite soaks up the sun, warm to the touch. My fingers form a karate-chop shape inside the crack, slightly torqued to create jams for both hands, the left over the right.

My toes are crammed in the vertical opening; the sticky-soled climbing shoes keep me in place. I slide my left foot twelve inches and then swiftly move my left hand higher with another karate chop. I keep alternating moves to the next piece of pro, as if climbing a ladder.

The Triangular Roof on *Moby Grape*, a classic Cannon Cliff climb.
Photo by Corey Hebert, Lee Hansche climbing, March 2008.

The short second pitch starts easily, with a prance to the bolt belay twenty feet from the Triangular Roof. While Ken hems and haws, I soak rays in a comforting Zen Belay. Finally, the rope tugs me into action. It's my turn, and I yank the rope twice to signal I'm climbing.

Pulling over the roof, I can see the need for hand jams above. Reaching high, I push off with my left foot, plunge my left hand into the crack and then stand. My right foot peels, tossing me back to the slab.

Shaking out my hands, it's time to chalk up and try again. Ken hauls on the rope, impatient with my lack of progress.

Why is this so hard? My arms are toast, fried from holding the hand jam. Clenching my fists, I'm ready for another try.

The granite is warm and solid, with no dirt or distracting bugs—only me and the two-inch-wide crack, a puzzle that has me stumped. Trying a new move, I locate a nub for my right foot high under the roof, mashing my left foot on the opposing wall.

I reach with my left hand and create a fist in the crack. Stretching the right hand high—Excellent!—to find a hand-hold. Poof, my left fist pops, and down I go, the rope tightening and catching me dangling over the roof.

Luckily my tippy toes touch the rock. Yanking on the rope for slack, Ken lowers me a tad. Thankfully, I don't look down or get freaked out. More pissed that I'm this out of shape.

Craning my head to inspect the moves again, my backpack whacks the rock, knocking me off balance.

It's the danged pack. Sandbagged on the crux, bogged down carrying the crap. No wonder I'm not flashing this move. Should toss the sucker to the hungry boulders below. But no, that's a dumb idea.

Frustrated, I realize there's another way to solve this puzzle by ignoring my free climbing ethics. Recalling the John's Brook bridge aid practice, I place my right foot in the sling attached to the Friend.

Now, it's simple to scale the roof. I'm drained but relieved to get over the crux, yelling for slack to keep the rope from pulling me off. To hell with climbing style, sometimes one has to break the rules.

Friends are made by Wild Country. The revolutionary cam design made climbing a lot safer. September 1987.

The rest of the climb is spectacular and tons of fun. We make it past the classic Finger of Fate and top off the climb. Sitting on a super-nice and sunny ledge, it's time to confess.

"Remember the Triangular Roof pitch? Well, I cheated, stepping into the sling to make the crux." Many would consider this intelligent, but the climbing world frowns upon using aid. I rummage for a granola bar.

"No way, Flinny, you punk." Ken reaches for my bar. "You forfeit snacks with your foul."

I laugh. "You can have the granola bar. I have chocolate." The sun glistens off Mount Lafayette to the east, the vista incredible. Root in my pack to pull out two beers, handing one to Ken. Popping the delicious reward, I clunk his beer. "Thanks for a great adventure. Too bad we can't fly down."

He chugs the entire can, handing me the empty. Luckily, there's more. Ken transforms as he opens another beer, grinning madly as he stares me down. "Have I told you about my parapente?" Boast mode is back.

"What the fook is that?"

He bounces to his feet. "You know, a hang glider married to a parachute? John Bouchard makes them at Wild Things. You heard about the hosers that jump off El Cap?"

"Heck, yeah. Researched them for an article in my Journal."

"Here's a story for you. Write this up! Last week, when I was at Cathedral Ledge, the day was stellar and perfect for flying. I dashed up to the launch point and cruised off. Sweet conditions for kiting, zooming around the cliff, totally radical."

Here we go. I have a feeling an epic must be brewing. Ken is never animated over something lame.

"All of a sudden, the danged wind shifts. I'm Zenned out, soaking rays, gliding in the updrafts. A gust blows me down closer to the cliff. Panicking, I jam the lines, trying to turn away from the wall."

He has his arms out, knees bent, Bruce Lee, ready to pounce. "And bam! The next gust shoots me straight into this big-ass tree. Boom, my rig crunches into the branches and slams into the trunk. Grasping, tearing, praying I don't pop off and plummet, bouncing to crater on the ground."

Finishing my beer, mesmerized as usual. "Holy poop."

"Big load of poop is right." Ken guzzles his beer. "There I was, dangling in the damn Charlie Brown kite-eating tree."

"How the heck did you get down?"

"Luckily, I had a knife and cut myself free. Climbed down the tree in the dark. Danged kite waited for days till I could get back to shag it."

"Were you calm and cool during this episode?" Laughing, visualizing him thrashing around, tangled in his lines. Ken fully unleashed, roaring at the audacity of the tree.

"Absolutely cool, man," he replies. He sits to take off his climbing shoes, wiggling his toes. And poof, normal Ken is back with me again. He looks over and adds, "Still better than rappelling, mate."

"No argument there. We're walking off, right?"

"Righter is righter!" Ken hands me his shoes, and I pull out our sneakers.

It's the usual thrash at the top, branches grabbing at my head, prickers lurking and snagging my pants, pushing through the scrub to the descent trail. It's an easy stroll, views along the ridge, winding down steep dirt-clogged ravines to the road.

We pass the famous Old Man of the Mountain, and the trail widens as we walk side-by-side.

"I need a big adventure," I say. "Your Nepali trip has me totally pumped. Time for me to fly."

Ken jumps over a boulder in the trail. "Good idea. Better than hitchhiking. Go to Annapurna if you can."

"I've always wanted to go to the Himalayas. But I gotta go back to my roots in Africa."

"Don't keep whining about it. Get amped up and motivate."

Back at the Boise Rock parking lot, Cannon's faint outline fills the sky as the moon rises. No rappel from hell, no flying into kite-eating trees. A lovely slog down. But Ken's right. Talk is cheap—time to fire.

FALL SLIPS by as I stomp on the gas pedal and finish school in early December. Most of my time is spent on my thesis, writing computer graphics software, and describing why it's fantastic—the next best thing. I dash around climbing a few times, but work and school take the focus.

The best part about my degree is the pay increase from $25,000 to $35,000. Not too shabby. Money wasn't the primary motivation, but it sure helps. I can't resist giving Dad a ring to tell him the good news.

"Hey, Dad, good to hear your voice. How is life in the big city?" Dad now lives in New York, moving up in the world by ministering to Manhattan's muckety-mucks.

"It's a bit busy, being such a large church, but I love the bustle here." He's an urban boy, that's for sure.

"Two updates for ya'. First, the company gave me a 40 percent pay raise, thanks to my Master's. Pretty nice." Dad can appreciate making more money.

"Great. Don't spend it all on climbing gear." He also knows I strive for the good things in life.

"Well, that brings me to the next topic. I'm planning a trip to Africa next year. Too many friends have blasted off and now it's my turn."

Dad is quiet as he processes this news. "You've been muddling with this for a while. Why now?"

"After four years of working, it seems that if I don't go soon, I never will. My hitchhiking pal Steve has some time off. We'll head to Egypt for three weeks, and when he flies back, I'll go south to Uganda."

"That will be amazing. Hey, can you stay longer after Christmas? Yona Okoth is visiting. He's the Archbishop of Uganda, traveling the States to drum up money for the church."

"How do you know him?"

"He's a dear friend who lived south of us in Tororo and was the bishop of our district. He fled the country in 1977 when Idi Amin's thugs assassinated Archbishop Janani Luwum. Yona escaped to Virginia as a refugee before returning to Uganda following Amin's ouster in 1979."

"It would be great if I can stay with him."

The phone makes a loud rumbling noise, and Dad comes back on. "Hey, David, my dinner guests just showed up. Great news about going to Africa."

"Thanks, Dad. See you Christmas Eve. I love you."

Things are looking good. It'll be great to meet Yona and get some tips for the trip. Lying awake in bed, I wonder if this is the right thing to do, just quit my job and launch off to Africa? My boss can't promise me my position when I return.

The Red House lads would say "When in doubt, run it out," climbing slang for taking action when uncertainty unfolds. Time to trust the universe. Manifesting destiny is what it's all about.

∾

HESITATION IS TOSSED out the window since it's time for a trip to Keene Valley with the Bitch-and-Moan Brothers. We cram into Ken's company car, rocketing across the Mass Pike, and I can't resist telling them.

"Hey, you guys, I'm going to Africa."

"Africa?" Jamie futzes with the cassette deck, trying to find a good Little Feat tape.

"Yeah. I'm done with the corporate world. Hitched all around North America, and now it's time for the big show. Buying a one-way ticket to Cairo. Then to Uganda."

"Whoa, that's an adventure. Why Uganda?"

"Mainly because it's where I was born. And to fully embrace my African heritage."

Ken jumps in. "How about Nepal? Go in late summer after the monsoon. Climb a real hill like Annapurna or Everest."

Jamie sums it up with, "Fire or retire, mate. Remember Camp Five on Annapurna, Ken?"

And off they go, the rest of the ride is filled with boasting, moaning, and a bit of bitching thrown in, as the journey to Keene Valley flies by.

Jamie chats about his stint at the New England School of Photography. He finally bailed out of Keene Valley since the whole climbing school thing fell apart. Reaching for his more creative side, he refocused on his passion behind the lens. Hope he takes a great shot of me skiing off some insane slide.

Our plan has a few missing details. First, we ignored the snow reports and discover the Adirondacks are bone dry. Our hope of skiing Gothics, blazed by the Ski to Die Club, is toast. The second missing detail is a place to spend the night.

To discuss our options, we end up at Monty's Elm Tree Inn in Keene, quaffing beers. The banter continues as we abuse and blame each other for the big failure. Jamie starts to pontificate on his prowess and excellence in doing bold and crazy climbs.

"I'm way more badass than you," he asserts in a blurry voice. "Remember when I soloed *Gamesmanship* butt-naked in the moonlight two years ago?"

The Spiders Web in Chapel Pond Pass, Adirondacks. *TR* is highlighted in the center of the wall. September 1987.

Ken, not to be defeated in this game, fires back, "You can't call that soloing, climbing twenty feet and backing down. You lunkhead! I soloed and skied *The Eagle Slide* on Giant last year. All on my tele skis!"

"Oh, yeah?" Jamie, of course, amps it up. "If you're that good, we should climb something sick. Prove it."

Seeing where this rant is going, it's time to dampen the enthusiasm —standing between the two, placing my hands on their chests for emphasis. "Now, slow down a bit, laddies. Let's grab one for the road and figure out where we'll sleep tonight. We can discuss a radical outing tomorrow, but let's focus on a camping spot."

"Not a bad idea, Flinny," Ken says, "but still, I can outdrink and outclimb Jamie-poo. Anytime ... with a cat ... in a tree ... in a box ... can't outclimb me. Sam, I am he!"

Somehow, I wrestle the Bitch-and-Moan Brothers into the car, and we head back to Keene Valley with a few sober notions of where we're going. The car ends up at the Red House. The old place looks lonely, with no one living there since we moved out. Soon we're bivouacked on the front porch, laying out sleeping bags and foam pads.

Naturally, beers are cracked as we stamp around, getting ready for the night. It's below freezing, but the cold is not an issue.

"Jamie, you're such a pansy," Ken says. "You brought a pillow? Wimp. I'll solo the Chapel Pond Slabs while you cozy up with your lame pillow."

"Heck with the pillow and the Slabs," Jamie fires back. "I'm going to the Spider's Web and aid climb some sucker. You're such a big talker."

"I can do it! I might let you second it. Flinny can feed us beers."

I'm alarmed as Ken accelerates the discussion in a dangerous direction. This is not going well. So much for distracting the Brothers.

"Hey, you losers," I interrupt. "It's past midnight. Don't you think tomorrow would be a better time for this?"

Jamie is fired up and starts to stamp-dance, declaring that he's going. "Get your harness ready. Let's do TR^2. The overhanging wall protects the climb, so there won't be any spicy ice to make it nasty."

Ken swigs the rest of his beer and stomps on the can. "Finally! I'm game."

Another crack-of-midnight adventure with the Bitch-and-Moan Brothers is in full swing, and it must be my fault for getting them amped up. I should have done more to mellow their bouts of boldness. Standing there as they gather their stuff, shrugging as they banter into the wind.

"You guys are nuts. Go on, knuckleheads. I'm staying here, wallowing in my warm sleeping bag. Go beyond the vertical on the Spider's Web, aiding up ice-filled cracks in your headlamps, and outwit each other with bold feats of dumb-ass-ness."

They don't hear me as the car starts and drives off. I stay cozy in my bag, snoozing happily, waking briefly at dawn as the lads return from their adventure. We're in for a crack-of-noon start today.

~

THE FOLLOWING week zips by with Christmas shopping after work. The malls are mobbed, but going late just before closing is at least tolerable. Luckily, I've nailed down Ken for another adventure and head up north for the last climb of the year.

The raucous pounding of rock and roll reverberates in Ken's apartment. Antics and banter fire us up as we celebrate our plan to climb Cannon Cliff. Since the forecast indicates snow, we'll do the route in true Scottish style. We can't resist the challenge of climbing the *Whitney Gilman Ridge* in December's full conditions.

Stumbling into his apartment, I thump down my duffle bag and grab a beer.

"Still going across the pond?" he asks. "What's the plan?"

"Fly to Cairo in June. Going with Steve, my Syracuse housemate."

"Cairo? To do what? Climb pyramids? Damned hot, with lots of sand. Scorpions too."

"Nothing but exotic buildings. History. Culture. As if you know what that is. I'm going back to my Uganda homeland."

"Heh. You should go climbing. Screw the history. Solo the *Diamond Couloir* on Mount Kenya. Now, that's a climb."

Cannon Cliff with the 300' *Vertigo* highlighted. February 2009.

"What a great idea." I'm excited about the big trip, but tomorrow's adventure is on my mind.

We don't party late this time and get to bed at a reasonable hour. Without all the usual drinking, I nod off to sleep quickly, dreams of snowflakes dancing in my head.

"Come on, Flinny," Ken shakes my exposed shoulder. "It's time to move."

Light glares in my eyes, waking up on the couch. My head aches mildly due to last night's revelry. Even at a spry twenty-eight, I've never been a morning person.

"Okay, I'm good." I yawn. "Making coffee?"

Cupping the hot mug in my cold hands, I'm having second thoughts. The coffee goes down nicely, and my optimism returns as the caffeine sparks my brain. After pulling on my long underwear and wool socks, I head to the bathroom for tooth brushing and contact lens insertion. All set, I bound back to the living room, ready to roll.

As we drive north, snowflakes whiz past my window and the snow piles up on the road. Ken grins from behind the wheel. "It's gonna go, Flinny; I can feel it. The snow won't stop us."

I reply timidly, "Right. I wonder what's happening in Franconia Notch?"

"Full conditions!" Ken fires back. "Imagine us climbing the *Whitney Gilman* in a snowstorm. We'll be heroes!"

My stomach rumbles, unsure if it agrees with Ken's vision. Snagging another bagel from the cooler, I stare out the windshield as the snow whips by. Taking a bite, I relax as he works his electrical magic on me, firing me up like a turbine. Only Ken can get me going at six in the morning to rock climb in a blizzard.

Its tricky rock hopping amidst the snow drifts on the steep approach to the base of Cannon. We shamble over to the start of the *Whitney Gilman Ridge*, where the snow-clogged route puts a dent in Ken's enthusiasm. It appears impassable, with ice plastered all over the rock. We meander along the base of the cliff, and Ken perks up.

"Let's do this one. It's *Vertigo*³, look. And snow free! Woohoo! We can do this."

I stare at the bleak, vertical wall. Almost the height of the Empire

State Building, I can't see the top as the snow whirls around, blown by the wind.

"What's it rated, 5.9? Harder than the *Whitney Gilman*, I bet. If you want to lead the bugger, I'm in like Flinn."

The approach over, the transition to climbing begins as we empty our packs full of gear. Soon, I'm alone, holding the rope as Ken navigates a crack in the cold rock.

Stamping my hiking boots forcefully, I'm careful not to slip off the icy boulders. My freezing toes cry out for warmth, but I can't hear them due to the wind careening and whistling through my helmet.

Watching Ken's bleak progress, my gaze turns to the gray, darkening sky beyond him. *How did I get suckered into this?* Mumbling to myself, tied to the belay anchor, releasing the rope slowly as Ken proceeds.

The sheer wall looms above as the wind picks up again and blows snow in animated swirls. Resetting my grip on the rope, I realize Ken has sandbagged me again.

Ken pondering Cannon Cliff's *Vertigo*, December 1988.

The festering clouds accompany our glacial progress on the wall; it's getting dark even though it's only noon.

"Yes! Finally, a reasonable Stopper. Climbing." Ken's voice trickles down as my hands automatically feed him more rope.

"Climb on. Can you hurry? It's frickin' cold down here."

His chuckle fades as it loses its battle against the howling wind. When it gets gnarly, I feel lost without Ken's positive energy. In these conditions, I'd usually step into the snow, feel the howl of the blizzard, get back in the car, and speed away from Franconia Notch in search of coffee and snacks.

The rope jerks, pulling me back to reality from my Zen belay. While Ken futzes around, I wait, growing ever colder.

Time flits by, snow swirling, wind chortling in my ears, mesmerizing, and I almost zone off again. Do a little jig on the icy ledge, the rope snaking around my hands, fingers whining about their frozen state. Finally, I hear the words I've been waiting for: "Off belay."

"Belay off," I answer, happily unclipping the rope from my figure-eight. Prancing around, waving my hands to warm them, unwinding the webbing anchor, then patting the fat belay tree to thank it.

The rope rises taut against my harness, and Ken's voice filters down. "Belay on, climb when ready."

"Climbing!" I bellow, happy to be moving and generating some heat.

The first pitch is tricky, wedging my boot into the crack. Since the climb is too steep, it's time to take off my mittens; the rock feels like ice against my fingers. Yikes, I try to concentrate on footholds to minimize hand contact.

Stiff from the arctic cold, my hands feel like ice blocks, but I scoot next to Ken, my toes still complaining. No trees, no sun, just ice, rock, and us. We grin at each other, convincing ourselves that we are men doing a manly climb in insane weather.

Grateful for my wool mittens; I wish there was a fireplace nearby. Somehow I get my hands to thaw enough to put Ken on belay.

He traverses right five feet and gleefully places a Friend in the crack, clipping it into the rope. He's off again, heading to the corner twenty feet away, yammering about the pendulum.

Vertigo on Cannon Cliff is found in the center of the
photograph, December 1988.

When climbing a vertical line, the second climber is safer than the
leader since the rope runs plumb between them. Both are equally
exposed to a fall on a horizontal traverse. There's no handrail. While a
traverse adds risk, a pendulum kicks it up a notch. This requires the
climber to swing on the rope horizontally from an anchor.

Since I've already come this far, what's there to lose? Ken is bolder
and crazier, but I can do this. As the wind gusts, I think, *Lovely, a
pendulum. Seriously?*

Slowly, my awareness creeps out of its frozen place in my toes, and I notice that Ken hasn't moved in a while.

"What's up, man?" I shout. "Can't you move any faster? It's cold."

A nasty gust of wind makes me retreat and wiggle my chin deeper into my Gore-Tex parka.

Ken yells back, "Verglas is what's up, butthead. Watch me; I'm going to pendulum."

I finally notice the steep wall encased in a thin sheet of ice. Didn't volunteer for this. If the full conditions haven't dented my enthusiasm, the verglas pushes me to the tipping point.

Ken backs toward me and flicks the rope a few times, ensuring the Friend's security. Starting his dance, he kicks off with his left boot and lunges, hands scrabbling on the ice-crusted wall, pushing with his wool mitts to help propel himself, swinging on the rope.

Halfway across, his momentum stalls. I can see panic set in as he frantically scampers back to the micro-ledge. With the rope anchored by the Friend, he looks reluctant to push his luck, hanging on the dubious protection. I'm paying attention and pull in the slack as he climbs back to the ledge.

The sense of futility grows in my frozen noggin as our reality sets in. Continued effort is a heroic virtue, but my patience has iced over.

"You okay, Ken?" yelling into the wind. "It won't go. Let's bail."

Another gust whirls more snow in my face as definite doubts grow. Ken yammers to himself, trying to jumpstart his mojo. If Ken is flailing, I'll thrash when it's my turn. As the wind mellows, I tune into Ken's dialogue.

"God damn, son of a bitch, damn ice, damn damn damn."

My frozen mouth tries to crack a grin. Another Ken rant is well underway. Quickly he stops, smacking his hands together, trying to warm them.

"Hold me, I'm going," and he jumps off the ledge, propelled by a gust of wind. The snow surrounds him, an ice spider hanging on by a thread.

Here I am, stuck on verglas *Vertigo*, wiggling my fingers in icy wool mittens, watching my crazy friend Ken fume as he dangles on the rope again. Another epic unravels before my very eyes. The wilder part of me loves the adventure, ignoring the ominous nature of our predicament. My cautious part questions the wisdom of being trapped in such a place.

"Let's get off this sucker," I yell. "We can rap down and buy ice tools at IME."

I'm done with this climb, using any trick to convince Ken to bail. My frozen toes are wailing, and the wind's whipping snow into my eyes, making me pine for goggles.

"Trying again, watch me. Third time pays for all!"

Ken goes for it.

He comes to a halt hanging three feet below, swearing and cursing. The Friend holds him safely, albeit tenuously, as he sways back and forth. He mutters something that the wind blows away.

Reaching for the Friend, he pulls the trigger, drawing it out of the crack. He backs into my exposed, freezing, but secure belay. I make room, keeping the rope tight until he ties in.

The pendulum on Cannon's *Vertigo*. Imagine the rock slathered in thin verglas ice. Photo by Lauren Wilson, September 2007.

"Belay off. What now?" My teeth chatter in the cold.

He smacks his hands together, scattering snow. A fog of breath forms off his nose as he exhales. "When you discover verglas, it's time to find a beer glass."

As we ready our rappel, I couldn't agree more with the vision of pints dancing in our frozen heads.

Even in good weather, getting off Cannon Cliff is never easy, much less in a brewing blizzard. Rappelling down the blank wall, the wind toys with me like a cat batting a mouse.

Coming to the end of the double rope, I stop on a narrow ledge with a cute little pine tree sprouting from a shallow crack. Swinging on the rope back and forth, I search for an existing rap anchor. Most crags have them equipped with rappel rings for climbers to use.

The top of the first belay is below me, too far away. I keep looking for an anchor but can't find a thing. Lurching back to the little tree, I gently clip into a manky sling around its one-inch diameter. Two feet tall, snug in the little crack, its branches worn away, the top green with needles, the tree is happy to be alive. I'm alone on a wind-blasted wall, snow swirling around, anchored to a teeny-tiny pine tree.

In times like these, it's best not to overthink things. Usually, a thorough analysis of my predicament is required, hemming and hawing to uncover the optimal solution. After two minutes of pondering, the options boil down to one: hang out and wait for my trusty partner.

Yelling to Ken, I jiggle the ropes, indicating he should come down. Hearing his muffled reply, the ropes start to bounce with activity. Facing the wall, balancing on the one-foot-wide ledge, dancing for warmth, my harness is clipped into the faded red sling. A slip would have me dangle three feet below. Or worse, a fall could rip the tree from the wall, sending me to splat city.

Trying to occupy my overly anxious mind, I whistle Bing Crosby's "White Christmas" and wait for Ken as he slides down.

"Watch the belay," I warn him. "Our only anchor is this friendly little tree. No time to freak."

"What the fook? Gotta be something. Ah, shit, that's where we're supposed to be." He points to the belay ledge fifty feet away.

"Couldn't find a thing. Feel free to look, but it's getting darker with the heavy snow and scarier the longer we stay here."

The wind blasts snow in my face.

Ken pendulums around the blank wall, his hands waving, trying to find a crack. Nothing. He returns and begrudgingly takes the extra sling attached to the tiny tree; all his bounciness is gone with the wind.

"Let's not dwell on it," I say, pulling the ropes down. "We must be grateful for this cute tree as it helps us reach the ground." Without cratering or surrendering to panic.

Ken grunts and I realize this is the first time he has nothing to say. Smiling at the small win as he descends, rapping off the tiny tree while I balance on the ledge, watching the snow drift down as dusk settles around me.

Keeping my mind cautiously blank, witnessing the snowflakes gently gathering on the pine tree. I'm curious how long the fragile limb can support the weight. I'm trying hard not to visualize Ed on the Mount Washington cliff that horrible night years ago. Stay in the moment.

The rope jiggles and I hear a faint "Off rappel." Slowly and safely I start my descent, remembering to exhale. It's hard to believe that the little tree does its job, stoically keeping me safe as I rap down to the talus slope.

Tromping to the car, we teeter on top of boulders, headlamps lighting the way. Sure, we bailed on *Vertigo*, but Ken and I climbed in style, smug in our version of success. I'm thankful for having such a motivated partner and grateful for the gift of our very own Charlie Brown Christmas Tree.

Batian peak on Mount Kenya, July 1989

CAMPFIRE

June – August 1989

"Be solid, dude!" Steve's famous last words still make me chuckle. After three weeks of bounding around Egypt, always a prankster, he pokes fun at my fragile tummy rejecting strange bacteria from another country. Regardless of how carefully I choose my food, the nasty bugs bring days of unpleasant diarrhea. Fortunately, my stomach feels normal again, at least for the time being.

The five-hour flight from Cairo to Nairobi is way better than bouncing around by bus through war-torn Sudan. As the jet travels south along the Nile, I'm psyched to snag a window seat. Unfortunately, cloud cover obscures the Valley of The Kings. The drone of the engines lulls me to sleep, and I awaken as we descend, the green savanna of Kenya filling my window view.

I hope to spot an elephant, my favorite animal, but no such luck. Departing the plane, my extra-long legs relish walking after being cooped up in the tiny seat. The open-air jetway is lined with papaya and coconut trees, and the lush tropical smells jostle memories of my youth and welcome me back to Africa.

The guidebook advises against taking the cheap city bus, renowned for thieves poaching mzungu kit, so I splash out for a taxi. The driver doesn't speak English, but my Swahili phrase book helps me translate the hotel address. I'm grateful for the quiet in the cab to readjust after the chaotic airport terminal.

Kenya unfolds outside the taxi window. Marabou storks lurk in the tall acacia trees, ready to pounce on any unfortunate critter squashed by a passing truck. The lush grassland that surrounds the airport contains an occasional tree. People mill around on the road; I hope no one gets hit.

As we enter the city limits, abandoned cars, trash, mud, junk, shabby shacks, potholes, drainage ditches, rocks, and debris lie strewn around. The city spreads out. Most buildings have two floors; where downtown, a few dozen with twenty stories tower over the others. When we pull up to my stop, all the activity reminds me of New York City.

"Mzungu!" bellow the children as I stagger out of the taxi, hesitating in front of the guest house, bleary-eyed from the bustle. Daunted by the strangeness of a new place, facing the ominous possibility of more stomach bugs, the crescendo of chanting chases me into the lobby —a comforting sea of calm. While Nairobi beckons adventure, it's time to rest and let a nap bleed anxiety away.

Later in the afternoon, feeling refreshed, I explore the city, tuning into the Kenyan vibe while observing the coarse poverty. Absorbing the pungent smells of rotting trash strewn in the muddy roads, rusty store signs sit askew, complete with the fading graffiti adorning the run-down buildings. I sink into the pulse of the place, losing my freaked-out, first-world thoughts.

On the back streets, the children chanting "Mzungu!" cause uneasiness to flow through me. Nobody cared that I was a tourist in Egypt, so I could wander around without being noticed. Since most Africans rarely leave their village, labeling me a mzungu makes sense. Born in Uganda twenty-eight years ago, little do the kids know I'm just another local with a fair complexion.

When I check my mail at the American Express office, an Aussie haggles to get reimbursed after traveling with Japanese tourists in Zaire. Dozing off to sleep, he woke to find his money, traveler's checks, and passport; everything gone. Somehow, he escaped through Uganda and returned to Nairobi, a feat with no cash. Not a rookie traveler. The moral is to always wear a money belt.

I cram myself into the office phone booth to give Dad a jingle. Amazingly, the calling card works over here. It should be breakfast time in New York.

"Good morning from Nairobi," I say when he answers.

"David, great to hear from you. Your postcard arrived from Luxor. Mom and I never made it past Cairo." Dad keeps a photograph of them on camels outside the Great Sphinx in his office.

"I thought Egypt would prepare me for Kenya. It seemed safer, the poverty similar, but something else is going on here."

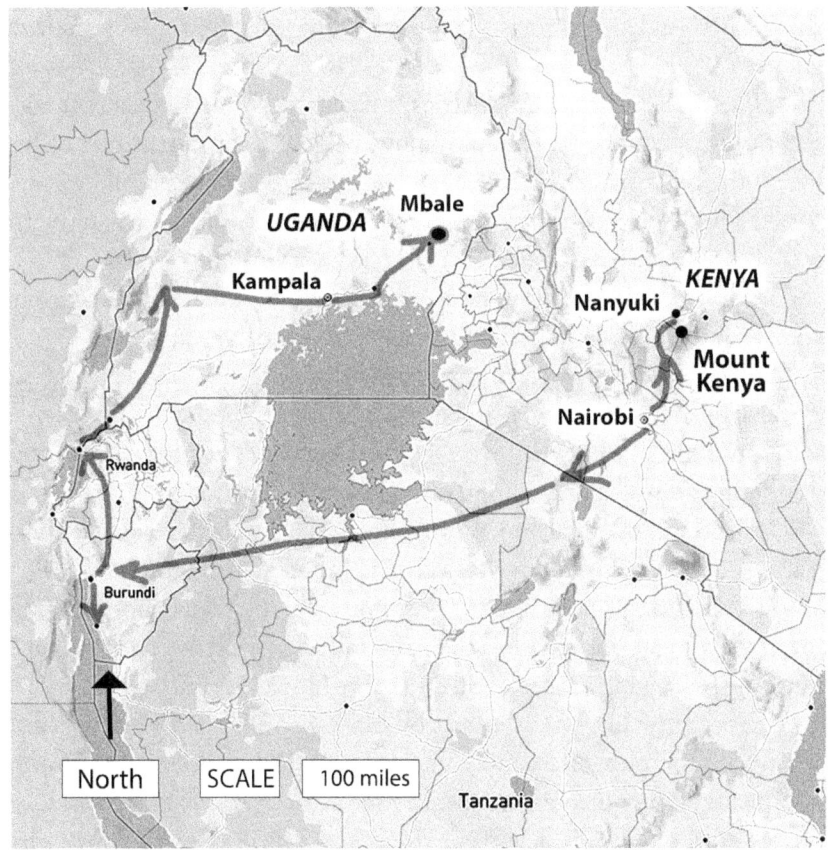

I was born in Kampala and lived in Mbale, Uganda until 1965. Twenty four years later, I came home. Drawn lines highlight my travels in 1989, based out of Nairobi, Kenya.

257

Dad loves this kind of stuff, fond of theology and world history. "Ah, yes. I didn't think it would change after we left Uganda. It's the tragedy of colonialism. Changes in power cause friction. The intersection of the First and Third Worlds colliding together."

"Do you mean all this is the fault of foreigners?"

Dad sighs. "Africa has always had conflicts, even before colonial rule. Most of the continent is like a teenager, growing painfully into adulthood. The first-world culture clash is huge. Not to mention the history of slavery. Summing it up, foreigners have all the fancy things, and Africans want their share."

"Yeah, there's lots of askari in the hotels and stores, especially the nice ones. Since many business owners are African, it can't be a race thing." My guidebook notes that Askari is informal Swahili for security guard.

"Theft is rampant in East Africa, a challenge for foreigners that take security for granted." He should know, having spent nearly 15% of his life on the continent.

"Thanks for explaining. It's not a big deal; no one's messing with me." People have been friendly; I can see Kenya with my own eyes.

Dad asks, "By the way, have you called Dr. Ker?" He's a family friend living in Nairobi that we knew from Uganda.

Pulling a notebook from my daypack to verify his phone number. "Got it. I'll give him a jingle. Still don't have a plan yet."

"Give me a call when you get settled. I'm worried about you wandering around alone. I hope you see Yona in Uganda."

"I'll be sure to visit him. Love you, Dad. Have a great day." Energized by our chat, I'm fired up to uncover more exciting stuff.

Heading to the guest house, I pass hordes of disabled people begging for money. Most impressive is the man with no legs selling newspapers, signaling he's trying his best. Still don't give him any money.

Shacks grow like weeds in nearby Mathare Valley, a notorious slum section of the city. Everyone comes to join the promise of Nairobi, hoping for an easy life, big money, and the gateway to the First World.

Steve would love it here. Our three weeks in Egypt went by so fast but his observations about life in the Peace Corps still resonate. He spent three years on a remote Filipino island and came away believing he made a difference only once. It's my turn to find out what's actually going on in the world.

Kenya is an island of relative sanity in Africa. Somalia and Ethiopia on its northern border are slowly blowing themselves up. Sudan, to the northwest, has never finished its war between Africans and Arabs.

Uganda is climbing out of twenty-three years of terror on Kenya's western border. Zaire, west of Uganda, is corruption personified. Tanzania, to the south, is paying dearly for its socialist principles after nationhood. Rwanda and Burundi are also beset by tribal wars. The West wants to believe in Kenya, and that's obvious in Nairobi, the land of a thousand aid programs.

Sipping tea outside the Thorn Tree Café, reflecting on my next move. The guidebook is right to rave about this place. It's a breath of first-world air, keeping my take on Africa at arm's length for an hour.

On a whim, I follow Dad's advice and ring up Dr. Ker, who invites me to stay with him. It's time to see more of Africa.

Getting around Nairobi means using a matatu, a Swahili word for a private taxi. Glorified minivans and pickup trucks with seats in the back, stuffed with passengers and all sorts of baggage, chickens, and children.

A matatu (private taxi) I used in Nairobi, Kenya, June 1989.

In colonial days, the British mzungu had their cars to bomb around in and Africans had little need to travel. The railroad was the first public transport, connecting the ocean port in Mombasa to Uganda's Kampala on Lake Victoria. Nairobi is stuck in the middle, a lowland swamp festering with malaria-laden mosquitoes.

In 1963, thanks to Kenya's independence, the matatu was born. A wild west of private vehicles blossomed to move people around the country. Anyone who could cobble together a dilapidated matatu could hustle customers along the roads. Tragic accidents due to poor maintenance finally led to government regulation in 1983 to improve safety. Respecting the potential danger of the matatu is necessary unless I want to walk ten miles. No hitching for me in this place.

"*Twende, twende,* (go, go)," the conductor yells as he slams the matatu twice with his fist. The engine splutters as the small truck builds speed. I'm on the west side of Nairobi, the only white guy traveling as a local. I did my best to find the most reliable vehicle. This truck barely has enough space for me to squeeze into the tiny rear cabin.

As the matatu gets close to my destination, I signal to the conductor, and he pounds the door to notify the driver to stop.

"*Asante sana, bwana,*" I say proudly, trying to assimilate with my "Thank you, sir." While Swahili is Kenya's primary language, it's more common near Mombasa and in Tanzania. The conductor probably grew up speaking Kikuyu and learned Swahili to assimilate in the big city, just like I did.

"*Mzuri.*" He thanks me with a toothy smile as I scurry out the door, my cramped legs thankful.

Walking up to Dr. Ker's house, I notice the askari waiting by the gate. He looks up when I say *"Harbari yako, rafiki?"*, Swahili for "What's up?" Or, more formally, "What's your news, friend?"

"Jambo," he says hello curtly. Askari are everywhere, guards who stand watch, protecting homes and businesses against invaders. It's unusual but not uncommon in Nairobi to install vertical iron bars guarding each window and mighty metal gates with intimidating high walls to keep bad guys out. There's a lot to ponder: askari, forbidding iron, and rampant poverty.

I push open the heavy, creaky gate and enter the compound.

Before me is a white two-floor house, roof of red brick tile whose color is fading due to rain or the passage of time. Immaculate gardens border the trimmed grass yard, where lemon trees, papaya, and orchids join the tropical flowers. Beyond a tall hedge, the chaos of shrubbery leads to a golf course fairway. Very different from the city scene.

Knocking on the door, bouncing on my toes as I wait. Shortly the door swings open, and a trim older man, my Dad's age, with short white hair and blue eyes, welcomes me inside. If he wore a suit instead of a button-down shirt and sweater, he'd be right out of Britain's royalty.

"Hi, Doctor!" I extend my hand in greeting. "I'm David; thank you for inviting me."

"Come in, come in. I'll put the kettle on, and we can have tea." He backs away and gestures for me to enter. Thumping my pack to the floor, I join him in the kitchen. This is much nicer than my guest house.

The Ker house in the Nairobi highlands. The gardener Dixson shows me around the back yard, June 1989.

The kettle whistles and Dr. Ker completes the ritual. Teatime is part of the old British empire, still ingrained in East Africa. "Here, grab some scones and clotted cream, and relax. I hope you drink Earl gray."

Sitting down gratefully, cradling the china cup, I inhale the tea's glorious aroma and scoop sugar to add punch.

Plowing into the scones, making a pig of myself. "Doctor, this is wonderful. I haven't seen civilization since I left New York. Sorry to stuff myself silly, but these treats are amazing."

Dr. Ker smiles as he sips from his cup. "It makes me happy; please have at it. If you don't eat them, I'll have to toss the leftovers to the golfers over the fence." He chuckles. "I realize we have a lot to catch up on, but is there anything you are keen on doing here in Africa?"

"I'm interested in seeing the Ruwenzori, Mount Kilimanjaro, or Mount Kenya. Do you know anyone who organizes climbing trips?"

"Hmm, let me ring an old chap who knows about the mountains." Dr. Ker grew up in England and has spent thirty expatriate years in East Africa. He's passionate about crop research on bug- and drought-resistant farming. Chased out of Uganda in 1966, he spends most of his time in Nairobi, working for a Canadian aid agency.

Settling into luxury, I soak in the quiet familiarity of home. After a splendid supper in the formal dining room, fatigue sets in. "Dr. Ker, dinner was delicious, but I'm quite knackered. I didn't realize a month on the road would be so exhausting."

He smiles, standing up to collect the dishes. "Happens to me all the time. Please, head to bed, and I'll see you tomorrow."

Dragging myself into the kitchen the following day, hoping for a much-needed coffee. Handing me a cup, Dr. Ker says, "I heard back from good ol' Cholly. He recommends the Kenya Mountaineering Club monthly meeting. We can dash over there tomorrow night and have a look."

"Sounds great to me," I say.

"One last thing before I head off to the office. Two Kenyans help take care of the house. Jennifer cleans and does the laundry for a few hours every couple of days. Dixson works outside doing yard work and carpentry. I informed them of your arrival, so they have no reason to call the askari."

"No problem. Thanks for letting me know. I'll say hello when I see them."

"Right then, off I go. See you at dinner." Dr. Ker grabs his briefcase and heads out to the garage.

Relaxing on an outdoor lounge chair, reading the local newspaper, I hear a rustling behind me. A woman and a small girl step out onto the back porch. Jennifer is calm and patient as she approaches, wary of introducing herself. Her daughter is naturally shy in the presence of white people. In an attempt to be friendly, I show her a super ball. That piques the girl's interest. The bouncy ball's pure energy makes her smile. Jennifer politely asks if I need anything from the store, but I thank her, not today.

The next evening, Dr. Ker drives me over to the KMC. It's a classic old building with rustic wood trim and elegant finishing, and the meeting room is stocked with chairs and the required slide projector. We listen to the formal agenda, and Dr. Ker is gracious and supportive. Finally, the droning ends, and I mill around, asking about upcoming trips.

Joe is an American, Andrew is British, and Francois is, of course, French. I can't believe my lucky charms that Joe, loaded with climbing kit, has a four-wheel drive Mitsubishi. He gets paid to photograph the truck out in the wilds of East Africa. The other two have no climbing experience, but their enthusiasm exudes. Plus, the more, the merrier, especially if someone gets hurt. Talk about manifesting destiny: a willing team with transport to Mt. Kenya, the biggest rock climb in Africa.

A matatu ferries me downtown as I forage for batteries. I'm looking to go rustic, no fancy boots or climbing gear, just my sneakers. This journey is taking place African-style—no first-world perks.

Naturally, it's time to visit the friendly Thorn Tree for a scone and tea. Stow my daypack under the table while flipping through the guide-book. As I prepare to leave, the pack has mysteriously vanished. Searching around frantically, but nothing. After checking with the waiter, he shrugs and says he's sorry. "*Samahani*, bwana."

I should have known better, lulled by the tranquility of a first-world oasis. Don't even bother to call the cops. Lost my Swiss Army Knife and Gore-Tex jacket, as well. Bummer. Off in search of a new rain parka.

Back at the compound by suppertime, I ask Dr. Ker about his upcoming trip.

"Looking very bonny, I must say! Management has granted the green light to monitor the disease trials. I've hashed out an itinerary for Rwanda and Burundi, leaving in a few weeks. Are you still interested in going?"

"Absolutely. I'd be honored. What an amazing opportunity."

I look forward to traveling with Dr. Ker and visiting his research projects across East Africa. His organization sponsors studies on maize and cassava resistance to insects, with the fieldwork performed by Africans. The warm climate attracts all life, including these pests. Thank God the research isn't looking into malaria or sleeping sickness; deadly biting insects aren't my thing.

THE FOLLOWING DAY, a strong man walks into the yard while I wait for the lads to show up. It can only be Dixson, from the Luo tribe near Kisumu, a Lake Victoria town. He has two wives, one back home and another here in Nairobi. After showing me the furniture he builds for foreigners, he appears to have a good gig at Dr. Ker's.

A few hours later, the Mitsubishi pulls through the gates opened by our askari. The lads jump out to greet us and help stow my pack. I give Dr. Ker a big hug and hop in. Joe backs us onto the street, and off we go searching for groceries.

We stick to the basics; rice, beans, chapatis, pancakes, oatmeal, pasta, cheese, and coffee—no fancy freeze-dried food. We have Joe's backpacking stove; scavenging firewood above tree line will be unlikely. After all the milling around, it's time to get cracking to Nanyuki.

Riding shotgun as the large vehicle cruises up the road, I read a story about the Mau-Mau caves in *Kenya Today*, the daily English-language newspaper. In the 1950s, Kenyans were fighting the British, hiding their meager weapons in a cave south of Nanyuki.

Tragically, they were ratted out, and the Mau-Mau rebels were bombed to smithereens. It appears that someone is hoping to turn the caves into a tourist trap.

Joe's Mitsubishi just before getting stuck on Mount Kenya, Andrew
supervising. July 1989.

Looking out the window, the run-down shacks and abandoned cars
flit by as we drive through the bush, jostled by potholes. Trying to figure
out my role in all this.

Am I one of the good guys? One of the bad? It's been a source of my
unease since arriving in Africa. The issues of poverty, power, rights, and
tribe compound my usual pre-climb anxiety.

We bounce into a Nanyuki market to snag some last-minute provisions. Surrounded by the children chanting "Mzungu," I attempt to
cross the divide and build a bond. My simple Swahili tells them I'm
heading to Mount Kenya.

"Mzungu!" Yell the older ones, and they drift away, leaving me to
wander aimlessly, not impressed with my boast of adventure. I focus on
my rafiki, the shy little boy who reminds me of my pal Micheal growing
up in Uganda. I wave goodbye as he runs off with his friends.

The village is similar to others we've been through, packed with two-story buildings that line the main street. Each structure has a rusty tin roof and steel bars over the open windows.

I'm puzzled by the lack of screens to keep out malaria-laden mosquitoes. The buildings look happy, whether painted yellow, faded green, or blue. Dust from the truck's passage billows up, wafting in front of people lounging against the pillars, watching us like marabou storks.

Within a mile, we turn right onto Sirimon's Pass road. Beyond the Mount Kenya park gate, the road ruts grow bigger. Joe puts the truck into four-wheel drive, but that doesn't work for long, and we ditch it in the mud. We hoist the heavy loads onto our backs and amble up the rutted road.

The renowned woodland heather surrounds us. High enough in altitude, we wander amongst the unique and lovely lobelia and groundsel shrubs that grow along the path.

Andrew and I join Joe and Francois at the top of the glacier-carved ridge. We've reached the volcanic basin surrounding Mt. Kenya, where the twin peaks of Batian and Nelion, poking through the clouds, create a majestic backdrop to the glorious vista.

The famous lobelia provide a welcome distraction from the drudgery of the slog; bogged down with too much crap. These rare plants only exist on the slopes of Mount Kenya and Kilimanjaro. Resembling humongous cabbages on short palm tree trunks, their leaves are pointy and sharp.

"Francois, look at this one." I squat next to the succulent, humongous artichoke.

"Beautiful. See how she captures rain inside her rosette leaves, storing water for dry spells. I study them at university. Botany is my focus."

"And look at that one with the wonderful blooms. Pretty." I touch the nearest leaf, the point sharp as a needle.

"*C'est jolie, oui.* The lobelia and groundsel bloom once in ten years and then die after displaying such splendor. *Tragique.*"

Straightening to settle my pack, continuing the trek on a slight incline. I may be here to climb Batian, but the lobelia capture my heart.

The groundsel collects water with its artichoke design, sunglasses
added for scale, July 1989.

A majestic scene unfolds after reaching the final ridge. Batian and
Nelion sparkle on the last rays of the sun. Clouds whip by like Star
Destroyers, followed by a mist that encloses the vista. The sparse landscape welcomes me, and a gurgling stream wanders its way back the way
we came.

Basecamp is struck outside the dodgy and damp Liki North Hut.
Because of the nice evening, none of us want to sleep inside. The location is stupendous, a flat valley surrounded by glacial ridges and
groundsel scattered among the rocks. Mount Kenya, a stout warrior,
watches over us.

Next to my chosen bedroom, a small lobelia bush has dropped its
leaves. I stash a few in my shirt pocket, as a memento for good luck on
the climb. After fluffing my sleeping bag, I confirm tomorrow's plan
with Joe. One of us will take the last spot on the rope while the other
takes the lead.

"Yeah, that's the best strategy," Joe agrees. "We'll go faster, minimizing time belaying François and Andrew. We don't need an epic up
there. No one's around to help with a rescue."

"Bringing raw beginners on a hard climb in altitude might not have been our wisest move," I add.

"Not optimal, but there's safety in numbers. Have a good sleep; see ya' in the morning."

Reminded of losing Ed on Mount Washington, I'm comforted by our large team. Walking back to my sleeping bag, the spaceship cloud has abandoned the mountain, promising a clear night.

Happy to be under the open sky instead of inside the grotty hut, the stars fuzzy with my contact-free eyeballs; I'm nervous and anxious, overwhelmed by the opportunity ahead. My eyes close in the quiet evening, anticipation brewing.

~

Mᴏʀɴɪɴɢ ᴅᴀᴡɴs ᴄʟᴇᴀʀ ᴀɴᴅ ᴄʀɪsᴘ. After a hearty bowl of oatmeal, we leave our extra kit in the hut and shoulder our packs to approach Batian. Following the *North Face Standard Route*[1], we climb eight easy pitches to a feature called Firmin's Tower.

Crawling out of the chimney, I say, "That pitch was tremendous, Joe, the best one today. You lucky dog, getting the lead. Off belay."

"Belay off," Joe replies as he unhooks from the rope. "I think we should consider crashing here. It's getting dark. We appear to be halfway up Firmin's Tower."

Back at the KMC, the vintage guidebook was a bit ragged. Its moldy pages suffered in the tropical climate, but it did its job, providing clues about the climb.

"Seems like a good idea to call it a night. Let's leave the crux and knife edge traverse for tomorrow." The sky darkens as Batian blocks the sun.

Climbing big mountains requires tradeoffs in comfort versus safety. Sleeping at the Liki North Hut would be more relaxed, but there's no way four of us can climb twenty pitches in one day. Even two people, moving quickly alpine-style, would struggle to make it.

That means a bivouac similar to the one Jim and I did on Mount Rainier, but this airy ledge is a whole other level of crazy. Navigating the narrow shelf, I stroll over to Andrew and Francois. Everyone needs to be included in a big decision.

"Hey guys, Joe and I think this is the best spot for the night. What about you?"

"Great idea," Andrew says. "Bonny view. How about tea? Francois, did you bring the cream and scones?" I can't believe he's so relaxed up here. Very stoic, as if he was born to do this. Good skills to have for a climber.

"Ha!" Francois smiles. "You love tea; I have a special for you: croissants!" My tummy rumbles happily.

Looking west to Mount Kenya's *North Face Standard Route*.

Joe walks carefully along the ten-foot-wide ledge. "We better use fixed ropes. No tumbling off into the night by mistake. That first step is a doozy."

Andrew fires the stove. "We only have a wee bit left to drink." He shakes his half-empty water bottle. "One liter each for tomorrow."

While the bleak water supply reality settles in, the eastern sky glows as the colors bleed orange and gold. At least we have two days of food, including the Kenyan version of ramen noodles, pasta, chapatis, cheese, peanut butter, and a few oranges. All very bland. Oh, and a boatload of chocolate and Francois's diminishing supply of croissants. I'm thinking about crab, pizza, and ice cream, watching the ramen noodles go into the cooking pot. Oh, well, it's the climbing life, right?

After wolfing down dinner, Joe and I putter around setting anchors for the night. We'll sleep in our harnesses, roped in. The ledge is wide as a car, leaving us a few feet before the long plunge to the talus slope below.

After our final round of water boils, we sit and relax, wrapped in our sleeping bags. The sunset glistens off Point Lenana to our right, the third-highest peak of Mount Kenya, more popular and easier to reach without ropes.

What cosmic attraction brought us together? Undoubtedly our adventurous spirit and love of nature. And a tiny desire for fame to be one of the few to stand on Kenya's highest peak. The universe is a wonderful place.

The sun is long gone in the western sky, and clouds obscure the horizon, but the midnight-blue sky is relaxing, with stars so clear and bright. Soon my eyes shut, my body trying to mold around the pesky stones jabbing my side.

"ARRR, what is this? Oh crap, snow."

Francois's French accent makes *crap* sound like *creee-aaaap*. My eyes awaken, my body groaning from the rock wedged under my butt.

Sure enough, there are eight inches of snow on top of me. Thank God for bivy sacks; my down bag would be soaked useless.

Francois enjoying the view with Firman's tower at the
end of the bivy ledge, Mount Kenya, July 1989.

It's no fun stomping around clearing the thick puffy powder. It's a struggle to balance on tippy boulders, thankfully roped, trying to reach the bathroom privy. Vertigo swirls around my brain as I try not to imagine slipping and careening off the narrow ledge.

Melting snow with the stove solves our water issue. Without this gift from the sky, we would have been forced to turn back. Just like on Rainier, a fantastic boon. Hopefully, we won't run out of fuel tonight.

Guzzling my tea, I wonder, "Thoughts on heading to the summit? There's a lot of snow on the rock, and the storm's still lurking around."

Joe nods. "Yeah, it's ominous, but the snow is melting quickly. I think we should go for it. At least to the knife edge."

Andrew agrees. "A shame to let a little white stuff ruin our fun. Powder adds spice."

"Okay, twende!" Joe settles our decision. "Rope up!"

It's taken my whole life to get to this place; it would be a shame to bail now. Boldness in the face of uncertainty is the only path forward. Since we're here, we need to try.

Most of the snow has been blown away or melted, but large drifts remain in the shade, and a gloomy mist settles beneath our ledge. I start up first, my climb is mellow—nice and blocky—and easy to protect. Within the hour, the team is up with me, and now for the next pitch.

Wiggling my toes in my thin sneakers for warmth, I give Joe slack in the rope as he moves into the ominous chimney. Supposedly this pitch is the crux, but the guidebook was notoriously vague about the details. It reminds me of Wallface, another chimney in cramped quarters. No frogs and moss to worry about here, just the usual rock and snow.

Joe stands under the roof, working diligently to gather his courage. It's hard to see from twenty feet away, but it looks like he can scooch around the roof to the right. Joe holds on with his left hand and stuffs his right into the chalk bag. His damp fingers root for dry powder, generating a puff of white dust when he removes them.

The overhanging roof—the crux—juts out six feet. When faced with this kind of exposure near to the ground, no sweat; thousands of feet off the deck, big sweat.

Joe extends his left foot and grabs the roof with his right hand. Shifting his weight to the right, he pushes off, ducking around the overhang. His face kisses the roof as he tries to move his feet into position. He thrashes around with his rack, placing some pro, and lets out a sigh of relief as it appears to hold.

"Watch me, slack, quick," he gasps, pulling the rope and clipping into the carabiner.

"Slack, please, slack," he yells as he lowers himself back under the roof, relieved to relax in a more comfortable place.

"Awesome pro, matey," I shout. "Go for it!"

Joe moves back to his high position, his left foot near the right on the wall, and quickly shuffles his hands over the roof. He pulls up, scrabbling for a hold.

Andrew and Joe (with the beard) soak rays on the bivy ledge. Point Lenana is in the background, Mount Kenya, July 1989.

Joe's right foot slips, and he pops off, wheeling backward, dangling under the roof, held fast by my belay.

"God dammit! Shit! Ahh, thank goodness for this pro. Flinny, lower me; now I see the foothold. Damn."

"I got ya'. You'll flash it." A belayer is supposed to be supportive, especially on the second-highest mountain in Africa, where the elevation sucks oxygen out of the air.

Thankfully, our lungs have adapted to the height, avoiding the horrible pulmonary edema, a lethal hazard from altitude sickness in the mountains. All we need now is for one of us to stop breathing.

Joe goes back under the roof, chalking his hands to ensure they stay dry, and poof, he fires. He scoots his right foot farther and gets his left foot on top of the roof.

"Woo-hoo!" we both yell in unison as Joe gleefully plunges the Friend into the crack. After he clips in, Andrew and Francois's tandem cheer echoes around the wall, and we don't look back.

273

"Off belay," Joe yells as the rope goes taut, followed by his "Climb when ready!" Andrew goes first, followed by Francois thirty minutes later. Joe belays me up the forbidding chimney, and I'm glad to be moving again.

Joining the others in a grand open theater, it's time for the summit attempt. Joe takes the lead and prances up the slab. It's not that hard, but I belay him for safety. The others are on their way next. My work is done; it's time to relax and enjoy viewing the pea soup surrounding me.

Pulling the lobelia leaf from my shirt pocket, I appreciate the soft, gentle texture that's not solid stone or cold snow. The tower slowly disappears below me in the mist, an eerie feeling as if I'm on a big beach as the fog rolls in.

My butt informs my brain that I'm crazy; this isn't soft sand, but ice-cold, lumpy rock. I'm drifting with the fog, wondering what the Red House lads would think. I miss them; memories of our Bob's Knob bivouac warm my heart but do nothing for my freezing bum.

I'm in the throes of a Zen Belay when a shout rings out, and Francois saunters back towards me. I return the lobelia leaf to my shirt pocket, puzzled.

"The weather's getting bad; Joe wants to fall back," Francois explains.

"Great idea. The visibility is worsening and we have two ugly raps back to the ledge." At least it's not snowing yet.

The route to the summit follows a knife edge, consumed by mist and fog. Imagine balancing on a sixteen-inch wide jagged semblance of a path, a perilous two thousand foot plummet on each side. The starving rocks below chant for us to join them.

Purists may frown upon missing the summit, but we've been on the crag since yesterday morning, and the weather is getting worse.

Slowly pulling in the rope, Andrew and Joe down climb towards Francois and me. The pitch is not hard, just exposed. The occasional gust of wind is scary; it's good that I belay them.

We discuss the descent and decide that I go first. Joe will lower the lads since neither has rappelled before. Now is not the time for them to learn.

Joe approaches the knife-edge ridge to the summit of
Batian, Mount Kenya, July 1989.

It's getting darker as the mist swirls while I rap over the crux and down into the chimney. At least there's no Diving Board vertigo to manage, simply the usual descent into nothingness.

Breathing deeply, trying to ignore the exposure and the fluttering in my stomach. Others may love zipping down a rope, but not a tired climber worried about getting everyone down safely.

"Off rappel," I yell and tug the rope fiercely. Joe lowers Andrew on the third rope while I establish the rap point. It's a thousand feet off the deck, and I'm glad I can't see jack beyond my toes. Mind over matter, ignorance is bliss.

Andrew appears out of the mist, and I welcome him with a cheery "Glad you made it, here you go," offering him the anchor before he unties from the rope. "How ya' doing?"

"I almost bashed my head getting down that chimney. Thankfully, the helmet did its job."

"Are you off?" I ask.

"I'm good. I'll try to find a wee snack for teatime."

Yanking on the green rope, it slithers up, and we wait for Francois. Luckily, he descends quickly, and in twenty minutes, he's sitting next to Andrew, exposed on the ledge but tied in safely.

Tugging twice on the green rope, I wait for Joe to release it. With a faint mumble, the rope goes slack, and I give it a pull. In a few seconds, *ffftwppt*, and the rest of the rope thankfully thumps down.

The two remaining ropes jump around; a knot ties them together to prevent rapping off the end. We hear muffled shouts; Joe must be yammering about his predicament. A few minutes later, he pops out of the mist.

"Welcome to our belay, fearless leader!" I say. "Now it's Tusker time." When in Africa, there's nothing better than a cold Kenyan ale.

"That damned roof has me worried," Joe says. "I hope the rope runs clean. Let's hold off the cold Tuskers until we're back on the bivy ledge."

He hauls on the red rope. It moves a foot and stops. Joe yanks some more, cursing. "Damn, afraid that would happen."

The rope is stuck in the rocks like a crab holding onto dinner.

"What do we do?" Francois asks. "We need the ropes, yes?"

"We'll figure something out," Joe says. "Let's not make it worse, getting the rope stuck tighter."

Wisps of smoke appear from Joe's ears as if he's steaming in quiet anger. But the mountain mist descending around us makes the situation dire.

"I have an idea," I say. "Joe, can you put me on belay with the green rope? Andrew, can you hand over the pro you carried? I'm going up."

"Uh, sure, one second," Joe replies as he works the rope into his figure-eight. "Okay, belay on, climb when ready."

Andrew fetches the pro and hands it to me.

"I'll climb to the roof and shake the ropes loose. Francois, do you mind rooting in my pack? I might need my torch."

He hands me the headlamp. *"Bon chance, mon ami!* You'll do it."

"Thanks, man. We'll get down." Luckily, this part of the climb is easy; I'm comfortable with a long run out to my first piece of pro, a nice Stopper.

The chimney lurks above with its claws clamped tight around the two ropes. I grab the blue one, feeling it jammed solid. Then the red. Stuck. Time to climb higher. Damn, I hate rappels!

A yank on the green belay rope lets Joe know I'm climbing again. The mist reflects faint light on the rock as I slowly climb up to the crux, easier without a pack.

Lowering Francois down the final chimney to the bivy
ledge on Firman's tower, Mount Kenya. July 1989.

Marla comes to mind as I focus on my balance, directing my attention to my feet. Smiling, I gently release the warm thought and make the move.

Placing a Friend to prevent a long fall, I clip into it for safety and focus on the stuck ropes, pulling on the blue and then the red. Grabbing them both, I try the flick trick again. Once, twice, almost. The third time, a hard pull on the red generates some movement. Sweet. Tugging harder, pulling more slack, then suddenly, the ropes whisk away, falling to my friends waiting below.

High up on Firman's Tower in the murk, I pause to breathe deeply before heading down. Tugging on the green rope, Joe pulls in the slack. Breathing slowly, lowering myself over the roof. After removing the Friend, my legs swing out into thin air, and I root for a hold near the trusty Stopper. Made it. This gratified climber exhales a massive sigh of relief.

Scuttling down the ramp, channeling my inner crab, the pull of the rope guides me to the belay. Thanking God, the lads give me a group hug.

Joe gathers the ropes, squinting into the wind. "One more rap to the bloody ledge. Hope the storm stays away; the weather is looking better."

Francois frowns. "Wish we could bail down to the hut. The croissants are all gone."

Andrew licks some ice off his glove. "It would be good to reach the ledge before dark."

"Let's roll," I say. "Ready, Joe? Go for it!"

I hand him the climbing ropes, letting him rap first. It's my turn to lower the other two. Hopefully, Joe can start the stove and have dinner ready.

The two ropes run cleanly when I finish the last rap, staggering along the narrow ledge to join the others. I'm toast, barely able to scarf down pasta before crashing into my sleeping bag.

～

Joe and I at the base of the *North Face Standard Route* on Mount Kenya. We're exhausted but happy to be down safely. July 1989.

A STABBING SHAFT of sun pokes me in the eyes, bringing me out of a tepid but dry sleep. Sitting up, I'm glad to see a dusting of snow, unlike yesterday's dump. The others are rustling; it's time to join them and soak some rays.

The way down takes forever as Joe and I alternate lowering the others. Good thing a third of the way is easy, a glorified scramble, almost too lame to bother with ropes. At the base of the climb, Joe hugs me, celebrating that everyone made it alive. I can't resist taking a grateful photo of Joe and me while Andrew and Francois scamper down to basecamp.

Tired as we are, the grotty ol' hut is warm and cuddly, now our best friend. The sparse firewood we find are scraps of fallen lobelia. Soon my dream comes true: the crabmeat roasting in the frying pan, the tasty smell wafting, and our stomachs awaiting the vital sustenance.

After demolishing the mac and cheese spiked with crab, satisfied and toasty warm, we share our next steps. Francois will visit the Carnivore

Restaurant in Nairobi with its vast outdoor grill. Zebra, water buffalo, ostrich, crocodile, and lion are ready for roasting. It's funny for a French guy to lust after wild game.

Andrew has to go back to work and Joe's off to the Maasai Mara National Reserve to photograph the Mitsubishi on safari.

Wisdom and insights usually unfold from an intense exploit. Lucky for us, there's no need for deep thoughts. Francois pokes the glowing embers as Mount Kenya's remaining snowpack glitters in the moonlight. Four mzungu relax around the campfire, regaling the climb, cherishing our bond, and celebrating life.

~

Mount Kenya peaks out behind the Liki North hut,
drying my sleeping bag. July 1989.

THE TRUCK DROPS me at my Nairobi sanctuary, and I wave goodbye as the others head out. The acacia trees whisper in the light wind while I pause in the driveway. The askari hutch remains empty in the daylight, and my pack waits, tipped over on the ground. Sadness ebbs through me. Brought together in a cosmic way, we had an intense adventure, and I wonder if I'll ever see them again.

I'm going to miss the lads; it's astonishing how well we got along and never got into a fight. Danger can bring out the worst in people, so I'm grateful for the unique experience and wish them the very best.

Heading into the comforts of the welcoming house, it's time to shed climbing mode and put on my traveling shoes. Back to the addictive urge to go mzungu, to keep wandering to the next town, one after the other, never looking back. But first, a hot shower is going to be lovely.

With our flight to Burundi tomorrow, Dr. Ker and I discuss last-minute details at the breakfast table. He mentions a large outbreak of meningitis in Nairobi. The airborne disease is hard to diagnose, and can kill in seven days. One of the askari at the house died from it last week. Horrible. Last month in Boston, I received a barrage of shots recommended by my doctor. Just in case, I check my yellow card, and phew, meningitis was included.

Jennifer is worried for her daughter. After the doctor dashes off to the store in the afternoon, she quietly asks for help with the meningitis vaccine. She earns one thousand shillings a month; the shot costs two hundred or ten dollars. In Africa, it's hard to resist such requests. Surrounded by many dire needs and worthy causes, I'm tempted to give away most of my money. Alas, sometimes, handouts can do little but instigate more begging. Dixson asked me for money several times, but Jennifer's daughter deserves it.

Dinner flies by, and we turn in for an early bedtime. I'm excited to see more of Africa and grateful to be tagging along with the doctor. He's been in the country forever, a professional traveler, and the lead climber on this trip.

The July morning makes for a lovely ninety-minute flight. The small jet takes off, and my nose is glued to the window, gazing down at the grasslands in search of elephants. When the plane leaves the Serengeti and approaches Lake Victoria, I ask Dr. Ker about where we're going.

First, we'll spend three days in Burundi, followed by a week in Rwanda. After that, I'm on my own to boogie north to Uganda. I'll return to Kenya in mid-August to join a week-long safari at the Masai Mara wildlife park. Need to hug an elephant.

The doctor mentions we'll meet many locals who use French. Fortunately, our key contacts speak English, so that's good. I pull out my Lonely Planet guidebook to see if there are other tidbits worth knowing.

The end of slavery at the turn of the twentieth century didn't stop first-world exploitation. After World War One, the colonists used Africans to control each other instead of shipping people to different continents. Ruanda-Urundi survived under colonial rule until 1962. Belgium extracted whatever wealth could be had and leveraged tribal rivalry to maintain order.

When freed, two countries were created, Rwanda (yes, with a "w") and Burundi (with a "b"). The new countries chose an English spelling instead of Belgian French. As with the rest of Africa, the people have it rough. The tropical climate is harsh; rampant diseases and the lack of electric power hold back any potential advances in agriculture and manufacturing, compounded by the constant battles for political power.

The Watusi run Burundi, who traditionally consist of pastoralists and travelers. Most of the population are from the Wahutu tribe, farmers who earn a living using manual labor on their tiny plots of land. The tribal-based power structure is flipped in Rwanda, where the Wahutu are in power. Since independence, both countries are still finding their way out of the awful situation imposed on them by a century of imperialistic rule.

This sounds eerily familiar to the history of Uganda and Kenya. It's sobering, and I ponder this as we fly over Lake Tanganyika's low mountains. Horrible events have happened in Africa; I'm not clueless. Mom and Dad came here to help, along with the Kers and many others. I never fully understood the depth of the tragedies that occurred during colonial times.

Closing the guidebook, it hits me that I was born before these countries were free. I wonder if Africans still loathe mzungu. I wouldn't blame them. Do they hate me?

~

WE LAND IN THE CAPITAL, Bujumbura, under bluebird skies. I'm grateful for sunglasses when walking out of the plane and onto the tarmac. We're met by Dr. Malithano, the project director, in charge of optimizing insect crop resistance. Both doctors hope the Burundi Agriculture Department will crossbreed the new maize with existing plants to create new disease-tolerant seeds. Dr. Malithano has been making significant progress with his low-tech approach.

Over lunch, he mentions Burundi's recent troubles. In March, the doctor and his wife—both from Malawi, south of Tanzania—nearly lost their lives when radicals started killing ex-patriots to destabilize the country. Fortunately, the government squashed the rebellion, and Burundi has been quiet for three months. Since Belgium left twenty-five years ago, there's been constant fighting.

Excusing myself from the table, I head to the loo, sickened. The news about war and genocide hits too close to home. I've been in an American bubble, bouncing around the globe, having a grand ol' adventure. I'm unsure what to do except learn, not to pull an ostrich, and stick my head in the sand.

Dr. Ker and I spend three days in a quaint but rundown African-owned hotel across the street from one of the French Novatel franchises. Bujumbura sleeps along the shores of Lake Tanganyika.

On a hazy, humid evening, we sit sipping banana beer, listening to the hippos honk, which sounds like Darth Vadar laughing. Other guests chat in French and a few in Swahili. The scene is romantic, with the rustling of the large mammals rooting in the lake and the festive lanterns reflecting pink and orange light on the papyrus reeds outside the porch. If you forget the past.

"Dr. Ker, how do you cope with being from a colonial power responsible for atrocities like those described by Dr. Malithano?"

He takes a long sip. "That's a great question, one that I always grapple with. Tribal battles are part of humanity, no matter the color of our skin. In the past, we Brits stirred up and manipulated the locals in our best interest. I try to show the Africans I'm here to help, not to exploit. That's my way to atone for the past."

"Don't they blame you anyway because you're a mzungu?"

"Some do; it's true. But I attempt to break through all the baggage, one individual at a time."

"Ah, I get it. Each person you meet is an opportunity to make it better."

"Exactly. I can't change what happened here years ago, but I can make today's impact more meaningful."

Finishing my beer and feeling better with the doctor's insights. "Is speaking the local language one way to help?"

"It's a great way to show your respect. Trying to integrate shows you're not demanding anything from them." Dr. Ker signals the waiter for *le facture*, the bill.

"Thanks for chatting. I've been grappling with this for a while." I'm certain that Mom and Dad felt this more strongly. They were present during the crucial phase of the colonial transition. A hippo grunts and then splashes into the marsh as we stand and head back to the hotel.

Over lunch the next day, I overhear some ex-pats talking about windsurfing. Intrigued, I can't resist listening. It seems one of the guys just "got his tubes cleaned." Doctors purged his stomach to remove nasty tapeworms, called Bilharzia, that penetrate one's skin from the water in nearby Lake Tanganyika. Wow, that's why no one goes swimming around here.

I'm lucky to zoom around Burundi in a government vehicle with the two doctors. The people living on Lake Tanganyika seem richer than those in the mountains. They catch fish and have decent soil to grow cotton, cassava, sorghum, maize, and coffee. The women wear vibrant and clean dresses. Neon colors are totally rad here.

Houses are built with homemade mud bricks created in the village kiln. Many have clay tile roofs instead of corrugated iron. This makes sense since clay is cooler in the sun and less noisy when it rains.

I appreciate the chance to absorb life as it happens instead of worrying about getting to the next town.

～

Dr. Malitano with the local project manager and Dr. Ker
investigating the maize disease trials outside
Bujumbura, Burundi. July 1989.

I'M STRUCK by the contrast of boarding a crisp, clean airplane and being whisked away on time; very civilized compared to the usual chaos when traveling in Africa.

We fly north to Kigali, the capital of Rwanda; the weather is stellar, and the flight a short puddle jump. The tiny country is nestled in low rolling hills between Zaire to the west and Kenya, Uganda, and Tanzania to the east. There's little wilderness left. Dr. Ker says Rwanda is the continent's most densely populated country.

The view from our hotel in downtown Bujumbura, Burundi. July 1989.

All the land is cultivated, and shiny iron roofs sparkle as the plane zips by. The country is small and landlocked, with few resources to provide for the large population. Little to draw the world's attention except for the gorillas in the north near Uganda.

Rwanda is drastically different from Burundi. The Rwandan franc is overvalued and very expensive. Dr. Ker and I are strapped for cash, so we stay at the posh Hôtel des Mille Collines since they take credit cards. A side benefit is a chance to kick back and relax in this oasis.

To top things off, the pool is surrounded by European guests in bikinis. I keep telling myself to go with the flow and enjoy it. Steve would be proud of me schmoozing with the ladies. The pervading sleepiness that calmly settles over me must be a disguise or perhaps a shield from the poverty outside the gates.

The Rwandans in Kigali don't mind speaking French when they hear my horrendous Kinyarwanda; it's one of the most complex African tongues to learn. Being a mzungu, they're surprised to hear anything other than French. I'm trying to show respect but perhaps they just don't care.

Lake Tanganyika is almost as large as an ocean, Bujumbura, Burundi.
July 1989.

We drive south to Butare, visiting other research projects. Since most of the dialogue is in technical French with thick Rwandan accents, I miss what's happening. That's okay. It's fun coasting along in the tailwind of the visits, soaking in the scenery, trying to make sense of it all.

The doctors drop me off for two nights at a Catholic Church retreat nestled outside Gisenyi. It's a welcome escape from the rigors of Africa, a place to recharge.

Gazing west over a calm blue Lake Kivu, squinting to catch a glimmer of Zaire, which echoes the American wild west. Many rumors drift out of corruption, despair, and serious bad craziness, a place for the most hardcore Western traveler. Not interested.

In the morning, bored from lounging around, I take a long walk up a well-traveled path to a high hilltop—accompanied by the constant shouts of "Mzungu!" as the children glimpse my tall white body through the banana trees.

When a youngster belts it out like a broken record, it lets me know my place, a stranger in their land.

Dr. Ker and members of the Rwanda Department of Agriculture. Near Kigali, Rwanda, July 1989.

And they're right, of course. We foreigners go round and round, flitting from place to place as if we're hummingbirds, never resting long enough to absorb life. It's time to sit and listen. Doing my best, but when in travel mode, the urge to go mzungu is hard to resist.

On the last day of July, the two doctors return and whisk me back to Kigali and the pomp of the Hôtel des Mille Collines. At dinner, I'm grateful for all they have done for me and pay *le facture*, French, for the damage.

Dr. Ker gives me a big hug and wishes me well. Now that I'm fully attuned to East Africa's vibe, it's time to head off solo in the morning.

The trip north to the Rwandan border is routine and surprisingly mellow—a most pleasant matatu ride, enduring crushed knees in the cabin, holding my pack. The driver is solid, and the other passengers are quiet but friendly. Not interested in me; I'm just another foreigner wandering aimlessly.

Dropped off at the last market in Rwanda, I walk a few miles to the border, where the Ugandan guards have guns, snappy camouflage, and mean looks.

House with tile roof on the way to Butare, Rwanda, July 1989.

They chuckle, seeing a skinny mzungu approaching. Doing my best to speak Lugandan, but once they see my passport with Uganda as my birthplace, they chat happily in English, welcoming me home.

With no matatus available, I wander the northern road in the sunshine, passing well-built buildings nestled beneath soaring trees, their branches laden with blossoms. Yellow, orange, and magenta flowers weave through the green leaves.

Many of the houses must have been built by the British, but no one seems to live here; almost a ghost town. Also found an abandoned golf course; signs of more vibrant days. If you didn't know the recent history, you wouldn't notice.

Fortunately, western Uganda shows little remnant of war, merely disuse. The country is beginning to rise out of the chaos, but it will take time.

When I arrive in Kabale, ten miles from the border, there's no electricity. The diesel fuel for the town generator has run out. The Highlands Hotel has its own, providing enough light to eat by. When the power is out, so is the telephone, so no calling home to Dad.

It's too bad I only have traveler's checks and no cash. The black market pays six hundred shillings per dollar for greenbacks, whereas the bank charges three times as much, two hundred shillings to a dollar. As costly as Rwanda. A bit miffed to miss the opportunity for a deal, but Uganda needs all the money it can get.

Kabale's shops have little diversity. A kiosk provides basic sundries of TP, cigarettes, gum, cheap mugs, and matches. The hotels are run down, with grotty toilets and rusty showers. Restaurants have limited menus.

I don't know many Ugandan words for food, but there is rice, beans, peas, *matoke* (mashed banana), chapatis, *mandari* (doughnut), and meat-based soup. You can find chips only in posh places such as Uganda Hotels and the Highlands.

Bouncing by bus, it's 130 miles north to Kasese in the morning. I spend eight hours wedged into a seat designed for children, and my thighs feel like petrified wood after being cramped for so long. Yes, it's an old school bus, packed with people carrying matoke but thankfully, no chickens.

The village was built in 1956 to support the nearby Kilembe copper mines. Wandering around the next day, people are friendly, but I'm getting tired of the "How are you"? Guess they teach this English phrase in school. Of course, the children have a field day chanting "Mzungu!"

Women use tumplines to carry large baskets against their backs. It's different from Rwanda and Burundi, where they carry them on the tops of their heads. Interesting; someday, I hope to figure out why.

Back at the guest house, I give Bishop Okoth a call to confirm my arrival tomorrow. A woman answers the phone and, luckily, speaks English. The bishop jumps on the line and agrees to meet me at the station.

In the morning, I hop on the train to Kampala. It's empty, and the hours flit by as I doze off, jouncing along the tracks for five hours and 250 miles. The journey gives me a chance to reflect, pondering my return to Kampala for the first time in twenty-four years. Grateful for Dad's photos; at least I have some idea of what to expect.

A truck boards outside my guesthouse. Buses or matatus are not common here in Kabale, Uganda. August 1989.

Easing off the train after arriving at the station, Bishop Okoth is a wonderful sight. I can't believe it's been seven months since meeting him in New York. He's a big man with a jolly smile and short, cropped hair with wisps of gray.

Dapper in his sport coat, he wears a purple shirt with the white collar of the church. Yona gives me a warm hug, happy to whisk me away to the bishop's house next to Namirembe Cathedral.

He knows about traveling around Africa. After a typical Ugandan meal of rice, matoke, and chicken, I'm early to bed.

The next day passes peacefully. When dusk arrives, the cicada drone overwhelms the eerie bird calls. Namirembe Hill is quiet; road noise rarely makes it into the house.

Situated at the top of a Kampala hill, the house's water is stored on the roof, and we must wait for the water truck when the tanks run dry. Electricity is constant, thanks to the Jinja dam, in contrast to western Uganda, where diesel generators are the norm.

While Mrs. Okoth is away at the family farm in Tororo, many orphans of the civil struggles help take care of the huge house. Yona gives them hope for a better life and a job to help them on their feet.

It's bad up north in Gulu; I recently heard a woman was shot. The government tries to create peace, but different groups are in opposition, stubborn in their thirst for power. Uganda has had a horrible time since the British left in 1962. Only recently, in 1986, Yoweri Museveni was elected president, and things seem to have calmed down.

The newspapers are fiery and healthy with their criticism of the government, signs of a free country. There's a struggle to revive the economy, but many critical copper, sugar, and coffee markets still have not restarted.

Another growing concern is the focus on academic education instead of vocational trade schools. Yona believes political scientists aren't what the country needs. Regardless, I feel peace would allow Uganda to avoid military burdens and start to foster redevelopment and jobs.

After a busy day tromping around Kampala, Yona and I sit on the veranda, sipping passion fruit juice and watching the sunset. Being on the equator, sunrise and sunset always happen at the same time, every day. The locals say six o'clock is zero hour in "Swahili Time."

"Yona, as I wander around Africa, the children love to call me a mzungu. I'm worried my presence is an insult."

He takes time to respond, putting down his glass. "Since white people are rare, the young ones react this way. In Africa, xenophobia is widespread, and people are concerned about being dominated by others. For instance, my family is from the Acholi, while Mbale is home to the Bugisu tribe. Since we can't speak each other's language, distrust is part of our survival instinct."

"And the colonists and today's African leaders exploit this fear of strangers?"

"Correct. It's our biggest challenge. As for you, please don't worry. Ugandans are learning to look beyond the past and avoid stereotyping someone based on their language or skin color."

"I've never felt threatened, thankfully. A bit scared at times. Guess I'm one of the good guys."

Yona and I at my Dad's New York apartment in January 1989.

Yona laughs. "Don't hand out shillings. The children will never let you alone."

A call from inside beckons us to dinner. "Thank you for your insight," I reply to Yona. "It really helps." He puts his arm around me, squeezing gently as we head in.

Near Yona's house is Mengo Hospital, where I was born in 1960. My parents came here from Mbale to be close to the British doctors. Nurses live here now, and the new hospital is much larger and fancier. I can't go inside, but it's a lovely peaceful spot.

Sitting under a jacaranda tree, the cicadas rub their wings, generating a mesmerizing hum as I travel back in time, imagining Mom, Dad, and me leaving the building many years ago.

Walking up the hill to Namirembe Cathedral, Uganda's primary Anglican cathedral, where Yona is bishop. I stumble on the gravestone of James Hannington from 1885, inscribed with "Tell the Kabaka I die for Uganda." He was the first Anglican bishop in East Africa, captured by soldiers for the king.

I was born at Mengo hospital in 1960. Today, the building is a nurse's residence in Kampala, Uganda, August 1989.

I relish Kampala's laidback and sleepy pace, which makes it hard to leave, but it's time to go home to Mbale. Yona understands and provides a solid breakfast, topped off with matoke, the ubiquitous Ugandan staple of mashed bananas.

After a warm bear hug from Yona, I walk the mile to the market, whistling down the quiet hill into the chaos of Kampala.

Waiting at the dilapidated shack for a matatu, people mill around, coming and going. "Busa, busa, busa," chants a driver, beckoning riders.

It's easy to leave Kampala, but need to transfer to another matatu in Tororo. It takes a while, but finally, I'm heading north to Mbale.

The brown-orange dirt road has occasional patches of asphalt, with potholes scattered randomly, but soon they thin out to allow for swifter passage. The Tororo rock fades behind, and the Wanale plateau looms over the small city, growing larger as we get closer.

The Wanale plateau hovers over the city of Mbale, where my family lived in Uganda from 1959-1965. August 1989.

Mbale has beautiful countryside, with the terrain varying from semidry woodlands to open fields of bananas and maize. Mount Elgon is nearby, hidden in the clouds, almost as tall as Mount Kenya, one hundred miles away.

The town is classic Uganda: store facades in decay, people walking this way and that. When I lived here years ago, this town center must have been gorgeous.

Cathedral Avenue provides the main thoroughfare, and St. Andrews Cathedral at the far end has the best view of Wanale. Walking back home after all these years leaves me in mild awe, almost as if I'm listening to someone else describe it.

In 1960, my parents helped build the community center, a place to house clergy visiting the cathedral next door. The building is deserted and lonely; no one is staying there. Dad helped confirm that I could use our old apartment during my visit. The original green walls are now painted creamy white, welcoming and cozy. The apartment is sparsely decorated but functional.

My mom is outside the community center next to Saint Andrew's
Cathedral, Mbale, Uganda. Photo by Seymour Flinn, December 1962.

The bathroom has the original squat toilet, and the sink appears to be working. I'm happy that the church has kept the place up after all these years. Not rundown like the rest of the town.

After storing my pack, I wander over to the cathedral where Dad used to lead services in Luganda and English. The wooden pews inside cry for oil to smooth their dryness. When it rains, cracks draw water down the walls, causing caulk stains.

Still, the cathedral stands, and people are happy. God fills them with faith and hope, praying for peace and a chance to return to their potential.

Yona and Dad kindly paved the way for my arrival. Several couples who remember my family treat me as an honored guest. Perhaps they recall the good times before the wars, or I'm one of the few mzungus who have returned, making me easy to remember.

I'm grateful that they take me on trips around Mbale, including up to Wanale, the gorgeous plateau above the town, stocked with banana and passion fruit trees.

The Wasikyes outside their home in Mbale, Uganda.
They are the kindest people who remembered me
from when I was born. August 1989.

Dusk is settling in as I return to the apartment at the community center. After a filling chicken and rice concoction from a street vendor, I splurge on beers, knowing the three lads will appreciate the drink. They are sons of church leaders I met this week, born after we left years ago.

Since they rarely see any Americans, we hang out and enjoy each other's company. I climb the stairs and open the door, exiting onto the veranda.

The Walimbras knew me from the 1960s. He is a
deacon in the Church of Mbale, Uganda. August 1989.

"Jambo, rafiki! Look what I have." Placing the bag on the table, I grab an empty seat and start popping the beers. I hand them out slowly since being formal is a thing in Uganda.

"You made it! Right before sunset. I'm grateful for the beer. Cheers!"

We clink our bottles and smile.

It's become a ritual for the last few nights. We chat mainly in English, although I try my pitiful Swahili.

I'm grateful that they welcome me. Maybe because I was born here, or perhaps it's just the beers. Regardless, I'm up on the veranda, soothed by the cool breeze that keeps the malaria mosquitoes at bay. Relaxing as we banter along, bonding as climbers would.

Suddenly, the lads get intense, lean into the table, and switch to Lugisu, the local tongue. Either they're making fun of me, or perhaps it's none of my business. Smiling and leaning back, taking in the scenery. I've climbed like a mzungu, and now it's time to travel like one.

SENIOR IMMIGRATION OFFICER

18 AUG

ENTEBBE UGANDA

20

his supplement, under seal, forms
a part of the passport.
Ce supplèment, sous sceau, fait
partie intègrante du passeport.

UPPLEMENT IS AN ATTACHMENT
RT NO: 100385135
RITY: NAIROBI, KENYA.
SEPT. 26, 1989

Visas

Entries/Entrées Departures/Sorties

Ambassade du Rwanda

A   Nairobi   FLINN

Nom et Prénom   R DAVID

Visa n°   1623/89

Valable du 18-7-89 au 17-8-89

Motif de voyage Tourisme

Nombre d'entrées Plusieurs

Droits perçus Ksh 200/—

Date 07-7-1989

Signature, Sceau

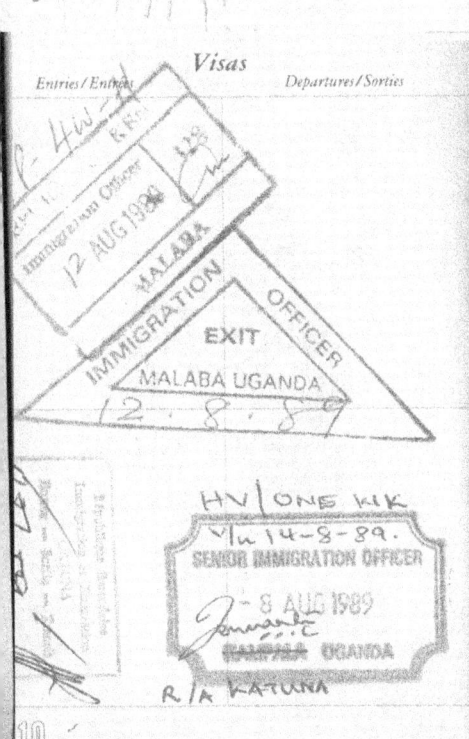

Visas

Entries/Entrées Departures/Sorties

Immigration Officer
12 AUG 1989
MALABA

IMMIGRATION OFFICER
EXIT
MALABA UGANDA
12.8.8

HV/ONE KIK
V/n 14-8-89.
SENIOR IMMIGRATION OFFICER
- 8 AUG 1989
KAMPALA UGANDA
R/A KATUNA

10

Visas

Entries/Entrées Departures/Sorties

VISA 601/89

SEEN AT THE PASSPORT
CONTROL OFFICE
NAIROBI, KENYA
GOOD FOR SINGLE JOURNEY
TO KENYA
WITHIN THREE MONTHS OF
DATE HEREOF. IF PASSPORT
REMAINS VALID
HOLIDAY VISIT
SIGNED
DATE 6-7-89.

OR.C.044074 PAID US $10.

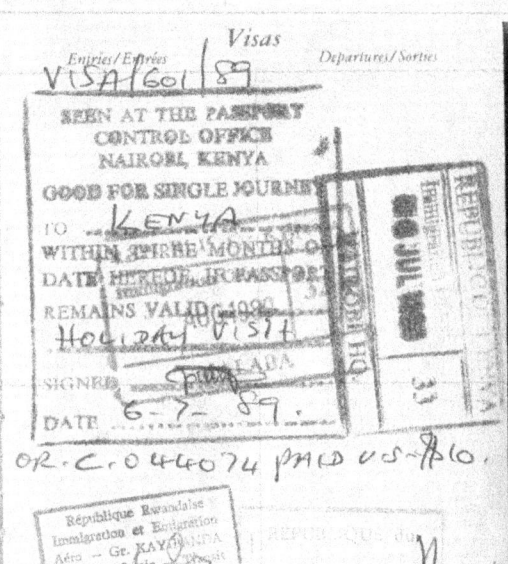

République Rwandaise
Immigration et Emigration
Aéro — Gr. KAYIBANDA
Entrée — Sortie — Transit
21 JUIL 1989

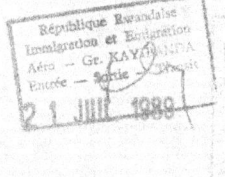

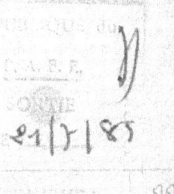

21/7/85

11

PLEASE LEAVE A REVIEW

I'm untangling a snarl in the rope, September 1987.

Thank you for reading this book. I would appreciate your honest feedback by leaving a book review. Even a line or two will really mean a lot to me. Please search for *Climb Like a Mzungu* on Amazon.com or Goodreads.com.

Upcoming: Travel Like a Mzungu

Travel Like a Mzungu is the next book in the "Live An Adventurous Life" series. The novel explores the motivations and desires of wanderers, highlighting exotics places and dramatic people.

I'm celebrating, Ama Dablam and Mount Everest in the distance.
Tengboche, Nepal, November 1989.

Please signup for my email list to learn more about *Travel Like a Mzungu*.

https://www.davidflinn.com

Seymour and Rosalie Flinn right after their wedding in August, 1959

ACKNOWLEDGMENTS

This story would not have been possible without my uncle, Irvine Flinn. Ever since I can remember, he has always been there for me.

The Syracuse University Outing Club's passionate leaders taught me amazing outdoor skills. It is wonderful to see this tradition continue today. Many of the SUOC characters in the book are my close friends, my valuable extended family.

The influential band of cavers, climbers, and water rats include Bill Arduser, Woody Carroll, John Chen, Paul Chen, Jeanne Conde, Rob Cotter, John Gilrein, Ed Grossman, Carol Hatch, Polar Human, Heide Novado Johnson, Deb Laun, Jim Lienhart, Jannette Pazer, Eric Pfirman, John Powers, Rick Riesdorph, Chris Rascher, Jim Ruch, Kelly Smith, Paul Stankiewicz, Matt Stillerman, R. L. Stolz, and Barb Wyscowski.

A big thanks to Steve DeSantis, my esteemed dorm and housemate during my college years. Without his boisterous energy, my foray into hitchhiking may never have happened. His willingness to accompany me to Egypt in 1989 set the stage for my return to Uganda.

Of course, my Red House tribe remains tight as we navigate our later-year adventures. Without these guys, I would never have pushed my climbing limits, taking me to where I needed to go. I'm grateful to Keene Valley establishments such as the Noonmark Diner, Valley Grocery, and The Elm Tree Inn in Keene. A huge thanks to Jim Wagner of The Mountaineer, who gave me the best job ever.

Landing at the Red House energized me to publish the *Adirondack Alpine Journal* from 1983 to 1986. Bob Hey served as my assistant editor, generating fabulous content and keeping me focused. Many local heroes believed in the mission and helped bring the Journal to life by providing articles or inspiration. They include Tim Broader, George Carroll, Jamie Cunningham, Nathan Farb, Carl E. Heilman, Mark Ippolito, Marek Kochel, Rich Leswing, S. Peter Lewis, Don Mellor, Dan Plumley, Alan Reno, Ken Reville, Marc Schenck, Jim Vermeulen, Tad Welch, Albert Wilson, and Jan Wiranowski. Many of these individuals also helped make me a better climber. They know who they are. Without them, I'd still be top-roping ice climbs in Cascade Pass.

Scott Wheeler energized my transition to the corporate world. I would not have been able to afford my Journal without his help. I'm grateful that he took a chance on a rogue cartographer. Not to mention the climbs we did were awesome.

When trying to bring this story to life, a huge thanks goes to my editor Elizabeth Barrett. Her guidance over these past few years helped me focus my writing style and improve the flow of the story. Her writing group in Newburyport, Massachusetts, gave me tremendous insight into my writing, guiding me to the creative nonfiction genre.

Critical feedback is always needed, and many have given me their thoughts over the years. In the final year of writing the book, Kathryn Elmer came to my rescue by reading, editing, and being an amazing sounding board throughout the entire process. A huge thanks to Karen Shaver, my first and most esteemed beta reader. Finally, my sister, Melissa Flinn, has been with me since our Africa beginnings. I'm grateful she's still willing to review my writing after all these years.

About the Author

The author on the John Muir Trail, August 2022

DAVID FLINN is a writer born in Kampala Uganda in 1960. After college, he published the *Adirondack Alpine Journal* in 1983, based in Keene Valley, New York. After years of bounding around, he lives on the ocean, braving nor'easters and planning his next mzungu adventure.

Visit davidflinn.com

facebook.com/flinny.author

linkedin.com/company/david-flinn-author

goodreads.com/davidflinn

youtube.com/@DavidFlinn

CLIMBING IN THE ADIRONDACKS

CLIMBING *in the* ADIRONDACKS   Mellor

White Mountain Guide

An Ice Climbers Guide to Northern New England   L. Peter Lewis & Rick Wilson

A ROCK CLIMBER'S GUIDE
Adirondack ROCK   LAWYER HAAS

DOWNWARD BOUND   "BATSO" Harding   Prentice-Hall

SELECTED CLIMBS *in the* NORTHEAST   ROCK, ALPINE, AND ICE ROUTES FROM THE CLIMBS TO ACADIA

The GAMES CLIMBERS PLAY   Ken Wilson   Diadem

Adirondack
Rock and Ice
Climbs

by
Thomas R. Rosecrans

CLIMBER'S GUIDE
TO THE
ADIRONDACKS

ROCK
AND
SLIDE
CLIMBS

TRUDY HEALY

ADIRONDACK MOUNTAIN CLUB

Climbing Notes

Approach

1. **Chittenango Creek** near Syracuse, New York. Visit an overview at https://www.amer icanwhitewater.org/content/River/view/river-detail/10880/main
2. **Moss Island** in Little Falls, New York hosts many great climbs. Please find more details at https://www.mountainproject.com/area/105830357/moss-island
3. **Uberfall Left** at the Shawangunks in New Paltz, New York. https://www.mountain project.com/area/107037539/the-uberfall-left
4. **Tinker's Falls.** https://www.mountainproject.com/area/109840006/tinker-falls-ice
5. **Lick Brook Falls** near Ithaca, New York. See https://www.mountainproject.com/ route/108751150/lower-falls
6. **Chouinard's Gully** in Chapel Pond Pass, Adirondacks. See more at: https://www. mountainproject.com/route/106644184/chouinards-gully.
7. **Seneca Rocks**, West Virginia. Visit for more information: https://www.mountainpro ject.com/route/109580580/the-gendarme
8. **Regular Route** on Chapel Pond Slabs in the Adirondacks. Visit https://www.moun tainproject.com/route/106411030/regular-route
9. **Pinnacle Gully** on Mount Washington, New Hampshire. Visit https://www.moun tainproject.com/route/105890658/pinnacle-gully
10. **Tuckerman Headwall** on Mount Washington. More details at https://www.moun tainproject.com/route/120054673/headwall-pillars

Belay

1. **Little Finger** on Rogers Rock. For more info, visit https://www.mountainproject. com/route/106092140/little-finger
2. *Climbing in the Adirondacks*, Book by Don Mellor, 1983.
3. **Diagonal** on Wallface, High Peaks Region of the Adirondacks. See more at: https:// www.mountainproject.com/route/107201641/the-diagonal
4. **Pete's Farewell** on Pitchoff Chimney Cliff. More information at https://www.moun tainproject.com/route/105985117/petes-farewell
5. **Regular Route** on Chapel Pond Slabs. Visit https://www.mountainproject.com/ route/106411030/regular-route

Crux

1. **Owl's Head** in Cascade Pass. More information at https://www.mountainproject. com/area/107894353/owls-head-mountain
2. **Equis** on the Lower Beer Walls in Chapel Pond Pass. More information at https:// www.mountainproject.com/route/107114275/equis

3. **Gamesmanship** on Poke-O-Moonshine in the Adirondacks. Visit https://www.moun tainproject.com/route/106074170/gamesmanship
4. **The Trap Dike** on Mount Colden. See for more information https://www.mountain project.com/route/107126372/the-trap-dike
5. **North Face of Gothics**, High Peaks Region of the Adirondacks. Visit https://www. mountainproject.com/route/107506193/north-face
6. **Jaws** in Cascade Pass near Lake Placid, NY. Visit https://www.mountainproject.com/ route/111966709/jaws

SUMMIT

1. **The University of Washington outdoor wall.** https://www.mountainproject.com/ area/105858218/uw-rock
2. **Fuhrer Finger** on the western slope of Mount Rainier. https://www.mountainpro ject.com/route/106636996/fuhrer-finger

VISTA

1. **No Man's a Pilot** on Wallface. For more details: https://www.mountainproject.com/ route/108411710/no-mans-a-pilot
2. **Central Gully** in Huntington Ravine, Mount Washington. See https://www.moun tainproject.com/route/105890662/central-gully
3. **Mount Silvertip** in the Delta Range, Alaska. More information at https://www. mountainproject.com/photo/108824648/some-of-the-major-peaks-in-the-deltas-as- seen-from-the-summit-of-institute-peak

RAPPEL

1. **Moby Grape** on Cannon Cliff, New Hampshire. Visit https://www.mountainproject. com/route/105884815/moby-grape
2. **TR** is found on the Spider's Web in Chapel Pond Pass. Visit https://www.mountain project.com/route/106001608/tr
3. **Vertigo** on Cannon Cliff, New Hampshire. Navigate to https://www.mountainpro ject.com/route/105888753/vertigo

CAMPFIRE

1. **North Face Standard Route** on Mount Kenya. Visit https://www.mountainproject. com/route/110309313/north-face-standard-route

Photography and Maps

Maps

All maps and 3D views were created by the author using Mapbox Studio. Two styles were used for printing: *Outdoors* and *Satellite Streets*. Most text and routes were overlayed using Adobe Photoshop.

Cover Photographs

- The front cover is the author standing on the Gendarme, Seneca Rocks, West Virginia, March 1983, from the David Flinn collection.
- Front-facing page (duplex cover) Mount Kenya, July 1989
- Back-facing page (duplex cover) The author on *Labatt-Ami*, Upper Beer Walls, Adirondacks, October 1987.
- Back page photo of the author by Tim Broader, John Muir Trail, California, August 2022.

Chapter Photographs

These full-page photographs are found on the facing page of each chapter. The author took all except for *Rappel* and *Crux*.

- ***Guidebook***. *The North Face Standard Route* on Mount Kenya, July 1989.
- ***Approach***. Ken in Huntington Ravine, Mount Washington, February 1986.
- ***Belay***. Bob on the *Regular Route* on the Chapel Pond, Slabs, May 1982.
- ***Crux***. Jamie on *Roaring Brook Falls*, February 1980, by Rich Leswing. Provided by the Jamie Cunningham collection.
- ***Summit***. Mount Adams from the summit of Mount Rainier, June 1984.
- ***Vista***. Tuckerman's Ravine from the Alpine Garden, May 1987.
- ***Rappel***. The author rapping in the rain on Whitehorse Slabs, New Hampshire, September 2006. Photograph by Paul Stankiewicz.
- ***Campfire***. The approach to Mount Kenya, July 1989.

Photographs

The author's collection provides the majority of the photographs in the book. Contributors include the following:

Belay

- Rogers Rock on Lake George by Justin Hodges.
- *Pete's Farewell* on Pitchoff Chimney Cliff by Rich Lessing, from the Jamie Cunningham collection.
- Wallface Cliff from adirontreks.blogspot.com.
- The Red House by Jamie Cunningham.
- The Mountaineer outdoor store picture provided by The Mountaineer.

Crux

- Lower Beer Walls by How Hulher.
- Ken on *Look, Roll, and Fire*, Hurricane Crags by Jamie Cunningham.
- Jamie at Mount Jo from the Jamie Cunningham collection.
- *The Trap Dike* by Carol Hatch.

Vista

- Wallface Cliff from adirontreks.blogspot.com.
- *The Diagonal* on Wallface by Kevin Heckeler.

Rappel

- Lee Hansche on Cannon's *Moby Grape*'s triangular roof by Corey Hebert.
- The *Vertigo* pendulum on Cannon by Lauren Wilson.

www.ingramcontent.com/pod-product-compliance
Lightning Source LLC
Chambersburg PA
CBHW060359130626
46553CB00003B/1309